CNN
The Inside Story

By Hank Whittemore

NONFICTION

THE MAN WHO RAN THE SUBWAYS: The Story of Mike Quill
COP — A Closeup of Violence and Tragedy
TOGETHER — A Reporter's Journey into the New Black Politics
THE SUPER COPS — The True Story of the Cops Called Batman and
    Robin
PEROFF — The Man Who Knew Too Much
FIND THE MAGICIAN — The Counterfeiting Crime of the Century
CNN: The Inside Story

FICTION

FEELING IT

CNN
The Inside Story

HANK WHITTEMORE

LITTLE, BROWN AND COMPANY
BOSTON   TORONTO   LONDON

FIRST EDITION

Library of Congress Cataloging-in-Publication Data

Whittemore, Hank.
    CNN: The inside story / by Hank Whittemore. — 1st ed.
        p.   cm.
    ISBN 0-316-93761-4
    1. Cable News Network.   2. Television broadcasting of news—United
States.   3. Turner, Ted.   I. Title.   II. Title: CNN: The inside story.
PN4888.T4W47   1990
070.4′33′0973 — dc20   89-14001
                                                                    CIP

10 9 8 7 6 5 4 3 2 1

HC

Published simultaneously in Canada
by Little, Brown & Company (Canada) Limited

PRINTED IN THE UNITED STATES OF AMERICA

To my brother, Jim.

To my children,
Eva and Lorna and Ben.

And to my parents,
Bill and Suzette.

Acknowledgments

THERE ARE MANY PEOPLE to thank for their help, directly and indirectly, in the writing of this book. John Savage got me down to Atlanta on a free-lance job and planted the idea; Barbara Pyle gave her insights into Ted Turner and introduced me to Michael Reagan, who obtained cooperation from Turner Broadcasting System and Cable News Network. It was essential to have the assistance of both Ted Turner and Reese Schonfeld, who each took time to answer my questions.

All during the project, Ira Miskin was always available to give advice; Alison Fussell helped to coordinate people and provided assistance at TBS; early transcribers were Jackie Jusko and Lisa Maxwell; Pam Knolla listened to hundreds of hours of taped interviews and transcribed them, along with keeping track of many details; Sara Bauman did library research; Dee Woods in Ted Turner's office was always helpful; and others who took time to assist were Vivian Schiller, Steve Haworth, Kitsie Riggall, Judy Henry, Jack Womack, Sarah Palatsi and Kathy Christensen.

Agent for the project was Lena Tabori, who took the early stages of writing to Irv Goodman, whose skill and support as editor carried me through. Michael Mattil did a fine job as copy-editor.

To all of the above, I am grateful.

Special thanks are due to Rick Brown, for providing insight and information.

Walter Anderson's friendship, support and counsel over the years have been invaluable.

I especially want to thank those connected with the story who shared their recollections. Other than those already mentioned, they included Paul Amos, Cissy Baker, John Baker, Frank Beatty,

Paul Beckham, Tench Coxe, Chris Curle, Ken Dickman, Lou Dobbs, Diane Durham, Gail Evans, Don Farmer, Phil Frank, Randy Freedman, Bob Furnad, Henry Gillespie, Don Lachowsky, Lois Hart, Fran Heany, Carl "Bunky" Helfrich, Gerry Hogan, John Hillis, Stacy Jolna, Ted Kavanau, Will King, Jim Kitchell, Steve Korn, Marvin Koslow, Don Lennox, Stuart Loory, Bill MacPhail, Jane Maxwell, Terry McGuirk, Roy Mehlman, Don Miller, Alec Miran, Dial Nagle, Sid Pike, Bill Papa, Burt Reinhardt, Bob Rierson, Arthur Sando, Bob Ross, Jim Schoonmaker, Daniel Schorr, Bob Schuessler, Bernard Shaw, Bill Shaw, Jim Shepherd, Flip Spiceland, Dick Tauber, Tom Todd, Sid Topol, Ed Turner, Jeanee von Essen, Dave Walker, Lou Waters, Jane Weathersby, Ann Williams, Dick Williams, Mary Alice Williams, R. T. Williams, Larry Woods, Gene Wright, Bob Wussler, Sam Zelman and Bill Zimmerman.

The final product, of course, is my own. This book is my version of the story of Ted Turner and CNN, no one else's, and I must take responsibility for its flaws and omissions. My thanks, again, to all who helped me pursue the truth and spirit of the adventure that they lived.

To the reader

THIS is a true story about people who did the impossible.

The book poses an overriding question: How did Ted Turner and a bunch of other mavericks defy the experts who said that CNN would never succeed?

Like most other stories of victory against great odds, this one contains answers for the rest of us.

CNN℠
The Inside Story

ONE

"I just wanted to see if we could do it — like Christopher Columbus. When you do something that's never been done before, sail on uncharted waters and don't know where you're going, you're not sure what you're going to find when you get there, but at least you're going somewhere."

CAN IT BE DONE?''

"Yes!"

"Do you want to do it?"

"Yes!"

With that brief telephone conversation in November 1978, Ted Turner set in motion the greatest adventure of his life.

The phone call, to a man he barely knew, had lasted less than thirty seconds. He had asked two quick questions and had gotten the answers he wanted.

It was that simple.

When he made the call, Turner was a few days from turning forty. The year before, he had won the America's Cup, the world championship of ocean racing. He had become a big-time celebrity in the media. He owned the Atlanta Braves baseball team and the Atlanta Hawks basketball team. His company had expanded from billboards to radio to television. It was worth perhaps as much as $100 million. He could retire for several lifetimes.

Now, as if in a high-stakes poker game, he was going to put everything back on the table again. (To many of his employees the move was sheer madness, the act of a crazy man.) Here, he was saying, take every bit of my earnings so far and deal the cards. All or nothing.

Turner made the call from Atlanta, Georgia, at the office of his independent television station, WTCG, Channel 17, housed in a cinderblock building on West Peachtree Street near the downtown district. Less than two years earlier, in December 1976, he had begun sending little WTCG's signal up to a satellite hovering 22,300 miles high; and from that outpost in space, the signal was being returned to earth in a wide arc blanketing all of North America and beyond. It spread from the Virgin Islands to Maine, from New York to Hawaii, from Mexico City to Alaska.

Now, instead of reaching only local markets in the Southeast, Turner's so-called SuperStation (a name he had coined) covered more than ten million square miles of the planet. His signal was being received by the fledgling cable-TV market. It was Turner's conviction that over the coming years the whole country would be wired for cable; and as cable grew, so would his "SuperStation That Serves the Nation." The advertising bucks would roll his way and Turner would keep building what amounted to a *fourth network* that could rival ABC, NBC and CBS.

It was an audacious challenge to the Big Three networks' long-standing monopoly of America's television audience. True, it would take time and stamina and even luck to succeed, but Turner was racing ahead to meet the future as it came rushing toward him. The future would be shaped by this miraculous convergence of space-age technology with the development of cable. Now he was poised for the marathon of a struggle against the giants.

He had known he would make such a call for nearly three years; and over the past several months, since the spring of 1978, he had been talking out loud about it. By now he was convinced that a national *news* network, delivered to the cable-television audience by satellite, was inevitable. If he failed to act on the idea soon, then someone else would. It was all a matter of timing, a question of who jumped first.

Turner had been intrigued back in April 1975, when Home Box Office, the pay-cable subsidiary of Time Inc., announced it would begin satellite transmission that fall. Soon after HBO's signal went up to the domestic bird and back down to the entire country, he started negotiations for WTCG to follow suit. It would become the first TV station distributed to cable systems via satellite. It took more than a year, until near the end of 1976, to launch the SuperStation; but well before then Turner had been looking beyond to an all-news channel.

He was simply looking at cable's menu of programming at this early stage of the game. Home Box Office was offering new movies, while Turner's SuperStation was now providing old movies along with sports and reruns of former network "family" shows. The only thing that cable TV or even regular broadcasting did *not* offer was twenty-four-hour news. All-news radio had been going strong, but no one had dared to suggest that Americans might want *television* news available around the clock.

What finally prompted him to make his phone call was much more powerful than any business decision. The one thing that gave the Big Three networks their sense of importance was certainly not the "trash" they put on the air to keep their ratings up. So what gave them their pride and prestige? What made them feel so essential to American life? News!

By the same token, the networks were in the *entertainment* business, living off the advertising money paid for their sitcoms and cop shows; and so, to bolster their self-image and soothe their conscience, they allotted time for news each evening — but only half an hour. Actually, just twenty-two minutes! That, they felt, was the limit of the public's appetite for news.

Turner had come to a radically different conclusion by reversing the conventional equation of supply and demand. He saw that the big, powerful networks were captives of market studies. They took poll after poll of the *demand* out there, and all their surveys plainly showed that news was a clunker. Without any more demand for news, they argued, why create any further supply?

Turner, however, saw market research as the wrong way of approaching business or people or even life itself. If you always had to ask someone's opinion beforehand, why create anything new or original? If, say, the airplane had yet to be invented, and you took a survey asking people if they'd pay to fly on one, how many would say yes? Not a lot! But what if you went out and just *built* the plane and *showed* people how it flew?

All you had to do was have the guts to put your money where your vision was and create the supply. Then if you could hang in there, the demand would follow.

TED TURNER

"I'll do it because a lot of people in high places laughed at me. Watch me. I'm like a bulldog that won't let go. Why do you think my own racing yacht is named *Tenacious*, dummy?"

PLAYBOY: "We give up. Why?"

"Because I never quit. I've got a bunch of flags on my boat, but there ain't no *white* flags. I don't surrender. That's the story of my life. Just think, if you were a rabbit, to survive you'd have to hop fast and keep your eyes open:

"'*Ride, boldly ride, the shade replied — if you seek for Eldorado.'*"

In that August 1978 interview, Turner had been referring to his commitment to reversing the fortunes of the Atlanta Braves. Not once did he refer to his idea for a cable news network, because doing so would have alerted the potential competition. Turner was almost pathologically unable to keep a secret, but in this case he had kept it under wraps. And now, in the face of all advice to the contrary, he had taken himself to the point where he would *have* to try to build an all-news television network.

Amid all the heady publicity about the Mouth of the South and Terrible Ted and Captain Outrageous, he had begun to think of his true calling as a kind of modern folk hero on the side of the common people against the northeastern television establishment. In that role, oh, how he'd love to show those snobs what it meant to be smart and scrappy and defiant and tenacious. He would show them how wrong they'd been to underestimate the needs and desires and, yes, the intelligence of "little guys" like himself who'd been stuck with no choice other than what the networks dished out.

Getting on the satellite with the SuperStation had been an extraordinary step toward providing an alternative to the networks. But *news*, Turner realized, was where the true battle for future television dominance would be waged. For three decades, the Big Three networks had become so smug and self-satisfied that by now they seemed unaware that their power over TV news could be threatened — especially if the threat came from some outsider in the South who had so little experience with journalism news.

So he decided to take every nickel of profit from his growing SuperStation, and from the sale of any other asset of Turner Communications Corporation, and pour it into this cable news network.

It was a business venture, sure, but it was really a mission whose possibilities went beyond all boundaries. If one satellite could bring world and national news to all of North America, then a second satellite eventually could bring the same information to still another continent. It was even possible to think about a single *world network* through which all nations, in effect, could talk to each other about their grievances and common problems.

If he clawed and struggled hard enough over the next few decades, by the end of this century he could change the course of television's history and become its dominant figure. In his wildest vision of that future it was he, Ted Turner, who would lead the country and, indeed, the whole world into the next stage of the Information Age. Televised communication for the entire planet! The global village!

In that mood, with that resolve, he made the call.

Reese Schonfeld worked at the New York Daily News Building, in the offices of the Independent Television News Association, a nonprofit syndication group he had founded. As ITNA's managing editor, Schonfeld was providing daily news packages to contributing TV stations around the country. For more than two decades he had worked as a newsman outside the structure of the Big Three networks, operating on shoestring budgets to compete with their high-priced, far-flung news departments.

If anyone had ever dreamed of creating and building an all-news television network, it was Reese Schonfeld.

He had just turned forty-seven. Over the past few weeks, in the fall of 1978, he had been hearing rumors that Ted Turner was talking about an all-news cable channel. Schonfeld had laughed it off. He had met Turner on several occasions and, from everything he'd seen and heard, it was clear that the guy had no love for news at all. He had made fun of news time and again. He *hated* news.

When Schonfeld heard that Turner was on the line, however, he had a sudden, gut feeling that the rumors might be true. This could be the call you waited a lifetime to get.

"Reese, How're ya doin'?"

"I'm fine, Ted. How are you?"

"I'm thinking about doing twenty-four hours of news for cable. Can it be done?"

"Yes," Schonfeld said.

"Do you want to do it?"

"Yes," Schonfeld said.

"Come on down and see me," Turner said.

The conversation was over.

Somehow, the long-awaited Grand Experiment of television news was being initiated not in New York or Washington but in the South. By the most unlikely source. Yet the man's sure voice, his concise conversation, seemed to carry conviction. In the past, when they had run into each other, Turner had joked around about news. And wasn't he some sort of right-wing southern redneck? A wild man with a loud mouth? What were his real intentions? To gain power to foist his views on the whole country?

Be careful, Reese Schonfeld told himself.

He booked a plane ticket.

He remembered seeing Ted Turner for the first time back in the early part of the decade, down in Atlanta, during a meeting of independent TV station owners. At the time, Turner already owned two stations. In the 1960s he had rebuilt his family's failing billboard business, parlaying it into a multimillion-dollar conglomerate. By 1970 he had acquired Channel 17 in Atlanta, which had been losing $600,000 a year; and six months later he had bought Channel 36 in Charlotte, North Carolina, which had been losing more than half that. Through a combination of high-powered salesmanship and belt-tightening, along with a philosophy that the way to succeed was to keep increasing the value of his product, Turner reversed the fortunes of both stations. In fact, he turned the first profit for Channel 17 within a year and a half; and in 1972, he acquired the rights for his station to telecast Atlanta Braves games.

Soon after that, Schonfeld saw him at the meeting of station owners and general managers. It had been an enormous coup for a tiny independent UHF station to have grabbed the baseball rights away from WSB, the most important station in the South, and the other broadcasters at the convention were amazed by what Turner had done. Schonfeld was simply part of the crowd, on hand to pitch news to the various station owners, when Turner stood to make a speech welcoming them to Atlanta. Beside him was his wife, Janie, and he put an arm around her.

"All you guys are comin' up and congratulatin' me on how

wonderful it is to have the Braves games," he said, "but you know, it's a lot like gettin' married. You work so hard to do it! You really work so hard, and then all of a sudden you wake up the morning after the wedding, and you say, 'Gee, did I really want to *marry* this broad.'"

Now the guys in the crowd were astonished, but Janie was smiling and they all laughed. It was incredible, Schonfeld remembered. He had experienced "the great Turner aura," as he referred to it, before the deluge of media coverage that followed.

Schonfeld loved news.

He lived news and dreamt news and woke up thinking about news. He was a king of the news junkies and spent his days chasing after it. He was a hit-and-run, sneak-attack newsman in the old *Front Page* style: find the story, get it first and bother with the frills later; or, better, don't bother at all and just keep scooping the hell out of everybody else with *more* news.

Like Ted Turner, he never looked back. He was too busy having fun and trying to beat the big guys at their own game.

At six-foot-three, an inch taller and thirty pounds heavier than the young entrepreneur in the South, Reese Schonfeld was a bear of a man with a wide, toothy grin. It was another thing he shared with Turner — a commanding physical presence that made you notice when he came into a room. The source of that presence, for both men, was sheer gusto. They were competitors with almost everyone around them. Turner and Schonfeld each had a boy inside him; their eyes glowed with a merriment that was part innocence, part unabashed enthusiasm, part devilment. Schonfeld, like Turner, was subject to wide, volatile mood swings. He could fume and grow so tense he'd begin to tremble, but then he'd straighten up and the storm would pass — or burst into a thunderous rage, filled with torrential abuse.

At the same time Schonfeld was a kindly, wonderful guy who'd be first to appear at your bedside if you were ill from excitement, tension and overwork. The only catch was that he'd probably driven you to that state in the first place.

Turner and Schonfeld both had egos as big and wide as all outdoors. Both loved to take risks while scheming to circumvent the hazards and making sure they'd win. Schonfeld himself was a gambler and loved any kind of betting. He had experienced the joys and pains of high-stakes winning and losing at poker, but he took calculated risks in life as well.

But they were different in how they viewed themselves and the world. Turner approached business and life as if he were playing in a sports event, while Schonfeld saw himself as dedicated to the news business as a professional. And for all his verbal skills, he had none of Turner's folksy way with a crowd or desire to gain the spotlight.

Fine with me, Schonfeld thought. *Turner can have every last drop of publicity, so long as he lets me do the job.*

It seemed as if they were being drawn to a common space; the question was whether they could accommodate each other. Could they join forces to bring into existence what neither man could create on his own? Or would they become like two thunderbolts trying, simultaneously, to strike the same patch of ground?

Maurice Wolfe Schonfeld was born on November 5, 1931, in Newark, New Jersey, a city whose social upheavals and political machinations would intrigue him for the rest of his life. If you had to think of a town that reflected his own temperament, Newark, with its wild conflicts and conflagrations, would fit the bill.

His father wanted him to be a lawyer. Schonfeld went to Dartmouth and got a BA degree in 1953, then returned to New York and earned an MA in government at Columbia University in 1956, before entering law school there that fall. But during the summer before law school began, Schonfeld took a part-time job at UPI Movietone, a maker and syndicator of news films. He became a copy boy and was hooked. By the time he earned his law degree in 1960, he had risen at UPI Movietone from copy boy to reporter to producer. Now it was too late for jurisprudence.

Robert Edward Turner III was born on November 19, 1938, in Cincinnati, Ohio, where his parents had met. A younger sister, Mary Jane, was also born there. His father, Ed Turner, was a Mississippian who had become a salesman after watching his own father lose his cotton farm during the Depression. It was in Cincinnati that Ed Turner started his billboard company from scratch; and when Ted was nine, he moved the family to

Savannah, Georgia, where he felt he could make more money. Ted was in fifth grade when his father enrolled him in the Georgia Military Academy; and two years later he entered another military school, McCallie, in Chattanooga, Tennessee.

From the beginning it was his father who had been the dominant influence in his life. He was a demanding man who, out of love for his son, pummeled him with discipline and tough tests to pass; and the two would have long discussions about what Ted should do with himself. The young Turner became feisty and competitive among his peers at McCallie, who nicknamed him Terrible Ted because of his high-strung behavior. When he was seventeen, Ted won the Tennessee state high school debating contest. Intrigued by military history, he almost tried for an appointment to the U.S. Naval Academy at Annapolis; but then, bowing to his father's wishes, he applied to Harvard — where he was turned down — and finally enrolled at Brown University in Providence, Rhode Island.

The act of obedience was followed by rebellion. After a freshman year of undefeated intercollegiate sailboat racing, he was suspended as a sophomore, following a drunken, rowdy fracas at a nearby women's college. He spent six months as a member of the Coast Guard and, at Brown again, decided to major in the classics. He was still pursuing his interest in great figures of literature and naval warfare when his father wrote to say he was "appalled" by the choice and that he had "almost puked" over it. In a long, well-intended but harsh letter, Ed Turner told his son that "I think you are rapidly becoming a jackass" who would be better off anywhere else than at Brown.

"You are in the hands of the Philistines, and dammit, I sent you there," his father wrote. "I am sorry. Devotedly, Dad."

Ted complied, in a sense, by breaking the rule against entertaining female guests in dormitory rooms and getting himself expelled before he could graduate. He spent two months bumming around Miami before rejoining the Coast Guard and, inevitably, going to work for his father full-time. By then his parents were divorced and his sister, Mary Jane, had died of lupus, a progressively degenerative disease from which she had suffered for years.

In the fall of 1960, just twenty-two years old, Ted became general manager of the Turner Advertising Company's branch in Macon, Georgia. Two years later his father bought into another firm, based in Atlanta, but fits of depression drove him to initiate plans for selling out. When Ted discovered this, he was shocked and furious. He was confused by the man who had taught him never to give up. He stood up to his father, which had always taken some doing, and threw back all of Ed Turner's own arguments against quitting in life.

Shortly after this acrimonious verbal battle, on March 5, 1963, Ed Turner killed himself with a pistol in the bedroom of his plantation home in South Carolina. Having lost his best friend and mentor, Ted Turner sped forth on a quest from which he would never look back, as if the same bullet were chasing him just behind his ear.

Instead of taking any money from the sale of the billboard company, he halted the sell-out transactions then in progress. He sold his father's plantation to help pay notes, and set about regaining parts of the family business. He became president and chief executive officer of the company and started to build it into an empire.

TED TURNER

"I came out of a Depression family, where my father started with absolutely nothing. He thought that the way to be successful was to make a lot of money and have a lot of riches and power. When he was fifty-three years old, he had a nervous breakdown and blew his brains out. I loved that man desperately; he was my father and we were very close; but I spent a lot of time trying to figure out what it was that he did wrong. He put too much emphasis on material success. I can tell you it's fool's gold. . . .

"I really grew up with a tremendous work ethic and it was pumped into my head to 'be a success, be a success.' And all during my life I had this gnawing feeling that maybe I wasn't going to *be* a success. My father died when I was twenty-four and he was the one, really, that I had expected to be the judge of whether I was successful or not. . . .

"So when I finally got on the cover of *Success* magazine, I held it up and said, 'Dad? Do you see this? I made the cover of *Success* magazine! Is that *enough?*'"

In New York, after leaving UPI Movietone in 1963 over an editorial dispute, Reese Schonfeld watched it collapse because of its inability to keep pace with advances in technology. Movie-tone's delivery of news film to independent stations by air freight had become ridiculous and obsolete. Soon afterward Schonfeld joined a friend, Burt Reinhardt, who was putting together a new UPI news service out of the rubble.

Reinhardt was born on April 19, 1920. He began his own career at age nineteen with Fox Movietone News; and as a World War Two combat cameraman in October 1944 he recorded General MacArthur's historic return to the Philippines on film. From the end of the war on, he was managing editor for the Fox service; and now, in 1963, he was creating UPI Newsfilm, another agency to supply national and international news. And he hired Reese Schonfeld as his national editor.

It was the first chance for Schonfeld to help set up an organization from the beginning, yet because of the networks' dominance in wealth and technology he knew that UPI Newsfilm was doomed. After only a few years, the company was consolidated with a British counterpart and renamed UPI Television News; and as managing editor of UPITN under Reinhardt's direction, Schonfeld was well aware that *this* operation would never last either.

Its life span turned out to be nine years, until 1974, during which time they struggled to compete with the more affluent Associated Press. It was a losing battle but also exhilarating, because they often came up winners in the scramble for exclusives. Schonfeld had a knack for hatching new ways of stealing stories from the competition. (If a dozen camera crews were heading for a press conference, he might place a strategic call to get his scoop beforehand, filming his UPI reporter delivering the story.) By the time he became vice-president of UPITN in 1973, still under Reinhardt, he had "done it all" in news — as writer, reporter, editor, producer, manager. He was a "working" newsman who had covered every political convention, civil rights march, space shot, race riot and Vietnam war demonstration. But his greatest goal, aside from the daily struggle to survive without resources, had been to find new solutions for breaking through the financial and technological barriers that made independent newsgathering so difficult.

In Schonfeld's view there was an unspoken conspiracy, between the three networks and AT&T, to keep other news organizations from using the crucial telephone-company land lines. The six hundred broadcast stations affiliated with ABC, NBC and CBS were the main suppliers of TV programming to seventy-five million homes; and these local affiliates had to receive the signals via wire. The three "networks" or "webs" of stations were literally linked together by those land lines crisscrossing the country; and as a result, they had become enormously powerful phone-company clients.

The networks paid for the lines at a twenty-four-hour rate, which, because of their heavy usage, included a staggering discount of about ninety percent. For AT&T, the arrangement worked out just fine because the networks provided a guaranteed income. Meanwhile, companies using only "occasional" time on the lines paid on a per-mile, per-hour basis. Three hours on land lines cost UPITN more than the networks paid for the full twenty-four hours.

Reinhardt and Schonfeld did battle with the phone companies for years. They sued AT&T to get the "occasional" rates lowered, and bitterly complained about the enormous monopoly held by the networks — all without success.

When microwave relay stations started appearing in the late sixties, AT&T and other phone companies saw their network-TV business on land lines being threatened. The Portland-to-Seattle run went microwave; so did the Milwaukee-Minneapolis and Dallas-Houston runs. And the networks, feeling even more powerful than before, put pressure on the phone companies to *lower* their twenty-four-hour rates or face further defections.

By 1973, that pressure paid off. The phone companies lowered their twenty-four-hour rates. The networks stopped using microwave delivery and returned to the land lines. And the "occasional" rates were raised.

It was a crushing blow to UPITN. Reese Schonfeld and Burt Reinhardt knew they couldn't cover the huge land-line charges; and microwave delivery was too expensive. From their vantage point, the dream of building an independent "fourth news network" for television was all but dead.

TED TURNER

"When I bought Channel 17, everybody just hooted at me. The station was really at death's door. I didn't bullshit anybody. I told them I didn't know anything about TV. . . .

"My accountants told me we were going to go broke in Charlotte. They also said the company was going to go bankrupt with
Channel 17. They said I was crazy. . . .

"I just love it when people say I can't do something. There's
nothing that makes me feel better, because all my life people
have said I wasn't going to make it. . . .

"The secret of my success is this: Every time, I tried to go as
far as I could. When I climbed the hills, I saw the mountains.
Then I started climbing the mountains. . . ."

In the early 1970s, Turner was putting together a whole new
team of guys who would go "all out" with him. Sid Pike became
WTCG's general manager and R. T. Williams made a deal
to build up some production facilities. Will Sanders took the
hairy job as vice-president for finance, while Paul Beckham
joined as corporate controller. Gene Wright came aboard as
chief engineer. Gerry Hogan, age twenty-five, who had signed
on to sell advertising, became sales manager within a year.
Terry McGuirk, who had joined one summer during college,
began working his way into special projects. If Ted Turner
could be likened to the roguish captain of a ship sailing into
unknown waters, then they were key members of his hearty
band of pirates. . . .

PAUL BECKHAM

"We had the money crisis the day I walked in. And the records
were just atrocious. My initial job was to straighten them out,
so we would know where we were and be able to make some
type of projection we could show to the banks. Ted was very
cost-conscious and profit-motivated. You get to the point where
you don't panic over the debts. As long as the value is there and
growing, you just move forward.

"One time I went with Ted to a bank where we were trying
to get a loan. The executive listened and finally said, 'That's
all very well and good, Mr. Turner, but what if you drop
dead?' In the next second Ted dropped to the floor and lay
there as if he was dead. Then he slithered up the side of the
desk, grinned at the banker and said, *'Fooled ya, didn't I!'* We
got the loan."

GENE WRIGHT

"There were maybe forty-three people in the whole corporation when I arrived. We had absolutely no equipment at Channel 17 and no real engineering or maintenance being done. We had all kinds of technical problems and kept going off the air. I bought a cot and basically moved in and stayed there.

"The operators would sit around playing banjos and smoking pot while the film would run out. Nobody really knew there *was* a Channel 17 in those days. . . .

"We had a bad transmission line. Every time the wind blew and the tower moved, our transmitter would cut off. Ted wouldn't buy a new line. Finally, when we were off the air several more times, he asked what another one would cost. I said it would be around $75,000. By the time he agreed, we had waited too long and our transmission line blew all the way up at the top.

"It took about seven days to get back on the air. I worked on the tower for that whole week and never got any sleep and my shoes were full of blood. If I had had time to look for another job, I wouldn't have been there. I thought he was crazy. . . .

"I'd say, 'We need another monitor.' Ted would say, 'Well, you *got* one.' I kept insisting that we needed 'redundancy' in the system. He said, 'Gene, you are the most *redundant bastard* I ever met!' I stayed around because of the challenge. After about three years of working seven days a week, with no vacation, we started making progress. Ted came through one day and he said, 'Hey, Wright, we haven't been off the air in a long time, have we?' I said, 'No, we haven't.' He said, 'God, redundancy's great!'"

Turner became a crafty salesman of UHF by painting its liabilities as assets. When potential advertisers pointed to the smallness of his audience, he agreed. Yes, he said, his viewers were few in number — precisely because their intelligence was so high. The reason? Well, because anyone who could figure out how to tune in a UHF station *had* to be smart. Even *he* couldn't find Channel 17 on his dial, Turner would say, but his mentally superior viewers could. When the advertisers shifted to the apparent liability that most of his programs were in black and white, Turner asked them to think about the "shock value" when their commercials suddenly appeared in color.

"Pretty strong, huh?"

BOB SCHUSSLER

"When I got to the Charlotte station to head up sales, I wondered what the hell I'd done. I mean, it was out in the country. We had woods on both sides and, in front, a pasture with cows. The second night I was there, I was watching our big movie in prime time. Our highest rating, by the way, was a two, which is about as low as you could get. So I'm looking at the feature that starts at eight. It's some Maureen O'Hara movie about the desert. Here it comes on, and you see these camels with Maureen O'Hara, and they're walking upside-down and backwards! This goes on for about three minutes and they shut it off. It's just black. For five more minutes. Then the movie comes on again, but the camels are still upside-down, so it goes off again. But this time, instead of a black screen, they run about seven minutes of straight commercials! Finally it comes on and we try once more — but now it's a different movie!"

R. T. WILLIAMS

"Everybody at Channel 17 was walking out the door in the beginning, quitting on us, because at that time no one even knew we existed. The joke was that we were number seven in a five-station market. There was another Atlanta independent and they were just killing us. But when their parent company pulled the plug, they suddenly went dark. Bang! And I get a call from Ted, who wants to do a 'Thank You, Atlanta' party. A one-hour special program. I hang up and go roaring into his office and tell him, 'Hey, Ted, we didn't win! We didn't beat 'em! They defected!' He says, 'Nah, we beat 'em. We won.' And sure as shootin', we put on a one-hour special. We had a couple of bands, with balloons floating down, and Ted was wandering around talking and thanking the people of Atlanta for their support! I'm thinking, 'What is this bullshit? I've gotta get out of here!' I look back on it now and remember that nobody knew who the hell Ted was at the time, but he *called* it a victory and so it *was* one."

Channel 17 had gone from fifth of five stations in the Atlanta market to fourth of four. When the local ABC affiliate began carrying network evening news at six o'clock, Turner put on *Star Trek* at the same time and got a quick ratings boost. He ran only the FCC minimum of forty minutes of news a day — at two or three in the morning.

Moreover, his station, he declared, was offering an escape from current network shows "with rape and murders going on all over the place." His own lineup included reruns of *Gilligan's Island, Leave It to Beaver* and *Andy Griffith.*

GERRY HOGAN

"In our first meeting he was amazing. Ted had the most unbelievable energy. He was like a hyperactive kid on Christmas Eve. He was running around the room and he'd walk behind me and spin me around in the chair. I said to myself, Well, what have I got to lose? I was twenty-five and I figured it was at least worth investing a year to see what happens. Every year from then on, I've said the same thing. It's like you're halfway up the hill and you've got to see what's on the other side. Every year something crazy or wild came up. . . .

"Eventually you take on an attitude that you're like guerrilla fighters. Or like a bunch of pirates going after an armada. You accept the tough parts, because there's a sense of mission. I got to the point where I really enjoyed living on the edge, which is what Ted always did. And he would do anything, like stand on a table or take a guy by the throat or kiss his feet. Whatever was called for in the situation."

Along with his growing roster of old television shows, Turner was building a movie library of about five thousand titles. And in addition to the Braves games, he also got wrestling rights away from the competition (by offering a better deal) and his ratings continued to climb. Although Channel 17's operating loss was more than half a million dollars in 1970 and again in 1971, he went into the black the following year; and in 1973, the profit was over a million dollars. The Atlanta and Charlotte stations became two of the most successful independents in the country.

There was also the new horizon of cable television. What spurred cable in the first place was the desire in rural areas for better reception of regular broadcast signals — a cable was strung, from an antenna on the highest point of local terrain, down to homes in a valley — and what opened up the field was a ruling by the Federal Communications Commission allowing independent stations to send their signals to farther, more distant markets. Turner was already paying for the rights to show his films and old network shows; but now, if he sent them beyond Atlanta (via microwave) to cable systems, the FCC ordered that additional fees or "copyright royalties" be paid by the cable operators themselves.

So now a broadcaster like Turner could expand through cable without having to pay the program rights-holders every time he sent their material to a new audience. Sensing the opportunity, he started sending his WTCG signal by microwave dishes to cable systems in region after region. The signal went from Atlanta to Alabama, to northern Florida and up to the Carolinas. The only rules he was breaking were old ways of thinking; but he was branded by other broadcasters as a renegade who had thrown his lot with the cable competition.

Well, Turner said, I don't think the way you do. But if you guys say broadcasters don't go into cable, then I guess I'm not a broadcaster anymore. I'm a cable guy!

When UPITN was folding in 1974, Burt Reinhardt moved to Los Angeles to work for one of its major owners, Paramount Pictures. He took charge of its educational division and began to nurture the development of home video. Reese Schonfeld, on his own, made a last-ditch effort to sell more syndicated news feeds to local stations around the country. One of his visits was to Ted Turner's station WTCG in Atlanta, where he saw Sid Pike, the general manager.

Schonfeld was trying to do more than sell Channel 17 a daily package of national news. What he desperately needed was a way to lessen the cost of the AT&T land line that ran from New York all the way down to Miami. Schonfeld's idea was to get some other station along the way attached to the line. Even if WTCG in Atlanta bought a few little news *inserts*, it would help to pay the cost of a syndication service.

Sid Pike laughed out loud at Schonfeld's pitch. "*News?* What do I want *news* for? We don't need news! We *counter*-program against news. News loses money! We *make* money. We don't *do* news."

Why, Schonfeld wondered, did I ever stop here?

"I work for a crazy man," Pike said, "and he buys so much

entertainment that oh, hell, we've got more movies here than we can run! I can't even play the stuff he buys *now*, much less put on a half hour of news! We'll *never* do news!"

Schonfeld wearily returned to New York.

His next job was at Television News Incorporated, known as TVN, which had been started by brewer Joseph Coors. A political conservative, Coors had set up his own syndication service to counterbalance what he saw as the liberal-slanted network news. That motivation never seriously influenced TVN's final product, however, and Coors began to succeed quickly. He used his brewery resources to drive his main competitor, UPITN, out of business in the United States; and when he bought up that company's domestic assets, he also got Schonfeld as part of the package.

The success of TVN was directly related to the way the Big Three networks were treating their affiliates. Those stations, now expanding their own newscasts, paid fees to the networks for excerpts of national news; but often the good stories were being held back and they felt cheated. Now Joe Coors, with his TVN service, was supplying the affiliates with material they couldn't get until after the networks' evening newscasts. That gap was already being filled for seventy-five such stations, including independents.

Schonfeld still had more schemes to try before he would quit fighting the networks. When he walked into TVN he was enthusiastic, this time, about satellites. A revolution was on the way. In the past there had been only international satellites for news feeds; but the real change would occur because of *domestic communications* satellites delivering television news to stations around the country. (Western Union had launched the first WESTAR in April of 1974 and RCA was ready to launch its first SATCOM.) Those satellites would literally fly over the expensive land lines and microwave dishes; and they would destroy, at last, the networks' transmission monopoly. (Seeing its own business threatened, AT&T had been lobbying against domestic satellites and delaying their deployment for five years.) Schonfeld told the Coors people, "You've gotta get into satellites," but they wouldn't listen, and TVN kept using the expensive land lines.

He liked Joe Coors, but felt the people working for him were amateurs and fools. They had come from Colorado — the New Yorkers on staff called them "the golden goys" — and they would tell Coors, "Look, if we've got any money left over, let's spend it on beer! At least that's something we *know* about."

Schonfeld knew that this service, too, was doomed.

Pursuing the future of TV news on his own, Schonfeld got in touch with Scientific Atlanta, a leading manufacturer of satellite hardware in Georgia. He needed all the facts and figures he could get. Sid Topol, the company's president, suggested he make a trip; and when Schonfeld flew down, Topol met him at the Atlanta airport and took him over to WTCG for an unscheduled visit with Ted Turner. "I think you guys should talk," he said.

(It would be the first face-to-face meeting between Turner and Schonfeld. In later years, neither Ted Turner nor Sid Topol would remember the brief encounter until reminded of it.)

For Topol, bringing the two men together was a business move. He and Turner had been discussing the fact that the domestic birds were going to be flying soon and that, when it happened, all the rules would change. When Turner could beam a signal up to a satellite and back down to North America, he'd have the potential of reaching cable-television systems around the country. Operators would need to install dishes to *receive* a satellite signal, but then the tiny cable industry would grow at a rapid pace.

In simple business terms, using satellite technology in conjunction with cable TV would be much more cost-effective than building a hundred microwave stations across the nation. Topol knew that Schonfeld had worked out the fee structure for satellite transmission and that he could talk to Turner about the cost. They met for a few minutes in Turner's office.

"I'm gonna put Channel 17 on a satellite and send it all over the country," Turner said. Schonfeld remarked that it would probably cost a million dollars a year to lease a transponder, one of the devices on the bird that was tuned to receive a specific signal and then transmit it back to earth. "You mean," Turner said, "I could reach the whole country for only a million bucks a year?"

"Yeah, but you'd also have to pay for the earth station that sends your signal."

"Yeah, I know. So what? I don't care about that."

"Well," Schonfeld said, "it would cost a million a year."

Turner paced around the room, fired up, and repeated that he was going to distribute his programming by satellite when it became possible to do so. As Schonfeld walked out of the WTCG building with Sid Topol that day, he thought to himself: *What an asshole! Who else in the country would want to watch his dinky television station broadcasting out of Atlanta?*

At TVN, where he was vice-president for operations, Schonfeld continued to press for the creation of a satellite-distribution network. This new way of delivering material to clients was the only alternative, he argued, to the costly land lines that had sunk UPITN domestically and that were sinking TVN deeper into the hole each day. He proposed, specifically, that the company buy receiving dishes — and then rent them to the TV stations, at low rates. But the Coors moneymen refused.

Schonfeld stormed into the TVN office for his final battle and got fired. Convinced that TVN would go down the drain the way the other syndication services had done, he went to his home in Tenafly, New Jersey, and developed a plan of action while waiting for the inevitable.

Meanwhile, two developments in 1975 brought the revolution closer at hand:

Following Western Union's lead with WESTAR I, RCA launched SATCOM I into a geosynchronous orbit above the equator. Here was the satellite by which virtually all TV programming would be transmitted to cable systems in the United States. There would be as many as twenty-four transponders and, already, Home Box Office had leased one of them for transmission of movies.

And the Federal Communications Commission was relaxing its restrictions affecting satellite delivery of news to independent stations. The requirement that passive, receive-only earth stations be ten meters wide or larger was being dropped. For most TV stations those dishes had been too expensive to buy and too bulky to install. So as the FCC allowed smaller receiving stations, the prospects for a syndicated-news network delivered by satellite grew stronger.

On October 1, 1975, when TVN announced it would go out of business in one month, Schonfeld picked up the phone.

He called every independent TV station in the country to round up support for his secret plan. He sent them a prospectus accusing them, with uncommon frankness, of having stood by while every syndicated-news service trying to serve them had gone under: Let's do it differently this time around; let's join together *not for profit.*

They would form a cooperative association which he, Schonfeld, would run from New York. The independent-station people would sit on a board of directors and tell him what they wanted to spend for news; then, they could trust him to spend those amounts and no more.

In the prospectus he quoted Ben Franklin: "We will all hang together or we will hang separately."

Many of the stations, including the New York rivals WNEW and WPIX, expressed interest. The clients would buy earth stations and, for the first time in history, would have an independent news service delivered by domestic satellite. Schonfeld would open a Washington bureau, but basically the service would gather news from each member station and distribute ninety-second packages to the entire group. Any station refusing to pay its bills would be out of the association. If members didn't like something, they could vote against it.

And just maybe, Schonfeld told them, we can stay in business this time.

On October 31, 1975, TVN closed shop.

Three days later, Reese Schonfeld began operating the Independent Television News Association at the WPIX office in the Daily News Building on Forty-second Street, starting off with seven charter members.

When HBO went up on SATCOM I, Ted Turner saw it as akin to the landing of early explorers in a New World; and he followed right behind, to see what parts of the unclaimed territory he could garner for himself. When he called Harold Rice, the RCA Americom vice-president of operations, his vision of both the SuperStation and Cable News Network was already taking shape. He wanted to be assured of not one but *two* transponders on the satellite aimed at cable-system dishes. Of course, the SuperStation would have to come first; without that, there would be no financing for any news channel.

The first discussion took place in late 1975, when Turner

called Rice down to Atlanta. "Ted was considering a distant-signal type arrangement," Rice said, "where he would pick Channel 17 off the air and retransmit it not just to one cable system but to the whole country. He felt this was a new opportunity, and he wanted to lease a transponder. He wanted to get it going very quickly. . . .

"In early 1976," Rice continued, "Ted talked about his long-range business planning. And he said that he had a concept, because radio networks had been very successful with an all-news channel, that this thing could apply also on television. And he had an idea that he wanted, at some point in time, to have an all-news television channel."

Few, if any, of Turner's associates knew about the plan to get involved with news — and over the years, no one except Rice would ever recall that Turner had talked about CNN at such an early stage.

TED TURNER

"I came up with the concept for Cable News Network even before the SuperStation was up on the satellite, because business is like a chess game and you have to look several moves ahead. Most people don't. They only think one move at a time. But any good chess player knows that when you're playing against a one-move opponent, you'll beat him every time.

"That's basically the way the networks were moving. But I've always thought several moves ahead. I pride myself on being able to look into the future and say, What is the future going to look like? What can we do to be at the right spot at the right time?

"Once it's obvious to everybody that something is going to be successful, the opportunity is gone. Then anybody else can do it, too.

"It was clear that after the SuperStation the next important service to the cable industry would be a twenty-four-hour news channel. At that point, however, cable penetration was only at fourteen percent of the TV homes in the country, so it wasn't economically feasible. There weren't enough cable subscribers to underwrite it."

The idea for CNN went to the back burner and Turner moved forward to launch Channel 17 by satellite. He would send his movies and reruns all over the country, but he needed to hold on to his sports to complete the mix. When he began telecasting the Braves games nationwide, advertising sales would soar; but then, he realized, the cost of the TV rights for those games would soar as well. Even worse, the Braves could be sold at any moment. What if they left town? Without the drawing power of baseball, the whole SuperStation concept could be in jeopardy.

Turner went ahead and bought the Atlanta Braves. He offered ten million dollars even though the team was doing poorly; but he arranged to make the first payment by using available funds that already existed in the Braves organization. It was the kind of deal that confirmed Turner's view that life is so fundamentally absurd that anything is possible — you buy something by using the seller's own money, then hurry up and turn it into a profitable venture so it will pay its way in the future. He then bought a controlling interest in the Hawks basketball team, which also might have left town otherwise; and he got the rights to telecast the Atlanta Flames hockey games.

Turner called Sid Topol of Scientific Atlanta and exclaimed, "Hey, Sid, I want to buy a station."

"Another TV station?" Topol said.

"No, I want to buy an *earth* station."

Topol's salesmen went over to Channel 17 and returned to Scientific Atlanta with a check from Turner. It was his down payment for a $750,000 earth station, or "up-link," that would transmit his signal to the RCA satellite. Turner formed a separate "common carrier" company called Southern Satellite Systems; but, he soon discovered, distributing his own product was against federal regulations. So he quickly got out of the carrier business by selling SSS for one dollar to a Western Union fellow named Ed Taylor, who agreed to handle the SuperStation's signal. For his fee, Taylor would collect ten cents per subscriber per month and become a wealthy man virtually overnight.

In Sid Topol's view, the moment that Turner placed his order for an earth station marked the beginning of "postbroadcast television." The satellite-cable linkage would "change everything" from then on.

Terry McGuirk was amazed by it all. Turner was getting involved in all kinds of things, from satellites to baseball, about which he knew little or nothing. But by now McGuirk was aware that Turner did best when he wasn't burdened by too much knowledge. The boss was a quick learner who went out and studied things for himself, if not always *by* himself. So in February of 1976, after they'd bought the Braves, McGuirk wasn't too surprised when Turner walked into his office and said, "Get ready to leave tomorrow morning. We're going down to Florida for spring training. And you're gonna play."

They flew down the next day and walked into the dugout while the team was at practice. Turner threw a uniform at McGuirk, who had been a college athlete, and said, "Put it on and get out on the field." McGuirk did so, and for the next three weeks he played ball with the Braves while Turner sat in the dugout and watched. Whenever McGuirk came back to the bench, he found himself assaulted by questions.

"Why," Turner asked, "did you run to second base? And what the hell is a balk?"

"He'd never done anything with a ball when he was growing up," McGuirk said. "Not even stickball. He had no hand-eye coordination and he really didn't know what was going on, but by watching me and asking questions he could get a picture of how easy or difficult it might be. We had a lot of fun — and by the end of spring training he had a good handle on the game of baseball, before he went on to do many other crazy things."

When Reese Schonfeld read about Ted Turner's new Super-Station he thought, *Well, it proves again what New York can do to you.* In sophisticated cities like New York and Washington, where local TV stations carried ballgames on any given night, it was difficult to remember that most areas had only the three networks. In much of the country you could watch professional basketball or baseball only when a network chose to carry it, which meant maybe one game a week.

I've been in this business, Schonfeld thought, *and I should have known better.*

Turner's move to the satellite had been a brilliant stroke. For those vast, mostly rural areas of the nation deprived of good local stations and home teams, it didn't matter that Channel 17 of Atlanta might be a dinky station. It was offering an alternative to the networks across the American heartland.

*   *   *

Turner hit the campaign trail on behalf of the cable industry, speaking at one convention after another and pouring his own money into promotion. As more homes were being wired, the SuperStation was gaining strength at a rate of 200,000 new homes a month.

To those fellow broadcasters who had turned their backs on cable, Turner was now a dangerous traitor. To the Hollywood establishment he was a Robin Hood, giving away their movies to the masses. To those controlling organized sports, Turner was invading their territory by allowing people all over the country to watch the Braves and Hawks whenever they chose.

Traitor! Thief! Pirate!

Turner loved it . . . and so did the public.

TED TURNER

"The FCC had to change the rules a little bit and now we've got everybody in the world suing us. The networks are scared to death of cable television and now that we're on satellite, they're *really* scared. We're sucking up the market. But NBC, ABC, CBS, the Motion Picture Association of America, the NBA, the baseball commissioner's office, the N.A.B., the BBC, the National Hockey League and an assortment of other people are trying to stop us. Can you imagine that? A little old raggedy station with a hundred employees and a bunch of torn-up furniture is going to destroy television and cause the motion-picture industry to collapse! I'm going to run for President just to stay in business. . . ."

— *Playboy,* August 1978

It wasn't easy for Turner's sales staff to convince major advertisers to climb aboard, mainly because there was still no way of calculating the numbers. Who out there was watching? One way to tell was through direct-response commercial spots; and *Time* magazine quickly discovered that SuperStation viewers all over the country were calling to order subscriptions. Another early advertiser was Bristol-Myers, which offered a consumer booklet and got heavy response.

"I went to the cable shows in the 1970s," said Marvin Koslow of Bristol-Myers, "because I was always frustrated, both as viewer and advertiser, by the fact that we were locked into a monopoly system. You had the three networks, that's all, and good luck to them. That's what you had to deal with. But we kept trying to find another way, an alternative.

"Ted was bright enough to see what the satellite meant. And instead of buying a football team with only sixteen games on the schedule, he bought a baseball team and a basketball team with hundreds of games to televise. Using basically the same franchise money, for the same dough, he got thousands of programming hours!"

In July 1977, Koslow and his family left New York to spend their vacation in northern Idaho. They stayed in a small town with a cable system. It was during that summer, while watching the SuperStation, that Koslow became convinced that Turner was riding the wave of the future. He also became a devoted fan of the Atlanta Braves.

Between the tail end of 1976 and the fall of 1977, Turner had become a big celebrity. At one point he had been suspended by Bowie Kuhn, the baseball commissioner, for prematurely initiating a contract bid for Gary Matthews of the San Francisco Giants. He won the America's Cup and was on the cover of *Sports Illustrated.* He was soaring.

During a convention in the fall of 1977, Turner was the center of attention. He attended the opening cocktail party with a blonde on either side of him as he wisecracked and had a tremendous time for himself. Also in the crowd was Reese Schonfeld, with members of his ITNA board of directors.

"Hey, Reese," one of them urged, "go pitch him! Tell him to join our service! Tell him he needs news!"

Schonfeld waited until Turner was loosened up with a couple of drinks — all it took, apparently, was one or two — and then he waded through the crowd to confront the so-called Mouth of the South. Turner waved his big cigar and grinned at the newsman from New York: "Hey, Reese! How are ya?"

People around them stopped talking to watch and listen.

"I was wondering, Ted, if you wanted to buy some news for your SuperStation."

"News? Aw, Reese, Ah can't do news! Ah got too much *other* product right now. And who wants news, anyway? News is nothing! *Nobody* watches news," Turner went on while Schonfeld thoroughly enjoyed the tirade. "Ain't you *tired* of all that news? Don't it just make you *sick* after watchin' that stuff? Listen, Reese, you know what my motto is? *No news is good news!*"

It was an act to shock and amuse the crowd, Schonfeld knew, as he played his role to the hilt and finally laughed along with everyone else.

As his ITNA service grew, Schonfeld became known in the business as the Electronic News Godfather, whose talent, experience and energy made him the prime candidate to challenge the networks head-on. He had competed successfully on a fraction of the networks' budgets; he had created his own TV news service; and he had been one of the first domestic users of satellites for distribution.

From his newsman's vantage point, he felt the networks had "stolen the birthright" of journalism by becoming an entertainment medium rather than an electronic newspaper. "It used to be that people *paid* for their entertainment," he'd say, "while the news was *supported* by advertising. But networking stole advertising money away from journalists to give free circuses to people!"

So the public watched network entertainment without paying for it. Advertisers threw billions into commercials, while news, near the bottom of the ratings, could not get those dollars. News had to be produced at a loss. The guys who ran the networks and owned the stations liked news only for the prestige it gave them; otherwise, they supplied the least amount of news possible.

Would they break into a popular program for a live report of congressional hearings on Vietnam? Not often. Could they expand their evening newscasts beyond half an hour? In the 1960s, the network-news expansion from fifteen to thirty minutes had been accomplished only after many corporate struggles; and now, opposition from affiliates made the move to forty-five minutes or an hour of news all but impossible.

Schonfeld reveled in surviving in TV news without the patronage of the networks. He and others in the independent field were alone in the news *business*, he felt, while network news employees were taking handouts from rich corporations. So his wildest dream was to have a chance to start up an independent network for news only and knock the Big Three onto their fat, glossy backsides.

The idea of a news service for cable television bounced around New York during the three years since Home Box Office had gone up on satellite. The thinking was to produce *eight* hours of live news, repeated once, each day. Time Inc., through HBO, went to Schonfeld for help in making an in-depth study; and he met with HBO's Gerald Levin, whose name had become synonymous with the satellite revolution and pay cable. But HBO was still struggling to expand, so the company was unprepared to spend the money required to start its own operation for worldwide newsgathering.

Well, Schonfeld said, why not try to do it with our ITNA news feeds? At least as a starting point?

Okay, Levin said, if you can sell us news then maybe we can go ahead.

"I'll talk to my board," Schonfeld said.

But the board members, representing traditional broadcast stations, were not ready to help any cable-TV operation. Why, they argued, should we let HBO take our news material? One member, a Metromedia general manager, vociferously objected on the ground that cable was "the enemy of broadcasting" because it posed a competitive threat to independent stations.

At that moment Schonfeld experienced something of a revelation: Cable might be *his* enemy, but why is it *mine?* He's in the *broadcasting* business, but I'm in the *news* business.

Whether broadcasting or cable did the job, Schonfeld realized, what mattered was informing the public. If the opportunity came, he could be a cable guy.

TED TURNER

"In 1978 I started thinking about a twenty-four-hour news channel again. By then several other services had gotten started, but they were very weakly funded. The cable industry was growing mainly with HBO and the SuperStation and Showtime, which was now in existence. But still no one had tackled news. . . .

"Even though the SuperStation had not really become a success with the advertisers yet, I could see that it was *going* to become a success. In my opinion we were going to be successful selling cable advertising — and without that, you couldn't have afforded the vast programming expenses that were gonna be necessary to do an all-news channel. That's why no one else had stepped forward.

"The easiest way would have been for one of the three networks to do it, but they didn't want to undermine their affiliate system. And it still wasn't clear that cable was going to be a success. They didn't *want* it to become successful. They loved having just a three-channel environment."

Terry McGuirk began to see another Turner phenomenon at work. In the spring of 1978, while sailing with Turner, he heard him talking to the crew: "What would you guys think if you could turn on your TV any time of the day or night and find out what's happening in the world?" On land, too, Turner was walking up to people to get feedback. When they rode in cabs, he would unload on the drivers; and soon the questions were becoming statements and even leaning toward sales pitches: "Don't you think an all-news TV channel would be terrific?"

Turner argued to McGuirk that news was "really in the Dark Ages compared to movies, sports and general programming" and that it was plain that news would be "the next great cable service."

"He was looking for a negative, for what might be wrong with his idea," McGuirk said. "We were as far away from a news-delivery system as you could get, so he was always willing to give it up to one of the major companies. If a big corporation was going to do it, we had no business getting in there. We were too small."

In Gerry Hogan's view, for Turner to get into news would be "as if some little company making seat belts suddenly decided to build a revolutionary new automobile that would change the face of transportation." In other words, a joke.

But by now, after trying to sell everyone else on his idea, Turner had sold himself.

DON LACHOWSKY

"I was vice-president of advertising for the SuperStation and my office was right next to Ted's. This was even before he began to call us by our first names. He yelled, 'Lachowsky! Get a yellow pad and come in here!' I said to myself, 'Oh, boy, what now?' So I grabbed a pad and went in. He said, 'I'm gonna do a twenty-four-hour news network. Write this down.' I'm writing it all down and he says, 'I'll tell you what it's gonna be. It's gonna be a half hour of news, like *Time* magazine. Then a half hour of sports, like *Sports Illustrated*. Then another half hour, of features, like *People* magazine. And a half hour of business news like *Fortune*. We're gonna repeat it every two hours, twenty-four hours a day.' That was his original thinking on it. He said, 'We're gonna do this half-hour format and freshen it up every two hours.'"

As word flew around the WTCG offices, many of Turner's employees became worried. The only news on the SuperStation was being shown at three o'clock in the morning, produced by R. T. Williams and hosted by an amiable, talented young man named Bill Tush. It was an inspired spoof of the news, along the lines of *Saturday Night Live* but totally original. At times, Tush would host the news with a German shepherd as his co-anchor. The dog, wearing a shirt and tie, chewed a mouthful of peanut butter and seemed to be reading wire copy. One time Tush delivered the news with a large photograph of Walter Cronkite's face held in front of his own face. During another newscast, Tush interviewed porn queen Marilyn Chambers, who started undressing him.

"Let's go now to the Unknown Newsman," Tush would say, as the scene shifted to a videotaped report from downtown Atlanta, where a reporter holding a microphone stood with a paper bag over his head.

So the salespeople did not think they could convince anyone that Ted Turner might be serious about news. The winds of mutiny began to stir, and an anonymous sign appeared on Turner's desk:

> PLEASE, TED!
> DON'T DO THIS TO US!
> IF YOU COMMIT TO A VENTURE OF THIS SIZE
> YOU'LL SINK THE WHOLE COMPANY!

Turner walked in, sat behind his desk and found himself staring at the sign. Whoever had drawn it up was right about the risk, because a round-the-clock national news operation would be a money-gobbling monster. It could easily drain all of the company's resources and still be hungry before it became self-sufficient, if it ever did. Everything could be lost: the Super-Station, the Charlotte station, the Braves, the Hawks, everything down the drain.

He left the sign right there, as if daring the naysayers to make him lose his nerve.

By the fall of 1978, Reese Schonfeld had heard rumors that Turner was talking about a cable news network. On this day he heard the same story from a friend who said, "You'd better go down there and talk to him."

"Hell, no," Schonfeld said, laughing it off. "Why should I talk to Turner? I *know* Turner. I pitch him every year! He says he *hates* news. He'll *never* do news."

"No, you should call him. I hear he's hot on this."

"Ah, I just don't believe it. No way."

"Why not give him a ring and *ask* him?"

Schonfeld stared at the phone in his New York office. He formed a mental picture of Ted Turner at the conventions, grinning and puffing on his cigar — with the babes staring up at him, the crowds gathered around — and launching into one of those funny diatribes against news.

No way would he make that call.

TERRY MCGUIRK

"It was about eight-thirty in the morning. Ted took me into his office and I sat there with him for two or three hours. And he just talked himself through it. 'Am I crazy?' he said. 'Why am I doing this? To make a go of it I'll have to commit $100 million! Have I totally lost my mind?' He slowly worked himself down, dissecting all of his thoughts. He was like a computer, chopping away at the problems and reanalyzing everything. He just threw all the cards up and redealt the whole hand again. As he worked through it, he answered all the questions and kept coming up with the same answers. So when he got to the bottom, he started working himself back up. I had said hardly anything during the entire time, but it was probably the most momentous thing that ever had occurred between us. Then he burst open the door and went running down the hall, pumping everybody up about it."

Having little or no background in news, Turner knew he needed a professional. He needed someone with experience — but outside the Big Three networks, each of which was spending $100 to $150 million a year on news operations. A guy from one of those news departments would probably think a twenty-four-hour service should cost even more! Turner needed to set up and run his own operation on far less. He called a friend, in charge of programming at the Cox stations, and put the question: Who would be the best person to hire? The answer was Reese Schonfeld, who was running his independent news outfit from New York on a shoestring budget.

Turner made the call.

"Can it be done?"

It could be done, Schonfeld thought, if they built an all-electronic newsroom, its systems tied together by computer, with row upon row of videotape editing machines. It could be done with a staff of three hundred, the bulk of the people at headquarters in Atlanta and the others mainly in domestic bureaus. They needed offices in New York, Washington, Chicago, Dallas and Los Angeles, at the very least. It could be done if they went outside the unions. It could be done if they contracted for international news feeds, while making exchange agreements with local stations as a way of getting access to coverage of breaking events across the country. It could be done if they devised a format to fill twenty-four hours each day and made a commitment to "go live" as much as possible.

It could be done, he felt, if they spent $15 to $20 million before launch and then a couple of million bucks each month to keep operating — but those figures were only guesswork. Turner would have to be patient, and hold on, for at least two or three years; he had to be willing to reach into his pockets for perhaps $100 million or more, until cable subscriptions and advertising fees began to cover expenses. And then, if they survived, Turner would need to put every nickel of revenue back into the news-gathering operation so it could expand and improve with more and more bureaus, not only in the United States but in various parts of the world. . . .

If they used satellites, for both incoming material and outgoing transmission, and if Turner's primary motive was to build the best damn news service the world had ever seen, the answer was yes.

"Do you want to do it?"

Are you kidding?

"I flew down to see him the week after our phone conversation. It was November 1978. He was gonna take me out to the plantation for the night, bring in the broads and really woo me — but he didn't have to, and he realized that, so he picked me up at the airport himself, drove me in, drove me back.

"It was a wooing process, but I was too easy.

"His opening line to me, and I always thought it was the most brilliant thing he ever said, was, 'There are only four things that television does, Reese. There's movies — and HBO has that. There's sports — and now ESPN's got that, unfortunately. There's the regular series kinda stuff — and the networks do that. All that's left is news!' Then he said, 'To show you how committed I am — you got a name for it?' No, I said, I haven't thought of anything.

"He said, 'Well, I'm not even gonna put my own *name* on this. I'm gonna call it Cable News Network! Not the Turner News Network — the *Cable* News Network.'

"And he had it all worked out. I had done the format and a budget for it, before going down there — it was all handwritten and I didn't even leave it with him. And we both understood that I was a free agent. We were just two grown men talking about an idea.

"But right in his office, he picked up the phone and pitched Russell Karp, who was then head of the largest cable company, Teleprompter, and he called Gerry Levin of Time Inc. He would make them each one-third partners, right then and there. Karp said no. Levin said he didn't think so. He'd have to do it by himself."

Turner paced around his office.

"The union situation in Georgia is easier," he said.

"I know," Schonfeld said.

"Can we do it here in Atlanta?"

"Yes," Schonfeld said, "but it would mean having to have a lot of our own satellite dishes."

Turner's eyes lit up, as if he could already envision an entire "satellite farm" of earth stations pointed at the sky.

"How many?" he asked.

"Seven," Schonfeld said.

"Is that all?"

"Six for incoming feeds from six different satellites —"

"Yeah —"

"And one more dish to send everything back out."

"Awwright!" Turner exclaimed.

Schonfeld discovered that Turner already had ordered a bunch of film chains and two-inch videotape machines. "Cancel 'em, Ted," Schonfeld said, "because we're not gonna use film and we want only three-quarter-inch machines. And a few one-inchers." Their news operation could use smaller tape now that the technology was being improved.

"How many three-quarter-inch machines?"

"Maybe two dozen," Schonfeld said, greatly underestimating the number of editing machines that would be necessary.

Turner called Gene Wright's extension. "Gene," he shouted, "are those two-inch machines cancelable?"

"Yes," came Wright's voice.

"Okay. Cancel all the two-inch machines! Reese says we need three-quarter-inch machines and some one-inchers! Can you order 'em?"

"Yup," Wright said.

"Good. Order twenty-four machines!"

Schonfeld was impressed. Turner could pick up the phone, call his chief engineer and simply say, "Do it." And the guy at the other end would go and do it, no questions asked. That was independence, that was control. No bureaucracy, no voting by any board of directors; just quick decision-making by one man and, no matter what the price tag, instant action.

Turner brought up the subject of getting well-known personalities as news anchors.

"I believe in stars," he said.

"So do I," Schonfeld said.

"Who's the biggest guy we could get?"

Schonfeld wondered whether it would be possible to get Dan Rather, who was supposedly in line to succeed Walter Cronkite as anchor of the *CBS Evening News*. For Rather, going with CNN would be a chance to be part of history-in-the-making, the way it had been for his hero, Edward R. Murrow. What's more, Schonfeld knew, Rather was angry at CBS for the way the network had been treating him. Maybe, by some wild accident of good timing, he would jump. What a coup it would be! To steal Dan Rather from CBS News!

"Well," he said, "I think the biggest guy would be Dan Rather."

Ted Turner stared back, his face blank.

"Who's Dan Rather?"

Now it was Schonfeld's turn to stare.

He explained who Dan Rather was.

"Okay," Turner said. "How much could we get him for?"

"Oh, a million dollars a year."

"A million bucks? Just to read the news?"

"Yeah," Schonfeld said. "That's what you'd have to pay him."

"Well, hell," Turner exclaimed, "I just offered Pete Rose a million dollars to play for the Braves, and he only works *half* the year."

It was all great, heady stuff, as Schonfeld rode with Turner back to the airport. On the plane he closed his eyes and heard that booming voice, over and over:

"Who's Dan Rather? . . . Who's Dan Rather? . . ."

The Western Cable Show in early December 1978 was held in Anaheim, California. Nearly two thousand cable-system operators gathered together in an upbeat mood over how their industry was growing. The hot topic at convention headquarters in the Disneyland Hotel was the explosion of interest in pay-cable programming delivered by satellite: Viacom's service, Showtime, was expanding its entertainment lineup; and Home Box Office now claimed two million TV homes subscribing to its movie offerings.

So far, cable penetration was estimated by A. C. Nielsen Company at about thirteen million, or eighteen percent of all television homes in the country. There was a long way to go, but the pace was accelerating.

In walked Ted Turner with his revolutionary idea for cable news. . . .

By now his Atlanta programming was being put out by cable systems in forty-five states, reaching nearly two million homes on a twenty-four-hour basis. The SuperStation was available, through Ed Taylor's common carrier, to any system wanting to pick it up from the satellite and rebroadcast it via cable. Turner was making his money from advertisers, charging them a modified national rate that was about thirty percent lower (in terms of cost-per-thousand viewers) than that of the networks.

With him at the convention was Terry McGuirk, holding the contracts for Cable News Network. They had decided to offer CNN at fifteen cents per subscriber per month. It was the only way CNN could survive; but even then, Turner had concluded, they needed a commitment of up to eight million of those subscribers. That would amount to a base revenue of $1.2 million each month, probably $800,000 short of covering CNN's monthly operating expenses. The balance would come from Turner's own pocket and, gradually, from advertisers.

Turner went before the board of the National Cable Television Association early in the convention week. The board members were entrepreneurs, like Turner himself; they were not, as cable operators would become in the next decade, corporate types with MBAs after their names. They were still "wearing red polyester" and they saw Turner as one of their own.

So he approached the assembled board members expecting their support despite any reservations they might have. He was counting on their faith — if not in what he was proposing, per se, then in him. He wanted them to heed the words of his own favorite slogan: "Either lead, follow or get out of the way!"

TERRY MCGUIRK

"We go off to the board with a contract and a letter that says we want them to commit to this. We said we needed a commitment of seven-and-a-half-million subs and, when we got to that point, we would do it.

"Ted stands up and tells them what we're up to — wham, wham, wham — and it's about three minutes. I hand out the contracts. Ted says, 'Please sign and we're off with the Cable News Network!' And the guys started chuckling and laughing: 'Do you mind if we *read* the contract, Ted?' He got them high on the idea, but they wouldn't sign right then. We literally couldn't do anything unless they put the CNN service on their cable systems. These guys were the leaders of the cable industry and they had to say, 'Okay, Ted, we endorse this. If you do it, we'll back you.' But they didn't believe he could do it."

"The risk to you guys is very limited," Turner was telling the board members. "We're not asking you to put up capital to do it. We just want your support for us to do it ourselves. I'm gonna sell off my station in Charlotte and use the money to finance this myself. For CNN we're gonna have maybe five hundred employees and fifty offices all over the world. Give me your support now and we'll start up in one year."

The launch date he gave was January 1, 1980.

"We're just asking you to agree, now, and if it doesn't work, we'll go out of business and you can quit without paying us. If it *does* work, your liability is still limited to fifteen cents a month for each subscriber.

"Anyway, this all-news network is exactly what the cable industry needs right now, and, uh, Terry? The contracts, please. We have letters of commitment for you to sign, so let's just pass 'em around. . . ."

They were falling over with laughter as McGuirk distributed the commitment letters and contracts.

"If you want to read it, go ahead," Turner said. "*Take* a minute or two, but I need an answer before you walk out of here."

"Can we have a couple of days?" someone asked.

"Well, I really can't wait. I need to know at least before the convention is over."

"Why don't we talk to you on Thursday," another guy said.

Having to wait until near the end of the convention went against Turner's style. He seldom, if ever, waited to make a decision, and he certainly never waited when faced with a choice like the one he was asking *them* to make. He, not they, would be taking the lion's share of the risk. But it was clear, for the moment, that they were neither leading nor following nor, for that matter, getting out of the way.

At the convention was Roy Mehlman, a thirty-five-year veteran of United Press International who was known as "Mr. News" of cable television. Just the previous summer, he had launched *Newstime,* the industry's first and only "slo-scan" service, delivered round-the-clock by satellite. *Newstime* used still photos along with audio voice-overs. As each photograph appeared on the screen, it dissolved from left to right; and during this "slo-scan" a narrator's voice had eight seconds to give the news that the picture represented.

Mehlman was well aware that Turner had been trying to drum up support for a news operation directly challenging the Big Three networks. It would mean a giant leap forward, beyond anything that television had ever done, and it would instantaneously relegate Mehlman's own slo-scan service to the horse-and-buggy era of cable news.

"How's it going?" Mehlman asked him.

"Well, Roy, I'm still waiting. What's your opinion? You think they're gonna do it?"

"No," Mehlman said, "I don't think so."

"Why?"

"I think you're charging too much."

"What are you talkin' about!" Turner said. "You charge five cents and what you've got is diddly-shit!" When Mehlman shrugged, Turner looked at him intently and said, "Listen, Roy, when I fly, you'll fly with me."

"Ted," Mehlman said, "when you fly a *lot* of people are gonna fly with you."

At this Western show, nobody flew with him. A few cable systems signed letters of commitment, but the figures were minuscule. At the convention it was said that cable TV was at a stage similar to that of movies in 1910 and television in 1950, but William Donnelly of Young & Rubicam (later a big supporter of CNN) knocked the idea of a news channel by saying it would be a drag on cable's credibility among advertisers.

Ted Turner, carrying the future in his head and empty contracts under his arm, returned to Atlanta.

"Hi, Ted."

"Hey, Reese, how're you doing?"

"I'm fine. How did it go?"

"Not well."

"Are we gonna go ahead?"

"Not for now. We gotta put it on hold."

"Okay, thanks. 'Bye, Ted."

Now that Ted Turner had floated the idea, potential players were buzzing around; and just as Turner himself had done, they were going to Reese Schonfeld because they saw him as the one man who could make it happen.

People from Scripps-Howard called Schonfeld, as did Joel Chaseman of Post-Newsweek. It was Chaseman who had led New York's WINS radio into its highly successful all-news format back in the 1960s; and now, as Post-Newsweek's corporate president under publisher Katherine Graham, Chaseman wanted to be first with all-news television.

"We're doing it," Chaseman told Schonfeld on the phone. "I'd like to put you on hold, Reese. Don't do it for anybody else until we've had a chance to talk to you."

For Schonfeld it was suddenly a great, wonderful time. He placed another call to Atlanta.

"Ted, other people are beginning to come in. They're starting to talk about this. What are you doing about it?"

"Still thinking."

"I don't think you can wait too long."

"I'll be getting back to ya."

Schonfeld reluctantly signed his ITNA contract in late January of 1979. It stipulated that he could not engage in the planning of any competing TV-news operation. The contract was retroactive, so it would be in effect for another nine months — until November. If Schonfeld wanted to help someone create a cable news service, he would have to do it secretly.

Turner was under increasing pressure to act.

RCA Americom had already announced its plans to launch another satellite, SATCOM III. The new bird would have twenty-four transponders entirely dedicated to cable, but most were already spoken for. Turner had obtained the legal right to lease a transponder back in 1976, but now cable-industry needs were exploding. He would have to exercise his option soon. Or the Cable News Network would have no satellite and, therefore, no means of transmitting its news.

So he took the first step in April 1979, by putting his Charlotte station, WRET, publicly up for sale. He would need the proceeds to help pay for the Cable News Network. In his mind, the launching of CNN was already certain; the only question was when.

He also went to Washington, D.C., to fight for the survival of his SuperStation, which would carry most of CNN's financial burden. Proposed changes in regulations would limit the power of stations to send programming to distant signals; and the biggest target was WTCG, which Turner felt would be "wiped out" if new restrictions went through.

At a news conference in the Hotel Madison, he announced a

greater commitment to "public service and discussions of significant issues" on the SuperStation and again lashed out at the three major networks: "They've had thirty years to improve the quality of television and they haven't done it yet! They need competition to make them better, and I promise to provide that competition!"

Turner accused the networks, along with broadcasters and Hollywood interests, of attempting to thwart the distribution technology that had made his SuperStation possible. He compared the alliance against him to the Mafia. In effect, he was saying, "Hey, you guys made the rules and I've been living by 'em. Now you want to change 'em again? Over my dead body!"

At the same news conference, he brought up the subject of his proposed Cable News Network. But he did not know when CNN would be launched.

FRANK BEATTY

"I was vice-president for UPI broadcast services based in Chicago when, one fine day, I discovered Scripps-Howard Broadcasting was going to do a news channel for cable. UPI Broadcasting was going to provide all of the source material for them — news, audio, pictures — and we'd have a big piece of the action.

"Then I saw in the trades a very small story that a guy named Ted Turner was gonna maybe start an all-news channel. I'd never heard of him, because I'd been in Hong Kong and elsewhere, and I'd never heard of the SuperStation. It didn't seem very credible that this Turner would do a news operation, but I went down to talk to him. I figured he's gonna have to buy a whole bunch of services and it ought to be UPI that sells it to him.

"I talked to his assistant, Dee Woods, and said I'd like to talk to Mr. Turner about his all-news channel. Within about five minutes he was on the phone. I said, 'I'd like to come see you.' He said, 'When?' I said, 'Well, how about Tuesday of next week?' He says, 'Great, great.'

"But when I got to Atlanta, something had happened. I went to see Ted and he was terribly distracted. He said, 'Can you come back in a few days?' I said, 'Yeah, if you're serious about doing this thing.' He was very upset. . . ."

Turner had just learned that Bill Lucas, vice-president of the Atlanta Braves, had suffered a massive brain hemorrhage. Under

Turner's ownership of the team, Lucas had become the highest-ranking black official in professional baseball, serving as director of player personnel but, in effect, acting as general manager and handling most of the trades and contract negotiations.

Turner became angry at the sheer suddenness of it all. How could a young, strong guy in full health, a former athlete, just collapse without warning? Lucas had been complaining of pains in his chest and arms for about a month, but a team doctor had repeatedly found nothing suspicious. Now, in a flash, at age forty-three, he was dying. Bill Lucas's life was almost over and its abrupt ending made no sense. The only way to *make* sense out of a tragedy like this was to recognize its absurdity.

"Death is inevitable," Turner had told an interviewer. "The first thing you've got to do is face the fear of dying, because that's the ultimate fear when you come right down to it — the fear of dying."

The truth, he felt, was that we are all living in an amusement park filled with scary rides and surprises, with funhouses and distorting mirrors — and when Bill Lucas suddenly lay on his deathbed, for Turner the rides started to fly around and the mirrors began to reflect that crazy, ephemeral quality of life which had forced him to keep moving so fast on the edge where it was so easy to fall if he looked backward or down.

The time to take action had come.

In New York, Schonfeld took the call.

"Hey, Reese! Do you know what happened today to Bill Lucas?"

"No. What happened?"

"He's got a hemorrhage! He's gonna die! And guess what? *None* of us is gonna live forever! So listen, Reese, let's *do* this thing! With or *without* support!"

Now it was real. Schonfeld called Post-Newsweek. He owed Joel Chaseman at least the courtesy of letting him know he was no longer "on hold" for him; but Chasemen was away on vacation. *Well,* Schonfeld thought, *I've met my obligation. I made the call.* Once again he booked a flight to Atlanta.

Bill Lucas died on Saturday, May 5, 1979, and Schonfeld arrived in Atlanta on the day of the funeral.

When he and Turner had lunch at the Stadium Club the day

after, he made it clear that his ITNA contract might force him to operate incognito for several months. "I might not be available until November, and until then I'll have to do this without anybody finding out, because —"

"Aw, Reese, you can work it out! I'll get my lawyer, Tench Coxe, and he'll find a way! Hey, ain't this wonderful?"

Turner's enthusiasm was infectious. He produced a contract in the form of a blue piece of paper, and Schonfeld, unable to resist, signed it on the spot. Then they left the Stadium Club and Turner sped Schonfeld over to the WTCG building to introduce his employees to the newsman from New York. Any intention of keeping a low profile was suddenly a lost cause. Turner, about as happy as a man could be, waved the blue paper over his head and shouted, "I want y'all to meet Reese Schonfeld, here, who has just signed up with the Cable News Network! He's gonna be the president of CNN! And I'm gonna be the most powerful man in America!" Turner paused, looking at Schonfeld, and said, "The *two* of us." Everybody laughed.

Later, in his office, Turner explained that in a few weeks he would go out to Las Vegas to attend the National Cable Television Association convention; and this time, he would not go in there begging. He would tell the board of directors that he was moving ahead full tilt. In fact, he would hold a press conference announcing to the world that CNN would be launched in one year.

The startup date would be June 1, 1980, come hell or high water. But this time, Turner would lead, and the cable operators could do one of two things: either follow or get out of the way.

"We'll both go to the convention," Turner said, "and —"

"I don't know if I can," Schonfeld said.

"You *have* to be there!"

"Well, my ITNA contract —"

"The hell with 'em, Reese! Now, listen, what big name can we get right away, to go out there with us?"

Schonfeld said he would explore the possibilities. Among them was Daniel Schorr, the former CBS News correspondent. "He's doing stuff for me now at ITNA," Schonfeld said, referring to commentaries by Schorr for syndication, "but he's free-lance and available."

"Well, Reese, let's get him!"

Schonfeld was pleased by the thought of having Dan Schorr

come aboard. If Turner was still regarded as the Mouth of the South, then Schorr's liberal reputation would balance things out. With Schorr in place, nobody in the news business would question CNN's integrity. In terms of the image presented to the journalism community, Turner and Schorr could be "matching bookends" while he, Schonfeld, would stand between them.

R. T. Williams, in the production department, was kind of dumbfounded by the whole idea of a news network. For the longest time, over two or three years, he had been hearing Turner talk about doing a *sports* network. Williams and his group at WTCG had built up a fairly large production arm, with crews covering golf tournaments and, of course, the Braves games. And they'd kicked around the idea of an all-sports network as a natural extension. Turner had seemed interested, although he'd remarked that sports would not have as much "credibility" as news. *Maybe*, Williams thought, *he still wants to run for president. All of a sudden, no more sports network. Now we're going to do news. Things happen pretty fast around here.*

It was nearly seven-thirty in the evening and the building was almost empty when Turner came by with the new CNN president and said, "Okay, Reese, R.T. will take care of ya. He'll get you a cab to the airport. You guys talk. See ya."

Turner strode off, leaving Schonfeld to stand there at the door. The man seemed overwhelmed, from being in Turner's whirlwind. Williams and Schonfeld looked at each other. "Hi, uh, let me give you a card," Schonfeld stammered. He pulled out his wallet and the contents, more than two hundred name cards and credit cards and slips of paper, cascaded to the floor. Schonfeld bent down to pick them up, but as soon as he'd gathered a bunch he dropped them again. And again. Williams, watching all this, figured that if Schonfeld were a drinking man he'd be smashed by the time his plane landed in New York. *I wonder*, Williams thought, *if he knows what he's in for.*

Welcome to the zoo, pal.

Burt Reinhardt in California got the news from Schonfeld in New York. "It's a dream come true," he said, wondering, *How often in anyone's lifetime comes the chance to start something like this from the ground floor?* Reinhardt couldn't wait to leave Paramount and get started.

All during May, until the convention that month, Schonfeld kept slipping out of his ITNA office to go make secret calls from the lobby of the Daily News Building. He enlisted the help of a friend, Stan Burke, who could line up talent.

"We need names," Schonfeld and Turner had agreed, so Burke got hold of people like Phyllis Schlafly and Bella Abzug to do commentaries for $15,000 a year.

Schonfeld made a deal with Dan Schorr's agent, Richard Leibner, and Schorr agreed to make the trip out to Las Vegas to meet Turner before the press conference announcing Cable News Network. Meanwhile, Schonfeld found himself in a major battle with ITNA's directors over whether he himself could go to Vegas. The board members were in an uproar, wanting him to avoid all association with Turner until his contract expired. Some of them were being as difficult and unpleasant as they could be, while Turner was urging Schonfeld on the phone to go out to the convention no matter what.

"Well, Ted, if they sue for breach of contract, it'll be your money they go after. I don't *have* a lot of money."

"We'll sue 'em back!"

In the end, by a narrow margin, the ITNA board approved Schonfeld's trip. The deciding vote had been cast by a man who wanted to get rid of him. *He's my enemy,* Schonfeld thought, smiling to himself, *but I really should thank him.*

FRANK BEATTY

"Bob Page, the general manager of UPI, was involved in Scripps-Howard's project for a cable news service. The two of us went to meet with this Turner guy in his office and he gets a call from Norman Lear, the producer of *All in the Family.* On the speaker phone, Lear was raising hell with him because he was carrying *All in the Family* over the SuperStation — which made it tough for Lear's salesmen to sell it to local stations. When the conversation was over, Ted turned to us and said, 'See? Norman Lear phones *me.* Are you guys impressed?' We said yeah, we were impressed.

"He started talking about his Cable News Network. He was going out to Vegas to announce it, and he said, 'You believe I'm gonna do it, right?' Bob and I said yeah, we do. He said, 'Okay, let's talk about who's gonna help me do it. How about you guys?'

"I was a little shocked, because we were down there to sell

him on UPI — but he was selling *us* to come work for *him*. Bob was in line to become president of UPI, so he said, 'Look, Frank, I can't do it, but why don't you? It would be a chance to be in on the ground floor of this thing. What have you got to lose? If it doesn't work, you can always come back to UPI.'

"Before making that decision, I was obligated to go back to Scripps-Howard and report to them about my meetings with Ted Turner. I said, 'You guys ought to get together with him, because you've got the news sources and he has the cable industry behind him,' but they wouldn't talk to him.

"I called Ted and he says, 'They don't believe I'm gonna do it? Well, I'm going to the cable convention in Las Vegas.'

"I said I'd keep trying to get Scripps-Howard to call him, but anyhow I'd see him out there. . . ."

DAN SCHORR

"I had some trouble understanding what it was about. I knew, at that point, nothing about cable. I had trouble grasping what it was. So I asked Reese a lot of questions and he went back to Ted for the answers. Finally he said that Ted couldn't answer them one at a time like that, but if I could come out to Vegas and spend a few hours we could talk directly.

"As it happened, I was supposed to give a lecture in the Los Angeles area the night before Ted's press conference. I was flying out on Sunday. And Reese, who seemed very hot to get me aboard CNN, called to say that he'd fly out to California with me. He flew from New York to Washington to get on the same plane from Dulles, so we could talk on the way out. Oddly enough, after he'd gone through all that trouble, we didn't sit together because I'd been booked in first class and there were no other seats available up there.

"So we got to Los Angeles on Sunday afternoon. We walked a lot and talked and then he said, 'I want you to meet an old friend of mine.' He introduced me to Burt Reinhardt. It was clear that he was also bringing Burt along on this venture. . . ."

Schonfeld knew that Schorr wanted a job. His main concern was to have him appear at the press conference in Vegas on Monday afternoon. If Turner was going to be taken seriously this time, he needed to show physical proof. The following morning Schonfeld would fly with Schorr to Las Vegas and deliver him in person.

Dan Schorr had earned a reputation as one of the toughest reporters on television. While working for the *New York Times* in 1953, covering a disastrous flood in the Netherlands, his work came to the attention of Edward R. Murrow, who invited him to join his famous team of CBS correspondents. Schorr first covered the State Department and then, in 1955, he opened the CBS bureau in Moscow. He arranged Nikita Khrushchev's first TV appearance (on *Face the Nation*) from the Kremlin; and after defying Soviet censorship, he was arrested by the KGB and expelled from the country. Later he covered stories all over the world before returning to Washington and becoming, as Walter Cronkite told CBS viewers, "our senior Watergate correspondent."

Schorr found himself on President Nixon's "enemies" list, which most newsmen at the time would have preferred over winning an Emmy Award, although he also had received three of those.

In 1976, after a quarter century as national and foreign correspondent, he resigned from CBS News in the midst of an historic confrontation with Congress over freedom of the press. When Schorr disclosed a secret report on CIA and FBI covert activities, in defiance of House rules, CBS suspended him pending the results of an investigation. Subpoenaed by the Ethics Committee, he refused to reveal his source, saying it would "dry up many future sources for many future reporters" and "betray myself, my career and my life."

Afterward, feeling that CBS had not backed him strongly enough, he declined an offer from the network to return.

Schorr, now sixty-three, had married at fifty. He and his wife, with their two children, had settled into a house in the Cleveland Park section of Washington. For the three years since his resignation from CBS, he had been covering Washington as a syndicated newspaper columnist and commentator on National Public Radio, as well as doing reports for ITNA. At this point in his life Daniel Schorr might pass up an offer to help start a new network for Ted Turner, with whom he had nothing in common aside from a personal streak of nonconformity; but that streak, along with the chance for a new career, happened to be what Reese Schonfeld was counting on.

The National Cable Television Association opened its thirty-first annual convention on May 20, 1979, in Las Vegas, with more than a thousand delegates on hand. Ted Turner arrived on Sunday evening with his own group from Atlanta.

DAN SCHORR

"The next morning Reese and I flew to Vegas. We checked in and went up to see Ted and a peculiar thing happened. Reese sat there and said nothing! And Ted kept looking at Reese. I don't think Ted exactly knew who I was. He only knew that Reese had said I was very important.

"Later I learned that the situation had to do with the fact that Reese was still under contract with ITNA. He had to be there but *not* be there. So I was negotiating with Ted alone. It amounted to a series of questions on my part, just trying to find out what this guy was about.

"I knew nothing about him other than what I'd read in *Time* magazine, about him having won the America's Cup and becoming very drunk, and that he had started a SuperStation, the nature of which I did not understand — bouncing a signal from a small station to a satellite and then to a lot of cable systems, none of which I had ever seen.

"But I *had* been told that one of the things he did on his station was a kind of lampoon of the news. So I was really bothered about why I would join this guy's news operation, if he was making *fun* of the news.

"Turner explained to me, however, that this was gonna be serious. It would be an *all*-news network and I'd have a serious role in it. He didn't really care what my role would be. I could define that for myself. He just wanted me on board.

"I kept expressing misgivings. 'Would you want me to read commercials?' I asked. 'No,' he said. I asked a lot of questions like that, but he didn't have a real idea about any of those things. He just wanted me. So he finally said, 'Look, I have a news conference at four o'clock this afternoon, at which I'm going to announce that starting June first of next year I'm going to start the operation of Cable News Network. If you will appear with me, if you want to work with me, let's sign something, *anything,* and I want you to go to the press conference with me. If you can't decide between now and four o'clock, there's no point in the whole thing.' He made it clear that what he really wanted was to have me at the press conference.

"We wrote a letter of agreement. He would pay a substantial amount of money just for my name, well before going on the air. And when I said, 'I don't want to have to do anything I don't *want* to do,' he said, 'Write that down and I'll sign it.' We agreed that I would not be required to perform any assignment that I felt went against my own journalistic standards. I must say, it was a contract clause I've never had before or since.

"He was a bundle of energy. He never stopped moving, almost with an animal quality, like a tiger, never *not* in motion. And he was distracted — a lot of balls in the air, a lot of phone calls, lots of ducking in and out of the suite. It was clear that he was leaving the content and substance of the operation to Reese.

"And as I sat there, I began to realize that here was a new generation of entrepreneur, a new kind of tycoon, and I began to have more respect for him in person than I'd had from reading about him. It occurred to me that Ted Turner was today's version of Bill Paley.

"Back in the late 1920s and early 1930s, as he was founding CBS, Paley had combined three elements — a knowledge of programming, skill as an entrepreneur and an awareness of the state of communications at the time. He had this idea to take some radio stations and put them together, and he called it a network! So I looked at this guy, Turner, and saw that he understood what satellites could deliver. He understood cable and its potential. He had some idea of what kind of programming he wanted to put on: 'If something's going on anywhere,' he said, 'we're gonna bring it right in live. People want to see it happening in front of their eyes.' Very bright. And, finally, he was a businessman.

"So he was doing right now what Bill Paley had done, by joining the knowledge of those key elements."

For the press conference they agreed on a number of different items to be announced. One was that Schonfeld would take over as president of CNN by the first of November at the latest; and, of course, they had Dan Schorr in person to confirm his two-year contract as senior Washington correspondent. Among additional "commentators" signed up were political columnists

Roland Evans and Robert Novak, astrologer Jean Dixon, psychologist Joyce Brothers and medical columnist Neil Solomon.

Altogether they would have fifty staffers acting as anchors or reporters or other types of newscasters appearing on the air. By the launch date of June 1, 1980, just over a year from then, there would be two hundred or more CNN employees working in up to ten bureaus across the country, with "overseas sources" around the world.

Schonfeld had listened to Turner's original idea for a format broken down into four parts — news, sports, soft features and financial stuff — run on a repeating but updated basis; and he had replied, "Well, Ted, I think the format has to be more flexible, to accommodate more breaking news, more live coverage, more up-to-the-minute news. Our thing is gonna be our ability to be there first, to show it on the air before anyone else."

Turner had agreed, so the format Schonfeld was about to announce was rather vague, allowing for all sorts of innovations over the coming months. He could tell the reporters, however, that the "heart" of CNN's day would be a two-hour newscast from eight to ten o'clock at night, Eastern Time. This would amount to "counterprogramming" against the Big Three networks in dramatic fashion, because it would attempt to draw viewers away from the most popular shows in prime time.

Also, they would put on a half hour of sports news at 11 P.M., Eastern Time, just when local broadcast stations were doing their late-edition newscasts: another strategic countermove.

The rest, in Schonfeld's mind, was loose. Financial news and weather would be covered, regionally and nationally. They would give news of the Olympic Games next year and cover the 1980 presidential campaigns. This was to be a *national* network, not a local one — because, for one thing, most cable operators had no capacity to produce local inserts.

Turner had his own announcements to make. Cable systems already carrying the SuperStation would be charged fifteen cents per subscriber per month, but others would have to pay twenty cents. Turner wanted CNN to be a "basic" cable service, coming into homes as part of the system's "first tier" of programming. He refused to allow it to become a "second-tier" service like HBO, which carried a separate charge to consumers.

Turner would announce, too, that since the Western Show in

December he had gotten about 750,000 cable homes' worth of "interest" in CNN. It was a tiny figure, but at least it represented a start.

He could report that twelve minutes per hour would be available for commercials — ten minutes for national ads to help pay for CNN, plus two minutes sold locally by cable operators. But there were no sponsors lined up yet.

Turner, Schonfeld and Schorr stood together outside the room where the press conference was about to begin.

"Well," Turner said, "I'm betting $100 million on you guys."

"Well," Schorr said, "I'm betting my reputation."

"Well," Schonfeld said, "I'm betting my life!"

Grinning at each other, the three men walked into the room.

Frank Beatty and Roy Mehlman of UPI were at the hotel in Las Vegas, each hoping that Ted Turner would be successful so they could join him.

In the 1960s, Beatty had invented a machine called Audi Pix, which was like a metal conveyor belt with news photos on it, giving the viewer up to twenty seconds to watch each one and listen to the narration before the next was projected. Mehlman's "slo-scan" service, *Newstime*, had been a bigger breakthrough: delivered round-the-clock by satellite, it would be reaching more than a million homes by the next year. But Ted Turner's twenty-four-hour video news, with live anchors and on-scene coverage, was about to make both services obsolete.

FRANK BEATTY

"When the press conference was over, Turner came out of the room and said, '*Now* do you believe I'm gonna do it?' I said to him, 'I believe.' He said, 'Come on, let's go up to the room and talk.' I said I'd be up there in a minute. Before I got there, I ran into the guy from Scripps-Howard Broadcasting and he says, 'Hey, get me together with Turner, will you?' This is the same guy who had refused to meet with him before. So I said, 'Okay, I'll try.' I rode up the elevator to Ted's suite and I said, 'Look, the guy from Scripps-Howard is here. He'd like to meet with you.' Ted said, 'To hell with him. He had two months to meet with me and you couldn't get us together. Now I don't need him anymore. I'll do it without him.' He goes into the men's room, whereupon he takes a leak with the door open, and he says, 'Let's talk about you. Are you gonna work for me? Are you gonna help me?' I'm standing there . . ."

ROY MEHLMAN

"The next morning I was having breakfast at the counter and Ted walked over to me. He put his hand on my shoulder and leaned down and said, 'How much?' That was his way of offering me a job. I said, 'Let me finish breakfast. I'll see you outside in ten minutes.' I was thrilled. I had been with UPI for thirty-five years and I had always thought that UPI would do it. But by now I had realized that they would never do it. And here I had a chance to get involved with the guy who *was* going to proceed. In effect it was a dream come true. . . ."

In the hotel, Turner stood in the midst of several cable operators at the convention. He was grinning and predicting that CNN would be "the greatest achievement in the history of journalism."

The cable guys told him how enthusiastic they were. We're going to sign up, they told him.

"Wait a minute," Turner said. "Didn't you guys tell me back in December that it wouldn't work? Didn't you say it wasn't time yet to do something this big? I mean, what the hell happened in the last five months to change your mind?"

"Nothing," someone said.

"Nothing?"

"Well, gee, Ted, back then you just wanted our *opinion* on the subject. You were *asking* us. But now you're saying that you're definitely going ahead. You're *telling* us. So it's a different ball-game. Now you're actually going ahead and *doing* it."

TWO

"The happiest times are when people get together and do something. . . . People have the most fun when they're busting their ass."

THE REASON I'm so smart is not because I watched TV," Ted Turner told an interviewer in 1980. "I never watched TV at night. I hated television. Until I got into it, I didn't watch a hundred hours a year. I watched the Super Bowl and the World Series. Can I tell you how many hours of TV *news* I watched in my whole life, before I started my own network when I was forty? I had not watched more than maybe a hundred hours in my whole life!"

"We didn't do the news seriously on my stations," he had told *Playboy*, "because we just didn't have the budget to do it properly. My father always told me, 'If you can't do something first class, don't do it at all.' It wasn't that we didn't want to do it. We couldn't do it properly, so we didn't do it at all. There's nothing worse than looking silly, you know?

"In those days I used to get kidded by my friends in the television business, who were saying, 'You might be doing okay in the ratings, but you haven't got any news.' And I would say, 'Well, you just wait. One of these days I'm gonna come on with news that'll make y'all green with envy!'"

"Have you read Alvin Toffler's book, *The Third Wave?*" he asked *Home Video* magazine, referring to a bestselling book predicting society's movement from the agricultural and industrial ages to one already forming based on information. "Toffler gave me an autographed copy. He said, 'Ted Turner, I wanted to meet you. You *are* the third wave.'

"I mean, I didn't *try* to be the third wave. I just happened to be there. When Toffler talks about cable TV and satellite-communication networks and fragmentation, he's talking about me, a guy who's *doing* it. We're the first to try to use the new communications creatively to reshape the world."

After announcing CNN in Las Vegas, Turner remained at the convention to appear on a panel with Marshall McLuhan, whose 1964 book, *Understanding Media*, had included the famous statement that "the medium is the message." It may not have occurred to anyone in the jam-packed auditorium that there was historical significance in McLuhan and Turner sharing the same stage; but while the older man had the concept of global-unity-through-television in his mind, the younger man had it in his grasp.

Between the press conference on May 21, 1979, and the launch of CNN on June 1, 1980, Ted Turner would undergo a kind of metamorphosis. "The thing that motivated me to find out what was really going on," he would later say, "was getting into the news business." It was also what prompted him to go from toying with the idea of running for president to wanting to save the world.

There had never been much room in Turner's mind for small-ness of thinking or boredom or, for that matter, modesty. It had been said often that he had "the attention span of a gnat." And as someone remarked, "Holding a conversation with Ted Turner is like trying to talk to a radio." He was a turned-on, gung-ho, self-driven man.

A case could be made that it all began when his father, who had pummeled him with admonitions to be a success, departed before he could comply; and that he had been living ever since with an endlessly expanding yardstick by which to measure his achievements and worth. According to this theory, Ted Turner had to keep redefining his own vision of success.

It may be that the driving force behind Turner's inexhaustible need to accomplish more and more was an extreme form of in-security and vulnerability. He identified himself instinctively with ordinary, regular folks, rather than with stuffed-shirt cor-porate types or jet-setters. That is why he insisted on cutting his own hair, driving a small car, forsaking limousines whenever possible and traveling coach on airplanes. He had a preference for being the outsider doing battle against those occupying the halls of power. He would line up the little, good guys behind him while he faced the big, bad guys in front of him, until the only thing left to do was lead the charge.

In deciding that he had to save the world from various threats to its survival, Turner was responding to his own need to keep recreating a sense of personal value. Erupting from such deep-seated vulnerability has been a firestorm of fierce ambition in search of grander, more noble conquests. He has needed to be *worth* all of that money and success and notoriety, by doing something *important* with it. And if you're Ted Turner living on the edge, time is always running out.

As Reese Schonfeld set forth to build, in a year's time, the unknown entity called Cable News Network, he began with the largest vision he could summon. A central goal was to "go live" at the scene and to allow viewers to become involved in the spontaneous, unpredictable unfolding of events. One morning he flew north with Turner for a session with members of the *New York Times* editorial board. They sat in a conference room, having lunch while fielding inquiries from *Times* executives. Whenever a specific question about how CNN would cover the news came up, Turner would turn to Schonfeld and say, "Well, I think I'll let Reese handle that one."

"We want to go live with breaking stories as often as possible," Schonfeld replied at one point. "Our philosophy is live, live and *more* live."

"But in reality," a *Times* executive said, "aren't you going to wind up covering a lot of little, two-alarm fires that don't amount to anything?"

Ted Turner, along with the questioners, looked over at his founding CNN president. "I'm afraid so," Schonfeld said, aware of the worried look on his boss's face, "but until the fire is over, you don't know whether it's a two-alarmer or the fire that burned down Chicago!"

"Awwright!" Turner said. "Strong!"

"What we want to sell in terms of live coverage," Schonfeld continued, "is a *role in the process* for our viewers. *We* won't dare leave the fire and neither will *they*, because nobody's gonna be sure what might happen next!"

It was not long before Turner adopted Schonfeld's vision and began to promote it in his own fashion. One of the key elements was that Cable News Network would avoid the slickly packaged look of conventional network news. Its live coverage would create, necessarily, lots of "ragged edges" and a certain loss of control. Schonfeld had faith that viewers would forgive and even appreciate any "mistakes" along the way. In the highly refined newscasts of the Big Three networks, bound by the limitations of twenty-two minutes per package, there was little opportunity for error and correction. In fact, the aimed-for image was one of flawlessness and perfection. But Schonfeld wanted the viewer to see "all the warts" as the news came in.

"We intend to reveal as much of the news process as possible," he said. "It's conceivable that we could operate from a completely 'open' newsroom, so the public can see how we work. We want to remove the mystery. And let people feel the excitement!"

In June he called Atlanta to put his idea for such an "open" newsroom into motion. It meant, simply, that the anchors reading the news would not be in a closed environment. Instead of being separated from the newsroom, the anchors would be part of it. They would be surrounded by the bustle of producers, directors, editors and technicians, along with the sight of cameras, lights, computers, video monitors. Schonfeld wanted it *all* there, expressing the whole range of emotions that he himself had always experienced as a newsman.

He wanted the ragged edges on view. But he was told it couldn't be done.

"It'll be too noisy," said Gene Wright, the engineer.

"Let's take a chance," Schonfeld said. "I mean, we're gonna be taking all *sorts* of chances on this thing."

"Yeah, but an open newsroom? The sound problems would be too difficult. You'll have no programming."

"Listen, Gene, I know you're a good engineer. But that means you've been trained that there's only one way to do things. . . ."

Schonfeld's frustration was compounded by the fact that he was still bound by his ITNA contract. How could he fight for his open newsroom, which itself had no precedent, when he was required to be working in New York? The most obvious answer was to find a replacement at ITNA quickly.

His first choice had been Burt Reinhardt, but the board members had turned him down because he was too independent. So Reinhardt was free to leave Paramount and get down to Atlanta by July 1, 1979, to become executive vice-president of CNN and the first active employee on its editorial payroll. The important point for Schonfeld was to have someone on the scene, to deal with Turner and his people in person.

In June he got Reinhardt to fly east. The two men sat on Schonfeld's porch and made sketches of what an "open" news-room might look like. When Reinhardt went off to observe the WABC News facilities in New York City, however, he was told that the idea was unworkable. A newsroom showing activity that was normally kept off-camera would be too disruptive during the live broadcasts.

Hearing this report, Schonfeld threw up his hands. "Oh, Burt," he said, shaking his head and leaving the sentence unfinished. He would have to slip down to Atlanta on weekends and fight for his idea by himself. In addition to arguing with Gene Wright, he would try to work on Bunky Helfrich, the architect.

Bunky Helfrich and Ted Turner were longtime friends, having gotten to know each other at age nine or ten in Savannah, Georgia. They had kicked around together over the years since then, mostly sailing, and Bunky would be joining Ted the following summer to defend the America's Cup.

Having been an architect for about twenty years, specializing in the restoration of old buildings in Savannah, Helfrich was already semiretired at forty and living on nearby Hilton Head Island, South Carolina. In June 1979, when he traveled up to Atlanta to see Ted and Janie Turner, he had no idea that his semiretirement was coming to an abrupt end.

The occasion was a party celebrating the Turners' fifteenth wedding anniversary; and the morning after, Ted summoned Bunky Helfrich for a ride. "Come on with me," Turner said. "I want to show ya some things I've got on my mind." So they hopped in the car and Turner, speeding off, said he was looking for a site where headquarters for both the SuperStation — whose call sign had just been changed to WTBS, to stand for Turner Broadcasting System — and Cable News Network could be located together.

Given the time frame for CNN's launch, they would not have the luxury of designing and building a new facility from scratch. Some existing structure would have to be purchased and remodeled, Helfrich realized. It also dawned on him that he was being recruited for the task.

When they stopped at the old Brookwood Hotel on Peachtree Road, Helfrich followed as Turner stomped through the lobby and up the stairs. No, the architect said, it's not substantial enough. So they jumped back in the car and Turner sped toward the Georgia Tech campus. He made a quick turn and came to the old Progressive Club, a former Jewish country club up for sale.

It was set back from Techwood Drive by parking lots on either side of a lawn with a circular fountain. A driveway went around the lawn to the front of a sprawling, red-brick mansion, whose two floors each contained fifteen windows across the façade. At the entrance was a portico with tall white columns, framing the main door. Surrounding the mansion at the sides and rear were twenty-one acres of lovely grounds, with trees and gardens and bushes and lawns. On the north edge of the brick clubhouse was the swimming pool, and there were tennis courts as well.

The whole place was deserted now, with no water or bubbling fountain out front. Helfrich could envision how the Progressive Club had looked during its heyday; it took a little more imagination to envision this same place as headquarters for America's first all-news television network.

But in a personal way, it seemed to make sense. There was a flavor here of one of Turner's favorite movies, *Gone With the Wind*. Turner himself was often cited as a modern version of the dashing Rhett Butler as played by Clark Gable, a comparison he thoroughly enjoyed, so why not enhance the image?

Tara on Techwood!

Turner pointed out the various ballrooms and lounges and dining rooms. Maybe they could put the administrative offices up on the second level, Turner said, while the SuperStation could take the ground-floor space. In the basement where the gymnasiums and locker rooms still existed, perhaps Bunky could find space for CNN's newsroom. The grounds sloped downward, so the basement's windows in back looked out on a green lawn, where the six gleaming-white receiving dishes could be set up to catch the incoming news feeds from those "birds" in the heavens.

A satellite farm!

What Helfrich saw, as an architect, was a facility whose 90,000 square feet of space would be adequate. He also saw a tremendous amount of demolition work ahead, to break down walls and remove columns. He saw an enormous job of restoration and rebuilding, not to mention the electrical work for lights, cameras, audio facilities, computers, videotape-editing machines, telephones — it boggled the mind.

Turner hadn't even bought the place yet. Once he did, and permits were obtained, with any luck demolition could begin by September — even as blueprints were being made — and maybe, just maybe, reconstruction could start in December.

Helfrich knew the pattern: Turner had set the goal and the deadline and the sense of mission; and now, as he always did, he was putting together the people who knew how to make it happen. If we can start by the end of August, the architect thought, we'll have ten months to get the Techwood building ready for CNN's launch.

Not enough time. Of course, you didn't tell Ted that. You just did it.

BUNKY HELFRICH

"Initially I met with Reese, who was pretty paranoid about breaching his ITNA contract, so our meetings were sort of clandestine. I met him a couple of times at the airport. We went into the men's room and talked.

"Burt came in right after that, so we used him as a go-between for a while. He was really the on-site guy at first. At one time Reese and Burt thought that we were going to put CNN on the ground-level floor of the Techwood building, but Ted said, 'Oh, no, CNN is new. We're gonna put it down below.' So they were relegated to the basement.

"One of the most beneficial things was the fact that Reese was a very flexible guy, willing to take a lot of risks in getting what he wanted to achieve. His overall concept was that he wanted the viewing public not only to get the news but generally to see how it came to be put on the air. He wanted to have the barebones type of situation, where you'd see the people running around carrying copy back and forth, and you'd have a bit of ambient noise.

"It was a completely new concept. And most people felt that it couldn't be done. They felt that the proximity of the anchors and the control rooms, and the noise in the newsroom, was

going to be more than TV could handle. Reese wanted everything to be happening, sort of like a theater-in-the-round, where
the anchors were in the middle and everything was going on
around them."

Desperately trying to keep the naysayers from crushing his vision before he began, Schonfeld kept holding secret meetings
with Helfrich in Atlanta. Finally, in August, he persuaded the
architect to join him on a trip to Vancouver, Canada, where a
local station was using a variation of what he had in mind. If he
could show Helfrich something even *remotely* similar to an
open newsroom, to demonstrate that the idea wasn't totally far-
fetched, he would gain an important ally who had Turner's ear.

There was still time, because Turner himself had gone off to
sail his sixty-one-foot yacht *Tenacious*, against three hundred
other ships, in the six-hundred-mile Fastnet Race off the southern tip of Ireland. By the time Schonfeld and Helfrich landed
in Canada, Turner was heading into a monstrous storm, with
seventy-mile-per-hour winds producing waves up to twenty-five
feet high. Other yachts, mostly smaller ones, were capsizing.
The storm was finally to claim fifteen lives. It was the worst
disaster in yachting history.

At the Vancouver television station, news of the Fastnet Race
was being fed to one of the monitors as Schonfeld and Helfrich
walked in.

"Why are you guys here?" a producer said.

"What do you mean?"

"You don't know?"

"Don't know what?"

"Well, your boss is missing."

"Missing?"

"Yeah. They think he's dead."

As Schonfeld and Helfrich went through the motions of observing the newsroom, they kept watching the latest news feeds
from Plymouth, England. It was a town awash in tragedy; the
race had become known as the Fastnet of Death. Yet suddenly
appearing on the monitor was Ted Turner, very much alive,
being interviewed about his own narrow escape aboard *Tenacious* during the gale.

"The common link between all fifteen deaths," an inquiry

would report, "was the violence of the sea, an unremitting danger to all who sail."

Turner had gone through it all by sailing defiantly into the force 10 winds and never allowing his crew to stop *racing*, at full speed, through the worst of the turmoil, until the storm was over.

They had survived.

Rescuers aboard helicopters had been unable to find *Tenacious* because, in fact, Turner's yacht had gone ahead by then.

He had won the race.

DAN SCHORR

"Ted had asked me to go out to Denver and make a speech at a cable convention. It was an evening in mid-August, and I was met by a tall young man named Terry McGuirk, who had a worried look on his face. 'This might be all for naught,' he said. I asked him why. 'Well,' he said, 'Ted's racing out in the Irish Sea and there's been a bad storm. He's missing.'

"I went up to my room in the hotel, wondering what to do, and turned on the television set. It was the evening network news. And sure enough, a lot of boats had been caught in the Fastnet storm and Ted Turner was missing.

"But when I went downstairs a few minutes later, McGuirk was smiling and saying, 'It's all right! Ted made it through and he's okay.'

" 'Wait a minute,' I said. 'I was just watching TV and they said he's missing!' Then I stopped and realized that, of course, the news broadcast I'd seen had been delayed because of the time zones. It was two hours old! And so this crucial bit of information — telling me whether I had a job or a boss or not, as I was going down to speak to the convention — could not be learned from CBS or ABC or NBC.

"In the convention hall I said to the audience, 'I've just come down here, and if you've been watching television, and if you heard that Ted Turner is missing, let me tell you that he's *not* missing. He's *found*. And he came in okay. The reason you might have thought he was still missing is because you were looking at *old-fashioned television*, which is delayed across the country, and that's one thing CNN *won't* do, because it'll be carried live everywhere.' "

*   *   *

If Turner had perished at sea, Schonfeld thought, then CNN would have sunk with him. For any other company or television network, the death of its leader would not have been fatal; but in this case, Turner *was* the network. Without him, the project would have been shoved into the file drawer. But now they were back in business.

The newsroom in Vancouver was much smaller than the one Schonfeld envisioned for Cable News Network. And, he told Helfrich, the layout wasn't really what he had in mind. The anchor desk was not in the middle. Instead it was in what they called a "quiet corner," with a tape machine behind it; and although they did shoot occasional cutaways of activity elsewhere in the newsroom, there was no real integration of elements. Schonfeld wanted the anchors in a "pit" surrounded by the supporting staff, so viewers would be drawn into the total environment.

"I see what you mean," Helfrich said.

"Good," Schonfeld said. If Bunky passed the word to Ted, then maybe the trip would pay off.

Earlier, in New York, Schonfeld had gone to work trying to find another replacement for himself as ITNA's managing editor. His second choice after Reinhardt was a legendary television newsman named Ted Kavanau, who had poured his guts and heart into the creation of Metromedia's *10 O'Clock News* in New York.

Kavanau was a heavy-boned, muscular man whose large feet, hands and head made him a formidable figure on the streets of the city. He wore a bushy, dark mustache. His skin was often pale yellow, even grayish. Friends would remark that Kavanau had never looked healthy in his life. An investigative reporter by instinct and habit, he had the look of a homicide detective on the beat. He was authoritative, alert, fast-talking, tough. Like many of the cops he had known — such as Frank Serpico, who had risked his life to expose police corruption — Kavanau was also a man who perceived danger at every turn, to the point where other newsmen felt he was paranoid.

Strapped to an ankle under his sock, to protect himself, Kavanau carried a gun.

Colleagues called him Mad Dog.

*   *   *

In July 1979, Ted Kavanau was living in the slums of Williamsburg, Brooklyn, depressed and broke and unemployed. He was paying twenty bucks a week to stay in a tiny room of a friend's crumbling brownstone. The neighborhood was ninety percent Puerto Rican and six percent black. The people here were hardworking and, like the poor in other parts of the city, the most victimized by crime.

Over the past few years, Kavanau had found himself on what he felt had been a "long professional slide" downward; and now, with nowhere else to turn, he had crawled into this little room to feel the terror and shame and loneliness of finally having hit bottom.

Kavanau wandered around the city with nowhere to go, wishing he still had his work to do. Without much money left, he shunned the subway and walked over the Williamsburg Bridge into Manhattan, often finding himself on Forty-second Street heading for the ITNA office to see his friend Reese Schonfeld, who would let him hang around and, once in a while, send him on a story.

No matter what problems Kavanau had, Schonfeld would never lose faith in his drive and ability. Now Schonfeld was talking about leaving New York to go down South and work for Ted Turner, the sailing guy, and he was even going out on a limb by recommending Kavanau to run ITNA in his place.

"I've put in your name to succeed me," Schonfeld told him, "but listen, the thing with Turner is gonna be all news. Why don't you come with me?"

"Well, Reese, I think I'd rather be broke and miserable up here than employed and miserable down there."

"It's gonna be great, I'm telling ya."

"Let me think about it."

As he spoke, Kavanau knew he already had made up his mind to take the ITNA job, if it was offered to him, so he could stay in New York.

Another friend who had put his faith in Kavanau was Metromedia executive Ed Turner, from Oklahoma, who had started *The 10 O'Clock News* for WTTG in Washington, D.C. That show proved to be a testing ground for a similar venture in New York; and in that city, it was Ed Turner who moved Ted Kavanau from executive producer of *The 10 O'Clock News* on Channel 5 to its news director, a decision that everyone who knew Kavanau's erratic temperament said was a dumb mistake.

(A legendary story was that Ed Turner and Ted Kavanau, in the midst of a union fight, grabbed hold of some thug and literally hung the man by his ankles outside a courthouse window.)

Kavanau proved the cynics wrong. After playing a key role as the show's first producer, he flourished for five years as news director. During that time it became the highest-rated independent newscast in America. He ran the news operation in a town where news was hot, serious stuff; and when he achieved success, it signaled one of the first cracks in the dam — a real challenge to the dominance of the Big Three networks.

Kavanau demonstrated an elusive but essential instinct for knowing what *was* news, in the first place. He could envision which stories were important; and then, he found ways of grabbing his audience's attention and holding it. At ten o'clock in the evening, against the best entertainment programming the networks could provide, he proved there was a public appetite to watch news. In substantial numbers, the people of New York turned from the network sitcoms to watch national stories along with local reports of killings and riots and fires and strikes and scandals and assorted other horrors. Here was all the wild, siren-chasing, police-blotter news that pulsed through Kavanau's blood and turned him into a wild man.

After a heated argument with Channel 5's general manager, over what he considered to be interference with his news department, Kavanau suddenly quit; and without realizing it, he was beginning his long slide downward. He went over to WPIX-TV, as managing director, and started another wild and crazy format. Unable to hold the operation together, he left to join WABC-TV as assistant news director for *Eyewitness News,* a more established organization, where he didn't fit in.

At that point he bumped into Schonfeld, whom he had known over the years, and poured out his woes. Schonfeld mentioned that the position of news director at KTVU, an independent station in Oakland, California, was open. Kavanau got the job and flew west.

Things started pretty well and he came up with yet another unique format, but then found himself pressured into firing someone against his better judgment. Disgusted with himself, again he walked out.

Back in New York, he moved into the room in the Williamsburg slum. He had no job, no prospects, nothing — but when Schonfeld asked him to go to Georgia, he still hesitated.

How can I leave New York again? And what can this thing down there with Turner really be? How in hell is some sailing guy gonna do news? Ridiculous! For me to disappear from New York and go to work for a little TV guy down in Georgia, I'd have to be even crazier than I already am!

So he decided to try for the ITNA job, although he laughed when a friend asked about it and said, "Are you kidding? They wouldn't take me. The ITNA board is made up of WNEW and WTTG and KTVU and WPIX. At one point or another, most of those guys have fired me!" In fact, he was not chosen.

Facing the prospect of staying in the Brooklyn slums, and having no professional future in sight, Kavanau went back to Schonfeld with a sheepish look on his face:

"Uh, Reese, you know that job down South? If you'll still take me. . . ."

By the end of July, Schonfeld was finally on his way to Atlanta to build CNN on a full-time basis. The deadline for going on the air was nine months away.

The ITNA board had rejected his first three candidates to replace him as managing editor — Burt Reinhardt, Ted Kavanau and Ed Turner — before agreeing on someone else. It was either ironic or fitting, or both, that those three men would be part of the small core of CNN's original news executives. Reinhardt was already in place; Kavanau would follow soon; and Ed Turner, now back at KWTV in Oklahoma City, was following the trade blurbs and getting the itch.

These men, along with Schonfeld, had learned their trade outside the Big Three networks. In that sense they were loners and mavericks, even misfits, which made them perfectly suited for the founding of an upstart cable news network being financed by a guy comparing himself with Christopher Columbus and Robin Hood.

During the building of CNN they would come to be known, simply, as Reese's Pieces.

In Atlanta, Reinhardt had begun with a desk and a telephone in the small brick building next door to the WTBS offices on West

Peachtree Street. He was a reticent, introverted, methodical man who would stay behind the scenes, shunning publicity and preferring to remain invisible. He was also a tight-fisted company man who knew how to get the most out of every dollar. In negotiating with people, he started at rock bottom and generally stayed there. He was the kind of green-eyeshade guy every organization needed; and, Schonfeld knew, when it came to spending money Reinhardt would act like a conscience to warn him.

At the same time, Schonfeld needed to "think big." He decided, for example, to have a news-oriented talk show at 10 P.M. Eastern Time on weeknights. Searching for a host whose name would carry instant recognition, he had begun negotiating to get David Frost or Phil Donahue or Geraldo Rivera to sign on. A well-known personality would be expensive, but worth the drain on CNN's budget. Ted Turner himself tried to hire Walter Cronkite:

> Dear Walter:
> It has been some time since you were sailing with us in Newport, 1977.
>
> I feel that when you learn the way we plan to deliver the news twenty-four hours a day on Cable News Network you will want to join us.
>
> I think we should at least talk. . . .

Cronkite responded with a polite note about how he would enjoy sailing with Turner at any time whatever.

At the moment, what Schonfeld needed even more was to build up the credibility, as well as the experience and knowledge, of his top management team. In Ted Kavanau he would have a man whose ideas cascaded one upon another. Mad Dog could move fast enough to do the work of ten producers at a time; and when he showed up, Schonfeld knew, CNN would receive an injection of high-voltage energy. But to challenge the network news departments, he would have to steal a few all-star executives from the networks themselves. How could CNN lure vice-presidents at ABC or CBS or NBC in the prime of their careers? What executive would be so foolish to leave the big time? Who, in a solid network position, would risk everything on a cable-TV news service that could fold before it ever got on the air? By the end of August, Schonfeld had found the answer.

He was focusing on two news executives, from NBC and CBS,

who had spent the bulk of their working lives at those networks. The beauty of it was that both men, Jim Kitchell and Sam Zelman, were at the point of stagnation or retirement. Schonfeld was going to call with something nobody else could match: one last fling!

First he had gotten hold of Kitchell, then general manager of news services at NBC, who had spent twenty-nine years with the network. Kitchell had directed the old *Huntley-Brinkley Report.* A technical wizard with the credits and credibility, he had put NBC's facilities and crews in action for coverage of the Cuban Missile Crisis, the John F. Kennedy assassination, the 1964 Olympic Games, the Apollo 11 lunar landing and Richard Nixon's trip to China. Since the early 1950s, Kitchell had directed NBC's coverage of national political conventions. That alone would be a tremendous boost, because right after CNN's launch in June they'd have to go up against the networks during the 1980 presidential campaigns.

It turned out that he was available and, moreover, his wife had family in Atlanta. They wouldn't mind moving down from New York. After much bargaining, Schonfeld wound up offering him the title of "senior vice-president" for CNN's operations. Kitchell tendered his resignation at NBC and would arrive in mid-September.

JIM KITCHELL

"I had dealt with Reese directly and indirectly over a number of years. He hated the networks and was a terrible thorn in their side — although, at one time, we had considered hiring him. He was probably the best assignment editor I had ever known. He had a superb nose for news.

"When I got there it was clear that we had two goals. One was to do twenty-four hours of news and the other was to go on the air on June 1, 1980. Those were the only guidelines. It was a challenge, to do something that nobody had ever done before, and I was intrigued by it. . . .

"Every one of us said, 'We're not going to be ready. Let's try to delay it.' And the answer from Ted was, 'No, we're gonna start on the first of June whether we're ready or not.' That was an incredible pressure, forcing us to work eighteen or twenty hours a day, but it was fun. . . ."

*　　　*　　　*

Schonfeld got in touch with Sam Zelman of CBS shortly after calling Kitchell. At the start of his Vancouver trip in August with Bunky Helfrich, he had suddenly thought to himself, *Zelman! Why didn't I remember Sam before now?*

In the Atlanta airport, he placed a call to CBS headquarters in New York. He had dealt with Zelman periodically for some years and considered him a friend. "Sam's my kinda guy," Schonfeld would say, and now as luck would have it Zelman was at retirement age.

"Sam!" Schonfeld yelled into the airport phone. "Don't do anything before we talk! Wait! I'm gonna be coming back from Vancouver and let's get together!"

Zelman had credibility and experience and, in addition, genuine class. With his big, warm smile and a mustache finely tapered at both ends, he exuded wisdom and charm. At CBS, he had been executive producer for election coverage. He produced *60 Minutes.* He established foreign news bureaus in the midst of every major military conflict since Korea — in Hong Kong, Saigon, Phnom Penh, Prague, Jerusalem, Paris, Mexico City, London, Seoul. He had seen it all; and after listening to Schonfeld he said, "A twenty-four-hour newscast? Well, Reese, my career is almost at an end anyway, so what the hell? It sounds great. When do I start?"

Now Zelman was scheduled to arrive as vice-president and executive producer, a week after Kitchell would come aboard.

SAM ZELMAN

"Many of us didn't express our doubts. I really didn't believe it would go on the air and be twenty-four hours a day from the very beginning. I thought, *Well, if we can get it on for* eight *hours a day, it'll* still *be something that's never been done in the history of the world.* I came from CBS, where there was a whole worldwide organization basically working to produce just one half-hour news broadcast each evening. And here, with much less money and far fewer people, we were going to put on news and *never stop.* Unbelievable!"

Still casting his net, Schonfeld came up with another catch: Bill MacPhail of CBS Sports, who had *already* retired from the network. MacPhail had spent nearly nineteen years with CBS Sports, having developed its first coverage of the National

Football League and the Olympic Games. Soft-spoken and conciliatory, he was a real gentleman whose contacts throughout the sports world would be of tremendous value. Like Kitchell and Zelman, he could not refuse the Fountain of Youth.

BILL MACPHAIL

"It was funny because, after Reese offered me a two-year deal, I finally said okay, provided I could run the sports department from New York. I was not about to go to Atlanta. And that seemed to be fine with Reese, so we shook hands.

"That night Ted Turner called and I really expected the sailing lingo: 'Hey, matey, welcome aboard!' But instead he told me, 'You've got to be in Atlanta,' and I said, 'Oh, I'm sorry, that was not the arrangement that was made.' And he says, 'Well, I'm sorry, but you have to be in Atlanta.' So I immediately called Reese and he said, 'Don't worry about Ted. I'll take care of Ted.' Twenty minutes later Reese calls back and says, 'Guess what? You have to be in Atlanta.'"

Schonfeld and Turner had go-rounds over whether CNN should be in the Progressive Club's old ballroom on the first floor or down in the basement. After agreeing to the basement, both Schonfeld and Reinhardt realized that the ballroom was clearly superior for tracking shots of an "open" newsroom. But Turner refused to budge on the issue, so they turned their attention to figuring how to remove some of the pillars from the basement.

They had continuing difficulties with Gene Wright, who still didn't buy the "open" concept. Schonfeld brought in a New York consultant, Irv Rosner, and said to Turner's engineer, "Gene, if you can't do it, I'm gonna have Rosner do it." After Rosner designed a layout, Wright suddenly reversed himself and became what Schonfeld called "a real can-do kind of guy."

REESE SCHONFELD

"There were some enormous battles. Kitchell said the sunlight would burn out the irises of the cameras and we'd have to spend $50,000 a year for new lenses. In the end, to solve it, I said, 'Okay, let's put up that brown glass,' a kind of filter you just put up for any TV production, to keep the blue out. So all these things were 'problems' that were solved quite simply.

"They said, for example, that you couldn't put the cameras on carpets, because the wheels wouldn't run. But in Vancouver, we had *seen* that it could be done.

"In the beginning it was tough because they were used to broadcasting, not news. And our budget was too tight for the normal ways. Wright wanted enormous generators, in case we had a power blackout, but I said, 'No! Get the cheapest generator you can find! Just to keep us on the air!' I figured that if the power went down in Atlanta, we'd just let the New York bureau carry the show. 'It may not *look* good,' I said, 'but I don't want to spend a million bucks for generators!' We'd go broke that way. 'This is gonna be a *news* channel,' I said, 'and it's gonna be belts and suspenders. And then, just in case something else happens, *maybe* we'll have a guy standing by to hold our pants up!'"

When it became clear to Schonfeld that he would need an assistant from here on, to keep track of the hundreds of details and decisions confronting him each day, he passed the word to Ted Turner and waited. At the moment, he and Reinhardt and Kitchell were working out of a one-story brick building beside the concrete WTBS studio on West Peachtree. They were sharing office space with Turner's cable-sales people. Zelman and Kavanau would be arriving shortly.

Schonfeld got word from Turner's assistant, Dee Woods, that a friend of hers named Diane Durham would be stopping by to talk about the possibility of working for him. "When can she start?" Schonfeld replied.

DIANE DURHAM

"I was working at the Merchandise Mart, as a secretary, when Dee called me. Before that I'd worked in a psychiatrist's office for ten years, doing case histories, which turned out to be the perfect training. . . .

"Dee asked me if I was interested in doing something new and I said, 'Oh, well, what the hell.' She said, 'Come over and meet Reese Schonfeld,' so I did. Reese gave me quite the usual disjointed conversation that you carry on with him. Then he said, 'Fine, come to work in two weeks.'

"The first day I walked in, God, I'll never forget it. Reese and Burt and Jim Kitchell were there. I saw that they had sketched out the whole newsroom one night on the back of a grocery bag. I was there a few minutes when Reese suddenly started dictating. He dictated to me for several hours without stopping. It was all about Grass Valley Switchers, about which I had no idea. I knew nothing. I mean, I'm walking in here totally cold. I'm a reasonably bright woman, but I didn't know what I was getting into.

"So I just started. Reese was the kind of person that wanted you with him all the time. From the moment I came to work at nine in the morning, until eight or ten o'clock at night, you didn't stop. It was incredible. I was with him all the time, and it got to the point that, when he looked across the room, I knew what he wanted to do and how he wanted it done. It just happened.

"Reese was very much like Ted Turner, in that the ideas flowed. Whether they were good, bad or indifferent, they flowed off the top, so people sifted through them and took only the good ones. You just went from one new idea to the next, like a free flow: 'Let's try this, let's try that.' And it had never been done, so why not? You never said to Reese, 'We can't do that,' until you *proved* you couldn't do it. You had to try, to the absolute ends of the earth."

In early October the small news group moved next door to an old, wood-frame, haunted-looking white house. The ramshackle home had been built in 1910, although it seemed more like a relic from Civil War days. Set on an embankment overlooking West Peachtree, it had a porch with white columns and, inside, two rickety floors above the basement.

At various times the white house had been a halfway home or shelter for people in trouble — alcoholics, drug addicts, former criminals, runaway teens — and in the bathroom, upstairs, was a list of names on a schedule for daily cleaning chores. Earlier in the century, by some accounts, CNN's new home had been a thriving house of prostitution. As evidence there were towel racks behind each bedroom door.

The inside of the house was dusty and musty. The floors and walls creaked; and with each passing of a bus, the whole place shook as if a mild earthquake were in progress. When the wind blew, the lights flickered or the power went out altogether.

On the day they moved in, Burt Reinhardt took a desk on the

second floor. His secretary, Janet Bowey, was keeping track of job applications coming in. By now he was getting more than a thousand résumés and videotapes each week from producers, directors, reporters and writers around the country — all piled in separate stacks, threatening to swamp Reinhardt by their sheer volume.

He was concentrating so hard that he barely noticed it had begun to rain outside. It was one of those sudden moments in a Georgia day when the sky turns dark without warning and the wind whips up and the rain pours down with a driving vengeance, forcing motorists to pull to the side of the road. Reinhardt's papers started to fly all over as the table shook and the house shuddered. Rain began dripping from the ceiling. Still he worked on, reading and making lists and talking on the phone, as the lights went off.

"Somebody get the power back on!" came a voice in the darkness of the old white house.

When the storm passed and the lights came back on, Reinhardt glanced down and realized there was a wide, deep puddle on the floor and that his feet were in the middle of it. His socks and feet were soaking wet. He started to shiver and wondered about his chances of getting pneumonia. Next time, he would wear his galoshes to work.

If those guys at the big networks in their posh offices only knew . . .

Sam Zelman had arrived from New York that morning, as they were carrying their typewriters and boxes from the brick building to the old white house. Now he was standing behind Diane Durham, waiting to use the bathroom and thinking, *This broken-down old house is just perfect for starting a little underground movement. . . .*

"So, Sam," Durham said, "I've never been to New York and I don't know anything about television. What wonderful TV stories do you have for me?"

Zelman looked around. Now that the storm was over, it had turned incredibly hot in the house. There was no air conditioning and they were sweating. A few months ago, he could not have dreamed that at age sixty-four he would wind up working in an old falling-apart house in Georgia where he would have to stand in line for the bathroom and wonder when the power would go out again.

"Well," Zelman said, smiling, "if I was in my office at CBS, up in the Black Rock, right about now my secretary would be coming into the suite with my tea or coffee, and danish, on a silver tray with doilies . . ."

Although the buildings on West Peachtree were near each other, they represented separate worlds.

In the concrete headquarters of Turner Broadcasting System, where Dee Woods screened all visitors to Turner's office, most attention was focused on WTBS, the SuperStation, along with other parts of the business: the Charlotte station, in the process of being sold; the Atlanta Braves, who had finished a poor season; the Atlanta Hawks basketball team; and the Atlanta Chiefs, the company's professional soccer team.

Sales to cable systems were being made from the brick building between Turner's headquarters and the old white house. But the TBS and CNN sales offices were on opposite sides of the hall. "The guys selling the SuperStation had been very skeptical about Ted starting this CNN thing," Frank Beatty said. "So when he brought in guys like Roy Mehlman and me, there was a lot of resentment. It was not very comfortable. Finally someone said we ought to be selling the same things, except Mehlman and I didn't know anything about the SuperStation and the other guys didn't know a thing about selling CNN." Eventually both efforts were merged, with Terry McGuirk in charge, as the sales teams traveled around the country.

Turner himself was still set to do a lot of sailing, first in the Southern Ocean Racing Circuit in early 1980 and then in the America's Cup later that year. If he had known sooner that the CNN venture was going to be able to start when it did, he told Frank Beatty, he would not have committed himself to the Cup again. But even without his heavy sailing schedule, the odds are that Turner would have let Schonfeld's group in the old white house go its own way.

Although he was seldom seen on the premises, Turner did make an effort to meet the top news people. He took Sam Zelman out to the Stadium Club for lunch and told him, "You know, all you have to do is keep up with what's going on. Anybody with a little money can make a lot of money. Like just the other day, I was reading that there's a fuel shortage. Well, we know that this world is running out of oil, and that we're having trouble providing all of our energy needs. My idea, and I'm doing it, is to buy up some peat bogs, because eventually they'll have to burn peat to create energy. So I have my eye on thousands of acres of peat bogs in Florida. And that's all it takes. You just have to be a step ahead of everybody else. I enjoy life," Turner went on, adding, "I find these interesting projects to do and the world's my oyster. And you're gonna like it here."

DEE WOODS

"I had met Ted back in April 1976, before we went on satellite with the SuperStation, and I'd learned since then that once he makes a decision he never looks back. He just continues to look forward, not necessarily just to next year but to five or ten years from now. And what he does, what he's really good about doing, is searching out the best people to do a job — so that then, instead of standing around, he can just let them do it. I think that is what he was doing in gathering these individuals over there in the haunted house. He had gotten the best people available to do Cable News Network and now they were getting everything organized and pulling it together. . . ."

Ted Kavanau stepped from the taxicab and stared up at the old white haunted house. Dropping his luggage on the sidewalk, he checked to make sure he was at the correct address.

This dilapidated, depressing building is the headquarters of a national news network with coverage from around the world? Are they kidding? It looks like it should be condemned! My God, I've just gone from one slum to another!

Standing there, about to run away in panic, he admitted something awful to himself: *The truth is, I don't think it can work. Right now all the experts say it can't be done, and I happen to be one of those experts! There is no way it can succeed. So why did I come here? It can't work and I can't afford to be associated with another failure. Professionally I'll never recover from it. Reese and Burt are down here on a failure course, headed for disaster, and I've been suckered into it with them. I should go back to New York, even if I have to walk!*

The trouble, Kavanau remembered, was that he was broke and

unemployed, with nowhere else to go. Lifting his bags and taking a deep breath, he marched to the door of the old white house.

Sam Zelman had kept a few of his personal feelings about this project to himself. For one thing, he was fairly certain that he and Kitchell and MacPhail had been recruited as much for their ability to help Turner raise money as for their experience in journalism. What he figured was this: *They're going to take our names and go to the bank and say, "Hey, we're not crazies! We've got people who've been in the news field and we need money to start a network." So they're taking our names, along with our credentials, to the bank.* It was a cynical view and Zelman knew he might not be doing justice to Turner or Schonfeld or, indeed, himself, but that was how he felt deep down.

More serious was his genuine doubt that CNN would get on the air as planned. Zelman remembered how, when CBS had expanded its Cronkite show from fifteen to thirty minutes, there had been pandemonium in the news department for weeks.

Yet in broadcast journalism the constant refrain had always been "If we only had more time!" *Now we've got until doomsday to do the story right,* Zelman thought.

As he started scouting for "talent" to be CNN anchors and correspondents, Zelman approached his task with a sense of reality. Unless they were people in crisis situations, he had very little to sell them. Here was an organization, after all, that hadn't even started. And its chances of success were, in his own opinion, slim. Why would someone give up a good career to join CNN?

His solution was to show them respect. He could not offer more money and could not assure them of a great new career, but he could appeal to their idealism and desire to grow. Zelman made it a point to tell people it would be a "hands-on" operation. They could go out in the field, then come back and do the writing and editing, because there would be no union restrictions. They could accomplish a lot and their ideas would be appreciated.

Respect. It was Sam Zelman's own solution to those nagging doubts, which disturbed him less and less as he became caught up in trying to make the whole thing happen.

Alec Nagle arrived in November.

When Schonfeld decided to make Ted Kavanau responsible for

getting "hard news" on the air, and for helping producers fill their shows with as much fast-breaking stuff as possible, Kavanau said he would need a "number-two man" who was creative, idealistic, spontaneous, enthusiastic. He mentioned a young man he had met in California, a guy who was now the executive producer of news at KGO-TV, the ABC station in San Francisco. For a couple of years before that, the young man had been in New York producing WABC's six o'clock *Eyewitness News* with Roger Grimsby. It was the city's top-rated hour-long newscast (*The 10 O'Clock News* was tops as an independent) and Grimsby was one of the most popular anchormen.

"We should try to get him," Kavanau said, referring to the young producer.

"Fine," Schonfeld said.

Now Alec Nagle was walking through the door of the old white house, dressed in a tie and jacket, with a vest, wearing glasses. He was a good-looking, clean-cut Ivy Leaguer with a shock of brown-gray hair that fell down across his forehead; and he seemed just the opposite of what Kavanau had described. Inside this ramshackle house, where Reese Schonfeld was plotting Ted Turner's guerrilla-style revolution against the news establishment, this recruit hardly fit the image.

His full name was Alexander Cooper Nagle the Third.

He had gone to Philips-Exeter Academy and graduated from Dartmouth College in 1967 (Schonfeld had gone there, too). Later he had earned a master's in journalism at Syracuse University. He had begun his news career in Philadelphia, at KYW-TV, as writer and weekend news producer. In San Francisco he had produced the TV news at KPIX before supervising late news at KGO and eventually taking charge of daily local newscasts. His credentials were good.

As Alec Nagle rather awkwardly introduced himself around, the big question remained: Exactly why had Kavanau been so eager to get him?

On the evening of Thursday, December 6, 1979, a satellite owned by RCA American Communications was launched by NASA from the Kennedy Space Flight Center at Cape Canaveral, Florida. The domestic bird, SATCOM III, was replacing SATCOM I for transmission of TV programming to cable systems across the country. Knowing that SATCOM III was crucial to his Cable News Network, Ted Turner had contracted with RCA for the lease of a transponder. SATCOM III weighed about a ton and measured eighty cubic feet. It was shaped like a washing machine with wings on its sides. With twenty-four transponders for as many channels, it promised to be a giant step toward massive expansion of the cable industry.

The satellite was launched aboard a three-stage Thor-Delta 3914 rocket. Its firing was perfect and already counted as the hundred and fiftieth successful Delta launch. For the first twenty-five minutes after lift-off, the space agency was officially responsible; then, after the craft's injection into elliptical orbit, control passed to RCA and its engineers.

Three days went by.

On the fourth day, SATCOM III was scheduled to be fired into permanent geostationary orbit 22,300 miles over the Pacific Ocean. At 1:15 P.M. on Monday, the tenth of December, ground-station engineers threw the switch firing the craft's "apogee kick motor" — a solid fuel rocket, built into the satellite.

During burn time, as expected, the beacon signal was blotted out. The RCA engineers waited to regain contact. And they waited some more.

As the minutes went by, their fears began to grow.

Where was SATCOM III?

Hours passed, but still no signal. The engineers hoped that a simple failure of the tracking beacon was making it impossible to home in on the satellite, but they also speculated that the worst had happened. When ignited, the solid-fuel kick motor was like a giant firecracker that couldn't be controlled. It may have blown up.

"We are searching the heavens," said Robert Shortal, an RCA vice-president. "Other companies with satellites are searching the heavens. The U.S. Air Force is searching the heavens. We honestly don't know what happened. It could have descended into some weird orbit and we can't find it. Or for all we know, it's on its way to Mars."

JIM KITCHELL

"Oh God, I died. There was great depression at the old white house. The word had gone out that CNN was dead, that we weren't going to make it. Everybody was pretty glum because, at that stage, most cable systems only had one dish, geared to SATCOM. So if we used some other satellite, there would have to be new dishes for all the cable systems in the country. That would be very heavy money, much too expensive. . . ."

At that moment, Ted Turner was attending the Western Cable Show in Anaheim, California, and telling the industry that CNN would be ready for launch in less than six months, as he had promised. Hearing that the satellite upon which CNN would depend had been lost in space, Turner shrugged: that was RCA's problem, not his. He had secured a "protected" transponder, so now the signal would be sent to a backup bird.

Exactly *when* another transponder would be available was not clear, but Turner had made a commitment and any delay was unthinkable. All his financial calculations would be upset. It would destroy the momentum of building up the news staff. It would cause everything to topple. It would give CNN's potential competitors a chance to catch up. He sent word back to Reese's Pieces at the old white house: "Carry on!"

The convention near Disneyland was taking place exactly a year after Turner had made his first, unsuccessful pitch for CNN, the one greeted here in Anaheim with pessimism and resistance. But now he was in a triumphant mood, full of optimism, despite all the talk about how SATCOM III's disappearance would set back the cable industry and possibly sink his own venture before it could begin. Turner dismissed all the gloom and doom with typical flourish. No matter what, he was moving ahead — because there was no other choice. By now, CNN's top editorial staff was in position; and momentarily, the hiring of more personnel was going to be escalating at a dramatic pace. Demolition work at Techwood had begun. The goal of having an all-news network headquarters completed in time was still within reach.

The missing satellite could be an insurmountable problem, but Turner brushed it aside for now. He was preparing to hold a press conference to announce his first major advertising breakthrough. Its importance was incalculable, because all the other advertisers were holding back; the rest of the herd needed one of their own to lead the way.

With Turner was Gerry Hogan, who had been negotiating with Marvin Koslow and his associate, Bob Turner, of Bristol-Myers for the past couple of months. The deal had yet to be completed and Hogan was becoming increasingly nervous as the scheduled hour for the announcement drew near. In fact, as reporters gathered in a fifth-floor conference room at the hotel, with Turner waiting in an adjacent suite, Hogan was still negotiating with Koslow down in the lobby. Whenever they came to a new set of possible terms, Hogan ran back up the stairs to inform Turner. At one point, nearly out of breath, he said, "Ted, this guy is really tough. I'm not getting anywhere."

"Well," Turner said, "see what you can do."

Hogan sprinted back down to the lobby again, bypassing the elevator to save time. He would have one more go-round. Koslow remained calm and unruffled. The offer was final.

Would Koslow come upstairs and speak directly to Ted?

No, Koslow replied, tell him he can take it or leave it.

Hogan raced up the five flights one more time and confronted Turner with the final deal. The press conference was now thirty minutes behind schedule.

"What should we do?" Turner said.

"It's not a good deal for us," Hogan said. "We've *got* to turn it down."

The blood seemed to drain from Turner's face as he bowed his head. At that moment he seemed like a vulnerable, small boy. Then he looked up. "We're gonna do it," he said. "Go downstairs and tell 'em."

Hogan returned to the lobby. The first major advertising commitment had been made: $25 million worth of commercials on Cable News Network, spread over ten years. The health-care company would sponsor "medical news" — a concept for television that, at the time, had no precedent.

What worried Hogan about the deal was the prospect of being locked into it for ten years; but in Turner's view, that mattered far less than the credibility gained. For the first time, a major company was recognizing CNN and putting its money into it.

Bristol-Myers wanted a "franchise" for sponsoring medical news, Koslow had told Hogan. If the network would produce special features on science and health, each a few minutes long, then B-M would be associated with those pieces. The deal started to expand Hogan's thinking until he realized that the concept of TV "news" itself was being redefined. Later CNN would come up with "fashion" news, "technology" news and so on. The possible categories were unlimited.

For Koslow the idea of "buying the world of medicine" on CNN had come from his experience with similar positioning in women's magazines, which had been devoting space to science and health for years. Television was still way behind.

MARVIN KOSLOW

"I loved the idea of Cable News Network from the moment I heard it, so I had to be careful not to pursue it too rigorously, because I'd lose my buying position. If they understood how enthusiastic I was, they would've killed me in the deal, so I had to pull myself back.

"I wanted a ten-year deal, because this was an opportunity to get involved with an arrangement that would protect us on long-term pricing. We argued that if our gamble turned out to be correct, if we'd picked the right horse, then we should have an opportunity in the future to do better than the marketplace."

Schonfeld had flown out to the Disneyland convention in time for the Bristol-Myers announcement and they all met in Ted Turner's suite before the press conference began. Schonfeld grew concerned when he heard Koslow demand that Bristol-Myers retain the right of approval over any anchorperson chosen as host for the medical news. The company had relinquished approval over editorial material and could not review the segments before airing, but this was a new wrinkle.

"We want someone who'll give it the look of credibility and authority," Koslow was saying. "It's a key issue for us."

Schonfeld called him aside, to another room. "Look, Marv," he said, "I'm a professional newsman. I can't give an advertiser the right to approve a newscaster. I've gotta tell you that if you insist on that kind of crap, I don't know what I'm gonna do, but I know I can't do *that*. You'll just have to trust me — you'll never, never have to be concerned about the credibility of a newscaster."

They returned to the suite and Koslow informed Turner that he had backed down.

"Awwright!" Turner said. "So let's go!"

He led the way into the press conference.

*   *   *

Turner and Terry McGuirk had breakfast with Harold Rice, vice-president of RCA Americom, during the Western Cable Show. They listened as Rice told them RCA was making every effort to get them satellite space. "We're going out to other carriers to see if we can lease some space," he said. "We're going to try to compress more message traffic. And we're trying to find the bird with the help of the air force and hopefully restore it. All these are options."

"I didn't know that satellites failed," Turner said. "I thought this thing was routine."

What he did know was that Rice had given him assurances that CNN would be "taken care of" whether SATCOM III was found or not. He had been told not to worry, but he worried anyway. Turner was aware that he had no legal document saying RCA was required to give him a transponder on SATCOM I. He was vulnerable. In fact, he was desperately looking around for some alternative. He talked to people at Showtime and HBO, to see if they'd lease him one of their transponders on the cable bird. But he was coming up empty.

Despite this uncertainty, CNN was moving forward at an accelerated pace. Back in September, McGuirk had received commitments from three multiple-systems operators: Storer Cable, Cox Cable and United Cable Television, whose combined totals would bring the number of subscribers over the million mark. The necessity of having the right satellite transponder, so these cable systems could be assured of receiving CNN in the first place, was all too obvious.

It was just as well, Turner thought, that he was going off to sail *Tenacious* in the Southern Ocean Racing Circuit in the Bahamas. A final answer from RCA would not be coming for weeks or as late as February of 1980, just months before airtime.

Underneath it all, Turner confided to McGuirk, he was concerned that RCA, as the owner of NBC, might try to protect its network from competition by blocking CNN from access to SATCOM I. It was possible.

In the old white house at 1044 West Peachtree Street, Schonfeld and Reinhardt were shifting gears as well: They had signed up former Treasury Secretary William Simon, Senator Barry Goldwater and consumer advocate Ralph Nader as additional commentators. They had made contracts with Reuters (for its news wire and commodities reports) and with UPITN (for its daily international satellite feeds). They had started the ball rolling on leasing space and building domestic bureaus in New York, Washington, Chicago, Dallas, Los Angeles and San Francisco. Overseas they would have operations based in London and Rome. They were even planning an office in Beijing, China.

The deals, promises, commitments and contracts, being made with Ted Turner's blessing and bank account, were growing. As the interviewing and hiring began in earnest, there could be no turning back. And next to come aboard was Ed Turner, who had worked not only with Ted Kavanau at Metromedia but with Schonfeld and Reinhardt, for a year, at UPITN. From Oklahoma, he had called the old white house on the day the satellite had gotten lost. Schonfeld was already spinning out backup ideas — such as using a different bird and selling personal, home dishes to CNN viewers — and Ed Turner had chuckled with amusement before realizing how serious the situation was. "But one way or another we're going on the air," Schonfeld had said, making Ed Turner's itch even stronger. He had gone full-circle in his career, through the "big time" in the Northeast and back to local-TV news in Oklahoma, but now it seemed as if all that experience had been a warmup.

ED TURNER

"Reese called me back and said, 'Why don't you come down and talk?' How could I refuse? I caught a plane and walked into a Hawks basketball game. Reese was there and Ted Turner was leaping up and down, cheering his team. When we were introduced, he thought I'd already been hired. So he congratulated me and said, 'We're glad to have you with us.' Then, taking note of our common last name, he asked me, 'Are you a dreamer?' I thought he wanted to know if I was some woolly headed lad you wouldn't trust with a typewriter, much less with a network, so I said, 'No, I'm not a dreamer.'

"He interrupted to announce what a dreamer *he* was.

"I thought, *Well, Turner, you're off to a real good start with the other Turner. That was the dumbest thing you could've said!*

"The next morning I met him in his office and the first thing he did was show me a videotape of himself on *60 Minutes.* It showed him winning the America's Cup and, during the trophy presentation, falling down drunker than a lord. And he thought it was hilarious! It amused him that he'd been caught for all of America to see, just smashed to his knees. I thought, *This is some character, who can so enjoy his own predicament.*

"And I signed on."

Schonfeld called Rick Brown and Jane Maxwell, whom he had met back in 1975 during the TVN days. Maxwell had joined the Joe Coors operation fresh out of college, starting as a receptionist, but she had used the job as a way of breaking into the news business. Brown, thirty, had been hired as a TVN editor on the assignment desk. Previously he had been a page at the New York Stock Exchange, a clerk in a brokerage house, a cartoonist, florist, musician, mailman. He had conducted tours in the NBC building, graduating to night editorial work for the *Today* show, where he had selected news stories, written scripts and edited film and videotape. On the sly, he had field-produced assignments and helped on satellite feeds to and from overseas. For the previous three years he had earned most of his living as a photo editor for the Associated Press.

Brown and Maxwell met each other at ITN, where they also met Reese Schonfeld before he was fired. On the day he left, Schonfeld told Maxwell that after the company folded he would call. When it did fold, Brown and Maxwell started dating; and after Schonfeld hired both of them at ITNA, the couple began living together. In October 1979, nearly four years later, they were married.

Now in January 1980, at CNN's expense, they flew down to Atlanta to talk to Schonfeld about joining. When they got there on a Saturday morning, he invited them to stay the night at his house in the fashionable Buckhead area. It seemed a bit too cozy for business dealings.

"I love Reese," Maxwell whispered to her husband, "but if we're being *interviewed* by him, how can we stay in his home? Shouldn't we create some kind of 'negotiating distance' between us?"

But Schonfeld insisted. Completely avoiding the subject of the CNN jobs, he invited Burt Reinhardt and some other guests to his house that afternoon; and later they all hopped into cars and went to a Hawks basketball game at the Omni Coliseum. Reinhardt took Brown and Maxwell in his car.

"I don't know you," Reinhardt said, "or understand what it is that you two do at ITNA, but Reese says you're both very good at it, whatever it is. And if Reese says that, I guess it's true. So I guess we should hire you. This new Cable News Network will be the place to be, you know. I don't know how you think about it, but if you come aboard, you'll be getting in on the ground floor of the wave of the future. So you should give serious thought to this."

On Sunday morning, Schonfeld drove them down toward the old white house to pick up Ted Kavanau at the efficiency apartment building, nicknamed Sleazy Jim's, where he was living. Then they all went over to Techwood to see the facility. What they saw was the shell of an old Jewish country club's mansion, with its white columns in front. (Each of the two large glass doors — later replaced by wooden ones — originally had a Star of David on it, prompting some wags to nickname the place Kosher Kolumns, until Ted Turner fired off a memo declaring that the place henceforth would be "headquarters.") Inside was a hole in the ground. The entire first floor had been removed, leaving just a cavity of dirt with pillars all around and nothing else.

"When we first took over this building," Schonfeld said, "we had to scoot out a tribe of winos." The derelicts had pitched camp in the shower room down in the basement, where Schonfeld now led Brown and Maxwell. "Isn't this just *great!*" he said, throwing his arms wide. "Isn't it *wonderful!* Look at how *big* it is!"

Maxwell, trying to envision all the desks and tape machines and monitors and newspeople, shook her head and replied, "Big? Reese, this is too small! Where's your *expansion* space?"

"Are you crazy?" Schonfeld exclaimed. "We don't *need* expansion space. This is great! This is big enough!" Maxwell and Brown looked at each other.

"Reese," said Rick Brown, "there's less than five months — are you sure this place will be ready in time?"

"Oh, sure," Schonfeld said. "Remember, we're in the South — and in spite of what you may have heard, things happen much faster than up in New York, where the unions can tie you up until your dying day."

After the Techwood tour they drove over to Sam Zelman's condominium, where Schonfeld and Kavanau made a sketch of the studio floor plan on the dining-room table; and later they went out to eat brunch. By midafternoon Schonfeld had not yet mentioned the CNN jobs to Brown and Maxwell. They were scheduled on a four o'clock flight back to New York.

Maxwell was not happy. From the beginning, the idea of coming to live in Atlanta had made her uncomfortable; and now she thought, *What is this? We've spent the entire weekend here — and nothing!*

Schonfeld bounded over and said, "Well, it's about time to leave the house. You have twenty minutes before you have to go catch your flight. So let's talk."

Maxwell stared at him.

Twenty lousy minutes.

They followed Schonfeld into his living room. Finally the three of them were going to talk.

At ITNA, Jane Maxwell had risen from weekend editor and producer to managing editor/assignment editor. She was now making $18,500. Brown, a producer overseeing incoming and outgoing news feeds, was making less. They understood why Schonfeld wanted them for CNN: they were not high-priced network talent and they knew how to do things cheaply.

Schonfeld said he wanted Maxwell to be domestic editor of CNN's assignment desk. He wanted Brown as manager of the tape department. The jobs paid $22,500 apiece. The work week would be fifty hours — although, as they knew, those hours always became much longer.

Brown was interested; but to Maxwell, it meant she was being offered a raise of only eighteen cents an hour. *Big deal, Reese,* she thought.

"These are the standard salaries we've decided on," Schonfeld said, "but listen, when we do this, it's gonna be so much fun! We're gonna kick the pants off the networks!" When Maxwell did not answer, he continued, "To get it off the ground, though, I have these budget constraints — and, Jane, I need an answer right away."

Maxwell said nothing, so Brown asked Schonfeld to join him in the hallway. "She's already being worked to death at ITNA, so she's not really thrilled about starting on the ground floor again. We need time to talk it over. I think we could let you know tomorrow."

"I need the answer before you fly back," Schonfeld said.

"Then the answer is no."

Schonfeld relented. "Why don't you two talk it over and let me know tomorrow?"

Reinhardt drove them to the airport. Brown sat up front while his wife was in the backseat. It had become clear to her that Rick wanted to take the job, but she couldn't bear the thought of leaving her roots and family, and New York itself, to move down South. They were silent in the car until Reinhardt made another stab at salesmanship. He was the antithesis of Schonfeld, however, and his attempts at conveying enthusiasm fell flat. Maxwell grew even more depressed. "Oh, damn," Reinhardt said. "I missed the exit." He kept driving and circled the entire airport. They ran for their plane, missed it, got on standby for another flight and went to the nearest airport bar, where Brown started making a list of pros and cons.

As they walked into their New York apartment, the phone was ringing. Brown picked it up and heard Schonfeld's voice: "Rick, I thought about it again and I need an answer now. Even if it means Jane saying no, I still want you to join up. Maybe she can get another job down here."

"Well," Brown said, "if Jane won't go to Atlanta, I'm not going either. But we haven't talked yet. I'll call you back within the hour."

It had been a ploy on Schonfeld's part. He wanted Maxwell at least as much as he wanted Brown, partly because of her experience at ITNA in dealing with news directors of local stations to obtain video news material. CNN would need even more help from stations. Schonfeld had decided that if he could lure Brown, he would get her with him; and he was right.

In their kitchen, Maxwell looked at Brown and said, "You want to go, don't you?"

"Yes. And I think you should go, too. Even if we stay just one or two years, it'll be worth it."

What the hell, Maxwell thought, *if Reese still wants me, I'll be the sacrificial wife and go, too. But not for long.*

She pointed her forefinger upward: "See this finger?"

He nodded.

"One year!"

"Or two," her husband countered, as she smiled for the first time. When Brown called Atlanta, Schonfeld hired them both and said to be down there in thirty days.

Getting Maxwell and Brown was part of a "raid" on Schonfeld's own Independent Television News Association. Also being lured away from ITNA was Mark Walton, who would become CNN's first White House correspondent. Mark Leff, who had been feeding European stories to ITNA by satellite from London, through Visnews, was tapped for the Rome bureau. Others from ITNA were Dean Vallas, Cindy Druss, Gerry Harrington, Mary Tillotson, David Browde and, eventually, Amy Birnbaum.

And then came the start of a raid on ABC.

Schonfeld had been going after George Watson, who was being replaced as Washington bureau chief for ABC News in favor of Carl Bernstein, journalist of Watergate fame. Watson was clearly unhappy. Roone Arledge, president of ABC News and Sports, was shifting him to a cushy job in New York, but, at forty-three, Watson wasn't eager to leave the firing line. So after Sam Zelman had begun negotiations, Schonfeld stepped in and offered Watson his top job in the nation's capital: vice-president and managing editor of the CNN Washington bureau.

At ABC's Washington bureau Watson had been running a staff of about three hundred fifty, while as CNN's managing editor he might have only seventy-five staffers at most, not to mention that he'd be exchanging ABC's power for that of Ted Turner, an unknown in the news business. On the other hand, by taking the CNN job, he could stay in Washington and become part of "an exciting new venture."

When Arledge realized that Watson was ready to jump, he spent an entire day urging him to stay in ABC's fold. Schonfeld brought Turner to Washington to help him conclude the CNN deal. As Dan Schorr had done, Watson was demanding that Turner's signature be on the contract — so if the new network crashed, he'd have a better "parachute" to avoid losing a year's salary.

At the meeting of the three men, Turner signed Watson's contract for about $100,000 — slightly less than what ABC would have paid him for 1980, but CNN's top annual wage. Reese Schonfeld was elated.

But Turner wasn't so sure. He had just reached into his own pocket to make the deal. "Is he good?" Turner asked when Watson had gone. "Is he important for us?"

"Yes," Schonfeld said.

"It was a good catch?"

"It was a *very* good catch."

In February, momentum inside the old white house began to shift gears. Schonfeld and Reinhardt had gone through thousands of job applications and now they were starting to hire people at the rate of ten per week. Most of those who would work at the Techwood headquarters were being told to arrive in March or April or even as late as May, but the commitments were being made right now. Contracts were being signed, the newsroom was under construction, the bureaus were in various planning stages and, clearly, there was no turning back without serious consequences.

Ted Turner, meanwhile, still had no word from RCA about its resolution of the satellite problem. Aware that what he had set in motion had reached a point of no return, he told Schonfeld to carry on while he went sailing off Nassau in the Southern Ocean Racing Circuit.

His assistant, Dee Woods, figured it was a perfect time to take a week's vacation; but instead of resting, she used the opportunity to attend a convention of TV programmers at the Hilton Hotel in San Francisco. It was a chance for Woods to learn more about the industry.

She mingled with the four thousand other delegates as they wandered among various exhibits in the hotel. In the RCA suite she found herself next to a group of men discussing the disappearance of SATCOM III. "You know," one was saying, "we're going to decide next week about who'll get transponders on SATCOM I."

"Who's on the list?" another man said.

"Well, we've got six services in the running for only two available spots. How can we choose? No matter which two we pick, the others would sue us! The legal risk is too high."

As a result, Woods overheard, RCA had decided to give out *neither* of the remaining transponders on SATCOM I. All the contenders would be offered leased space on a different satellite, which would be of no practical use for delivering CNN's programming.

"In other words," a man said, chuckling, "RCA has found it easier to screw everybody a little than to screw some people a lot!"

Dee Woods walked from the room.

In the hall, she ran.

DEE WOODS

"I called Terry McGuirk and told him, 'You've got to get in touch with Ted! Right away!' It was just an accident, overhearing that conversation, but I knew it hadn't sounded right. Terry called the Bahamas and Ted flew back to Atlanta. He got to the office before I did. The woman who was taking my place, well, she wasn't prepared for the pressure. She couldn't handle it. When Ted gets really pushed and excited, I'm the one who seems to be able to take it best. I've always been a high-energy person and so is Ted, but I'm also a calm, steady person and don't get hysterical, so we fit together well. Ted is very vocal, he's volatile, and with his high energy he talks loud. This poor woman, when I called the office, she was in tears. Ted got on the phone and said, 'Where are you?' I said, 'I'm still in California.' He said, 'You get back here now! I've got to have you here!'"

Turner was on the warpath. The next day he flew up to New York for a confrontation with RCA's lawyers. He was accompanied by McGuirk, Schonfeld and Ed Taylor (who owned the common carrier for CNN's satellite transmission), along with lawyers Bill Henry and Tench Coxe. Like a general leading his troops into battle, Turner strode into an RCA law library and faced Andrew Inglis, president of RCA Americom, and a group of stern-faced corporate attorneys.

TERRY MCGUIRK

"The lawyers were trying to intimidate Ted, but he went nuts on them. He said, 'All you guys, get out of here! I want the chairman of the overall parent corporation down here, right now, because I'm gonna break this company into so many small pieces that all of you will be looking for jobs!' He said there was no use in his talking to them, because they'd all be fired in ninety days.

I mean, he went on like that for nearly an hour and just scared the hell out of those executives. He blew 'em away."

In fact, Turner was calculating every move.

"Does your chairman know you're meeting with me here today?"

My God, Schonfeld thought, *here is the difference between an owner and an employee.*

The RCA executives in the room, for all their lofty titles and big salaries, were still subject to a higher authority. While Turner could make decisions right on the spot, they had no such power; and he would not let them forget it. He poured on the pressure.

At one point an RCA attorney spoke up: "Listen, Ted, we've looked at your contract with us. You've got no backup. You've got no legal ground. You'll just have to live with it."

Turner nearly flew apart. He had committed all his assets to CNN's survival, he said. He'd go all the way down, through the bottom, and never give up. He would take mighty RCA down with him, too!

"I'm a small company," he said, "and you guys may put me out of business." He paused. "BUT FOR EVERY DROP OF BLOOD I SHED," he roared, "YOU WILL SHED A BARREL!"

Faces turned white. It was, Schonfeld thought, the best meeting he had ever seen. Turner had not been out of control for a moment.

While not exactly backing down, the RCA lawyers asked Turner for a private conference and offered him a possible solution. In so many words, they told him: "Go ahead and sue us. And sue the FCC, too. We can't give you a transponder on SATCOM I while we're denying it to other parties, but if you win in court we'll be *forced* to give it to you."

In the RCA Building elevator on the way down from the meeting, Turner was elated. He had survived a crucial skirmish; the battle for the satellite wasn't over. Schonfeld and Ed Taylor were in the crowded elevator with him.

"We made a secret deal!" Turner exclaimed in a booming voice, capturing everyone's attention. Schonfeld nearly fainted; God only knew who else was overhearing the whole thing, in RCA's own elevator! Schonfeld tried blabbering some meaningless chatter to drown him out; but Turner continued, louder and louder, as his audience hung on every word. . . .

"I was sweating blood," lawyer Tench Coxe would recall about the RCA ordeal, because there was no assurance that he could win a lawsuit against such a corporation. The actual contract giving Turner a satellite transponder had made it clear that everything had been "subject to a successful launch." Coxe was doubtful that a suit for breach of contract would succeed. With CNN's future at stake, he was reluctant to go into court arguing that a satellite lost in space had been "successfully launched."

TED KAVANAU

"A meeting was held in Ted Turner's office and everybody figured we were dead. Without the satellite, we were finished before we began. He'd already made this huge investment and now he was confronted with what to do because it was all going down the drain. Everything looked black as hell.

"Turner has plenty of weak points, but I have fantastic respect for him because he's a great fighter. There's no question about it — a great leader and very daring. He took all the risks you had to take to make the thing work. He never got cautious, never backtracked. He went forward no matter what, with everything on the line.

"I guess this is a little poetic, but it had become like a crusade . . . a crusade against the networks — these monoliths, with all their power — and against anybody else who stood in our path. They had to be swept away or shot down.

"Well, he had this huge *broadsword* on the wall of his office, and whenever he wanted to make a point, he would take the broadsword and swing it around. So in this meeting he took the sword, held it up and shouted: '*We will not be stopped! No matter what it costs, we're gonna go on!*'"

The day after the RCA meeting, Turner placed a call to Andrew Inglis, president of the RCA satellite division. Recording the conversation for possible future use, and pacing his office as he talked, Turner was by turns pleading and threatening. He conveyed the desperation of his situation while making clear that if his ship was going down he wouldn't let it sink alone. Turner wanted to get as much "on record" as possible, but his main purpose was to make one last attempt to avoid the cost, time, uncertainty and sheer tension of a court battle.

Inglis: Hello.

Turner: Hey! Andy? How are you doing?

Inglis: Hi, Ted.

Turner: How are you doing?

Inglis: Well, uh, uh, what can I say?

Turner: Okay, the main thing, Terry called me right after it happened. I was out in the Bahamas and I dropped everything and, uh, came back. And let me set down our criteria first and see if you know exactly where we stand. . . .

You ran into problems and I know you've had a lot of problems and everything, and you know we have been a great customer and have tried to be as understanding as we could of your problem, and now we will just have to lay it on the line and tell you, so you can be understanding of *ours*, 'cause I know you are our friends and everything and you don't want to see *us* go down the drain, just like we don't want to see *you* go down the drain. Okay.

First of all, we *cannot* go on any other satellite with the outgoing transmission of the Cable News Network but the one that is carrying the *cable* traffic. . . .

The thing that is so unfortunate about this is that every day that has gone by, we have spent hundreds of thousands of dollars. Every day. We have signed firm leases in New York, Washington, the equipment is ordered — I wish you could come down here. . . .

Now, this is a *catastrophe* for us, because we have had people leave ABC, CBS and other companies to come to work for us, and we are in the process, we still have to hire another 150 people in the next ninety days and there is no way anybody would quit a job to come with us now, because they know there is no way the thing can succeed. . . .

> In order for this to work, we have to assume that in a relatively short time we would be able to get the small and large cable systems, and we *have* to be on the cable satellite or we have to lose the whole project. . . .

Turner referred back to his 1976 contract with RCA in order to cite a clause that could give Inglis "a leg up" in favoring CNN over other cable networks clamoring for relief:

> Turner: We never wanted to make any trouble because, you know, what the hell, we've been friends. . . .
>
> I'm hoping we won't have to do this, but it is something that we could certainly sue under, our attorneys feel like, and get some kind of relief, or at least cause all kinds of trouble — not that we want to *do* that, but this is something for you to think about. . . .

The clause had required RCA to give Turner's company a chance to use a remaining transponder on SATCOM I before anyone else could do so. Of course, that option didn't seem important when SATCOM III was scheduled to carry CNN instead; but now that the new bird was missing in space, Turner was seizing on the option as a lifeline to get on SATCOM I.

> Inglis: Ted, I think you are stretching a point, but —
> Turner: Okay, but all I'm saying is that we are going to have to, unless we can work this out, we are going to have to pursue, we stand to lose thirty, forty, fifty million dollars —
> Inglis: Okay, Ted —
> Turner: — perhaps as much as you lost when the satellite went down, except you were insured and we're not. . . .

He launched into various ways RCA and CNN could use combinations of satellites to satisfy their needs, but his main point remained that if CNN's outgoing signal could not reach all the cable-system dishes, the whole project was pointless. How, Inglis interjected, could RCA fairly choose only two scheduled companies without being sued by the others? Turner made it clear that he would cause trouble even if RCA, out of fairness, made no choice at all.

> Turner: Now since that satellite has gone down, we can't start the Cable News Network. We are going to have to *can* it and *sue* you for everything we possibly can, if that's the case. Maybe we won't collect anything, but, we will have lost, well, the loss is just too great to measure at the present time. It could drag the whole company down the drain, quite frankly —
>
> Inglis: Let me, uh, uh —
>
> Turner: Because we did everything that we could under the situation. We ordered the transponder, we had to have protected service on the cable satellite, in order to start the Cable News Network, and we did that. I mean it wasn't your fault that the satellite went down, but . . .

He argued that his 1976 contract "predates any other problems" and that RCA could "use that for an excuse" to favor CNN. If not, he warned again, "It is certainly going to be the basis for a major lawsuit from us." Later he added, "I've got to throw the lawyers into motion because, see, our problem is one of time. It is only ninety days to launch. Time is of the essence, because we are proceeding ahead, and we are spending lots of money, and making further and further commitments, hiring people and disrupting a lot of lives. We have already hired over a hundred people and I'm going to have to let them go in thirty or sixty days.

"I have to be on SATCOM I *now*," Turner added, "and I have to be on the new SATCOM III when it's launched! I *have* to be or I'm canceling and suing! I have no choice, if it can't be worked out!"

Urging Inglis to head off the legal battle, he changed tone and said, "Let's try and work this out on a friendly basis." He brought up instances when he had helped RCA and pleaded, finally, as if worn out, "So help me with this, okay? Because, I mean, it would be a shame for me to go down the drain at this point in time. . . ."

*　　*　　*

A few minutes later, Turner spoke on the phone to Tench Coxe as the recorder was still running. Coxe said he was ready to talk with Inglis and "tell him there is absolutely no question about what is at stake here and we have no choice but to go all the way." The lawyer added, "We think that RCA has improperly behaved and violated its duties as a common carrier, by throwing everybody into a barrel to shoot at each other."

"Well," Turner said, "we had better throw the wheels into motion." He urged Coxe to raise a possible conflict of interest "in the fact that RCA owns NBC," which viewed CNN as "a real threat."

"This thing has got to be resolved real soon," Turner told Coxe, "because if we don't have some sort of satisfaction this week we are going to have to stop going ahead. We have no choice. We can't go ahead and get people to leave other places. I wouldn't quit *my* job anywhere to go with an operation . . ."

Weary and despondent, he left his sentence unfinished. Then he said, "I mean, here we have spent all this money," but again his voice trailed off. The conversation with his lawyer was over, and it was time for action.

One week later, on February 28, 1980, in the U.S. District Court for the Northern District of Georgia, Tench Coxe filed suit on behalf of Turner Broadcasting and Cable News Network. Charging RCA Americom with breach of contract, he asked for an immediate injunction requiring RCA to give CNN space on SATCOM I.

THREE

"The best advice is never to do anything. You'll never get in trouble if you never do anything. But you'll never get anywhere, either. 'Faint heart ne'er won fair lady.'"

OVER THE ENSUING WEEKS of spring, the little white house would be jammed with people, their cars overflowing from the parking lot onto the nearby streets. As the bedlam grew, the inside of CNN's temporary headquarters would begin to resemble the dormitory in the movie *Animal House*, teeming with newcomers. They came mostly from local stations in nearly every state and were under no illusions about getting paid very well or feeling secure in their jobs. The whole idea of expecting long-term employment here was a joke.

Arrivals were given a manual, in looseleaf binders with fifty-one pages of double-spaced typing, called *Inside CNN*. It was the result of a collaboration by Alec Nagle and Peter Vesey, thirty-four, who had come to Atlanta from KSD-TV in St. Louis, where he had spent five years as director of news and operations. The manual served as an introduction for new staff members, covering every possible angle of the operation down to a glossary of terms "so we can all speak the same technical language" at the outset.

It even introduced the setting:

In general, Atlanta is a pleasant city with an impossible road system and friendly natives. Twenty-six streets in the city have the word "Peachtree" in their name. That's confusing. The thing to remember is that there is *one big* Peachtree Street, running north-south. . . .

Nagle couldn't resist including his personal stamp of enthusiasm:

We are creating an alternative to the three networks. They've owned the airwaves, and therefore television, for a long time.

Now comes CNN, using satellites and cable systems, and we've just started a new ballgame.

We will be putting on news when the other networks are offering entertainment. We'll be the alternative for millions of viewers. If we attract them and inform them, if we do our job, we will be successful.

And television will never be the same.

Welcome to the Great Adventure!

Among those coming aboard were Jane Caper, hired to take charge of the "commentators" whose reports were to be inserted during the daily schedule; Myron Kandel, financial editor in New York; Tom Knott, who would supervise production of the medical pieces sponsored by Bristol-Myers; John Holliman, given the task of delivering a national farm report out of the Washington bureau; John Baker, joining the team of executive producers in Atlanta; and John Ward, who would be Jim Kitchell's director of operations for the newsroom. On and on they came, but even by the first week of March only seventy-five of three hundred staff members had been hired.

The explosion was yet to come.

Mary Alice Williams, thirty, had signed on in the last week of February. A month earlier she had been fired from her job as anchor of the WNBC-TV *Morning News* in New York, where she'd been told, "Baby, you'll never be a star." What Schonfeld and Reinhardt wanted was not a star but someone capable of acting as both anchor and bureau chief. Williams took the New York job and, along with it, responsibility for CNN's twenty-four-member staff at the World Trade Center.

She came down to the white house to start preparing.

MARY ALICE WILLIAMS

"It was hilarious. There was a card table in the room where we worked and we'd have coffee cups setting there, and every time a bus would go by the table would shake and the cups would go flying all over. There was so much laughing. But our loyalty and our spirit and our guts went into it. We sat there trying to figure out how we were going to fill twenty-four hours of television news with credible and reliable information, every single day, without any role model, and with everybody on the planet having asserted for the last two decades that it couldn't be done. . . ."

JOHN HILLIS

"I came from the ABC affiliate in Raleigh, North Carolina, and when I walked in, the energy of the place was just frenzied. People were running in and out, résumés and videotapes were stacked high along the walls, and it was really like D-Day being mounted in there. It soon became clear that I possessed most of the qualifications for a young producer that they were looking for — namely, that I had two arms and two legs and was breathing — so I did five minutes with Reese and then ten minutes with Burt, who looked up at me and said, 'We are not gonna pay you a lot of money!'"

In the basement of the white house, a totally separate revolution was under way. Under the supervision of Rob Barnes, a WTBS employee who had become CNN's director of data resources, two young men were designing a space-age computer system for the newsroom. As producer Jim Shepherd described the scene, "Down in that dank, dark, termite-infested room were these two crazed guys, Peter Kolstad and Ed Grudzian, building our computer system. It was the first job for TV news that these guys had ever done. They were also fairly broke, so poor that they had to burn their own circuits onto the chips down there."

Helping Kolstad and Grudzian from a newsman's perspective was Peter Vesey, who was slated to become Washington bureau chief under George Watson's management. In their introductory pamphlet, Vesey and Alec Nagle had described the basement work as if it already had been achieved: "CNN has the world's first completely computerized TV newsroom. It will be used for everything: from the wires, the assignment desk rundowns, news scripts, producers' formats, TelePrompTer, to the tape lists, graphic rundowns, and notes to specific people. There are no conventional typewriters in the newsroom. Only the computer terminals. It will eliminate a ton of paper. Daily."

Kolstad and Grudzian had founded a company called BASYS in San Diego. They had created a large computer system for radio-news operations, but never for television news. Nobody else had done it either. In early September, they had gone to Las Vegas for the annual convention of the Radio-Television News

Directors Association. Amid the opulence of Caesars Palace, they were setting up their booth when Schonfeld and Reinhardt suddenly appeared, quickly introducing themselves, and said, "Can you give us a demonstration?"

"We can't really do that right now," Kolstad and Grudzian said. "We're not ready yet."

"Well," Schonfeld said, "we're not going to be around much longer."

"There's really not much we can do. We still have to get this booth set up."

"Look," Schonfeld said, "we're starting a twenty-four-hour TV network. It would probably pay you guys to take the time to do it for us."

The two men stopped what they were doing to give a brief demonstration. Schonfeld and Reinhardt thanked them and moved on. By the end of the convention Kolstad and Grudzian had forgotten their names. All they remembered was that one had been a short man named Bert who had looked a bit like Humphrey Bogart and that the other man had been tall. And that both were from New York.

Kolstad and Grudzian began referring to Reinhardt and Schonfeld, partially because one was short and the other tall, as "Bert and Ernie" from public television's *Sesame Street.*

Later on, the two young men from BASYS were among those who submitted proposals to CNN for designing an "all-electronic" newsroom relying completely on computers. In the process they met up with "Bert and Ernie" again; and they got the contract because, simply enough, their bid was the cheapest.

"We'll keep the price low," they said, "if you let us *create* it at the same time. We'd love to use CNN as the guinea pig for developing a computer system while you build the newsroom. Then, after we help you guys, we can go out and sell our system to other people."

The emerging package of software, called NewsFury, would be the first of its kind in broadcast journalism.

FLIP SPICELAND

"I got off the airplane from Springfield, Illinois, where I'd been doing pick-up work after quitting a California job — to this day, I don't know how Sam Zelman found me — and I grabbed a cab and went to the little white house, which should have been condemned. As the driver pulled up I said, 'You made a mistake. Here's the address I want to go to,' but he said, 'This is it.' I said, 'Well, I'm looking for a *television* place. It should be the Cable News Network with TV cameras, not an old white house. So I've either given you the wrong address or you've gone to the wrong place.' He said, 'No, this is the address you gave me.'

"And I said, 'Oh, my God, what have I done? I'm out of work, I've flown down here, and it turns out to be this old rickety house that Sherman forgot to burn.' So I go in and find Zelman, who had been a voice on the phone, and he hooks me up with Schonfeld and Kavanau. They hustle me out real fast and pump me with questions about being a weatherman and then they wonder if I have any questions to ask them. I had only one:

"'Is this thing gonna be around six months from now?'"

The answer, from most experts, was absolutely not.

Conventional wisdom was that CNN would never get on the air at *all*; that if it somehow *did* get off the ground, it wouldn't last any more than six months; and that if (by some further miracle) it did survive longer, then Ted Turner would go bankrupt within a year.

DON LENNOX

"I had worked at KABC all-news radio and Channel 7 in Los Angeles, producing and writing, and now I was down in Sacramento, between jobs, selling condos. . . .

"When Turner announced that he was going to start an all-news television network, everyone in the business thought it was just totally preposterous. But I had a kind of endearing feeling for the guy, because I'd always been a champion of the underdog, and I realized what kind of hold the networks had on television news. You either work for them or goodbye. You can't just open your own mom-and-pop TV-news store, which essentially was what Ted was doing.

"I kinda followed him and noticed he would be transmitting on the new satellite that RCA was putting up. When SATCOM III got lost, I thought, 'Well, there goes CNN and Ted's big deal.' And when he *sued* them I thought: *God, he's suing RCA! Come on! They'll chew him up and spit him out!*"

*   *   *

On the morning of Tuesday, March 4, 1980, Ted Turner called a press conference at the Techwood headquarters. Visitors to the half-finished newsroom were given yellow construction hats with CNN labels. Wearing a light suit and holding a cigar, surrounded by construction activity, he announced a federal consent order assuring his all-news network of a transponder on SATCOM I.

But for no longer than six months.

And if the suit against RCA was lost, so was he.

"This is not the solution we would like to have had," Turner told reporters. "But it's the best we could have done. It will allow us to get off on time. I think the people of America need this in-depth news service, and I've been willing all along to risk everything I have to provide that service. And we're gonna provide it.

"Barring satellite problems, we won't be signing off until the world ends. We'll be on, and we will *cover* the end of the world, *live*, and that will be our last event. We'll play the National Anthem only one time, on the first of June, and when the end of the world comes we'll play 'Nearer My God to Thee' before we sign off."

To this point Turner had invested $34.5 million, the amount he had asked the court to award him in damages if no permanent RCA transponder could be obtained. The figure was a clear message to potential rivals. From the outset, he had seen himself facing an array of potential opponents. They included, of course, ABC and CBS and NBC, but also several large media groups such as Time-Life, Post-Newsweek, Scripps-Howard and Times-Mirror. These organizations had been, and still were, actively studying their chances before committing their vast resources.

Turner saw them as hungry, snarling, saber-rattling giants who, either despite their power or because of it, had become shortsighted. They were unable to see what he could predict with certainty: that cable television would flow into the mainstream of American life and that, sooner or later, a channel strictly for news would *have* to be provided.

The biggest argument against twenty-four hours of news each day was that there wouldn't be *enough* news. A round-the-clock service would be an insatiable monster devouring every scrap of news at a pace no operation could hope to match. How could any news team produce so much programming? You would need a "factory" churning out edited stories by the ton and, inevitably, the results would be sloppy.

Meanwhile, the monster with its bottomless appetite would swallow all your footage, leaving only "video vapor" and the anchors stranded for hours in front of a camera, reading wire copy. Much of this news would be of little interest to the majority of viewers, whose boredom would be registered quicker than a weary anchor could say, "Recapping our major stories at this hour . . ."

But now those who had hung back because of such arguments were raising their voices. With his temporary victory over RCA, Turner was within ninety days of getting on the air. The question, suddenly, was no longer whether an all-news cable channel was possible but whether he himself was equipped to produce it.

BURTON BENJAMIN,
VICE-PRESIDENT AND DIRECTOR OF CBS NEWS

"It's certainly an interesting idea, but the question is how they'll execute it. I don't think people want to just watch some guy rip and read the news off the wires. But once you start moving crews into hot spots, the money's heavy. On a big story, say in Cuba or Iran, you might have to send two or three crews. One trip like that and you could feed a family of four for a year."

RICHARD SALANT,
NBC BOARD VICE-CHAIRMAN

"Each of the three commercial networks, whose service I am sorry to say is a great deal less than twenty-four hours a day, is spending around $100 million, this year, to cover news. Turner has allocated less than a fourth of that amount. And there's the rub."

J. CHRISTOPHER BURNS,
VICE-PRESIDENT, WASHINGTON POST CO.

"Post-Newsweek formed some conclusions about the realities of the marketplace. The reason Ted Turner decided to go ahead with it, in the form that he's doing, may be that he doesn't understand the problem. He's not paying attention. The cable industry doubts that Ted Turner knows his ass from a hole in the ground about news. If he had looked at it carefully, he would have changed his offering. But, in time, his going ahead will help those of us who can do it better. That may turn out to be expensive for him."

Turner told friends he would make J. Christopher Burns eat crow. He would send him a dead bird, on a plate, with a fork.

Most experts were scoffing at CNN's projected yearly budget of $30 million. "We run through that in two or three months," Roone Arledge of ABC said. "Why would anybody choose to watch a patched-together news operation that's just starting," wondered Bill Leonard, president of CBS News, "against an organization like ours that's been going for fifty years and spends $100–$150 million a year?"

Turner had answers that could only be tested in reality. He felt the network executives were wrong to boast about how they spent so much money. The fact was that they were *overspend-ing*, as a way of life. Their view of what an all-news operation would cost was based on that. And it was a big reason why they had been so afraid to take the risk.

In hiring Schonfeld and, in turn, a bunch of other mavericks who were lean, mean and hungry, Turner was pointing to a different way. He compared himself to a "five-foot basketball player" who learns to beat the giants on court by making quicker moves and stealing the ball at every chance. The people joining CNN right now were the same kinds of players, eager to start the game.

"We're gonna cover national news," Schonfeld told Alec Nagle, "as if we were handling *local stories*. We'll report the big stuff out of Washington on the basis that these things really affect our viewers' *ordinary lives*. We're not gonna try to prove how *smart* we are. As a result, they won't feel like they need a Ph.D. to understand it."

"In other words," Nagle said, "we're gonna do the *national-local* news!"

Schonfeld was startled. Nagle had grasped the concept right away and, in one breath, he'd coined a term for it.

The younger man would be supervising the 8–10 P.M. Eastern

Time show, to be called *PrimeNews 120,* from the Atlanta head-quarters. That two-hour broadcast was going to be the center-piece of CNN's twenty-four-hour day.

In early March at the white house, Nagle was still absorbing ideas and focusing on the "big picture" of CNN. "He's on my wavelength," Schonfeld told Ted Kavanau.

Nagle spent hour after hour with Kavanau and Zelman as they screened hundreds of videotapes in search of anchor talent. By now they had developed a "rating system" for prospective an-chors and correspondents who would be seen on the air. They awarded points for various qualities, on a scale from one to ten; and if someone averaged a seven, then Schonfeld and Reinhardt would be called upon to make the final decision.

One of the highest ratings was given to a young woman named Kathleen Sullivan, who was anchoring the news at KTVX-TV in Salt Lake City. Zelman was hot to get her. "She's magic," Nagle said when he saw Sullivan on videotape. "She makes love to the camera!"

It was Sam Zelman, the veteran from CBS News, who had a real knack for spotting the right people. He was calm and reflective, a kind of "intellectual godfather" at the white house, and at one point Nagle told a group of young staffers, "Keep looking at Sam, because he's gonna save us. I just know that one of these days, when we get into trouble, Sam will bail us out."

Zelman also had an eye for making newscasts *popular* as well as informative; and during the process of "noodling" with vari-ous formats to fill twenty-four hours, Nagle listened intently to the older man.

"Even though *we* will have more time on air," Zelman told him, "that doesn't mean the *viewer* will have more time. So we'll have to be careful. Just because we've got time to spend half an hour on a story, that doesn't mean the viewer's *attention span* is going to be that long. I think it's going to be just as short as it's always been — so we may have to make the stories them-selves just as short, too."

It was a strange paradox, having all that time to fill but still needing to keep individual stories brief.

"One way to get around this," Zelman continued, "is to repeat a story throughout the day but, each time, add new information from another angle. So even though we give just two-minute bites, our viewers will eventually know much more about the subject than they could get from any other TV news."

They discussed how newspapers allowed readers to jump from one story to another, while television — as it was currently conceived, at any rate — could not offer that option.

"People can scan through an entire paper in twenty minutes and know pretty much what's going on in the world," Zelman noted, "but they can't do that with television. Our viewers won't get to the next story until we finish the one we're telling. So we have to make our news go fast."

Nagle, on his own, began to write up elaborate formats for how to present continuous news. He churned them out in the form of long, detailed memos — "Newscast Raisons d'Être," he called them — which had the effect of getting others to think about the subject. Figured into his thinking was the tricky matter of anticipating the audience in each of the time zones across the country to Hawaii, along with what the Big Three networks would be running in the same hours:

> *6–6:30 AM* — I frontloaded this half hour to get on the air with a splash with hard news. . . .
>
> *6:30–7 AM* — This half hour is severely backloaded, to try and grab the audience waking up. . . .
>
> *7–7:30 AM* — All of a sudden we're not the only game in town; the nets are coming on with their morning shows. . . .
>
> *7:30–8 AM* — I understand there's a big tune-in factor at seven-thirty, so we've got to make this opening segment sexy. . . .
>
> *8–8:30 AM* — We have a chance here to pick up some audience. CBS has switched to *Captain Kangaroo*. . . .
>
> *8:30–9 AM* — By now our audience has changed as the Eastern Time Zone and much of Central is on its way to work. Our audience will tend to be older and more female. . . .

RICK BROWN

"Alec came up with what he called the 'pre-denounce' theory, to get people thinking. They'd ask how we were going to fill the time, so he'd put out a memo saying, 'This is what we're going to do.' People would say, 'No, that's *not true*,' and Alec would pretend to be very surprised. 'Well,' he'd say, 'I was just writing what I thought we all *knew*.' So they'd call a meeting to denounce his memo. He'd wink and say, 'It's great! I finally found a way to *get through* to these assholes!' So his theory worked. It meant he could put out a memo that was attacked by everybody before it could get off the ground as policy.

"They 'pre-denounced' it, Alex would say, but meanwhile everybody was arguing and thinking, which was exactly what he wanted us to do."

The experts saying that "it can't be done" were focusing, primarily, on cost. No matter how lofty anyone's vision might have been, the story of CNN inevitably rested on money.

SuperStation WTBS, by now being carried to over seven million cable homes in the United States, was acting as the "cash cow" for CNN; and that financial underpinning would have to remain strong for at least a couple of years. The all-news network would need plenty of cash, including bank loans, until its advertising and marketing arms could lift it out of red ink.

Turner had committed himself to spending much more money than he could afford, even while the doubters were saying that he wasn't budgeting enough. The burden of trying to accomplish "more with less" fell directly on the shoulders of Reese Schonfeld, who, with Burt Reinhardt's tight-fisted help, would have to find ways of proving the experts wrong without causing Turner to go broke at the same time.

On the second floor of the old white house, where Jim Kitchell was planning all the technical operations, Schonfeld faced the paradox directly and personally. For years, he and Kitchell had been on opposite sides, one independent and the other an NBC company man. While Schonfeld was glad to have Kitchell's network experience, he was less than thrilled to be dealing with the latter's network *mentality* — a habit, from three decades of having NBC's big budgets at his disposal, of spending through the roof.

Kitchell, meanwhile, had dealt with Schonfeld periodically over the years and frowned on his somewhat "sullied" reputation in the news business. He remembered Schonfeld at meetings to decide which network would do "pool" coverage for the others. If a news event was covered on such a cooperative assignment, then a syndicator like ITNA would have the right to use the footage; but Schonfeld would often ride "piggyback" on the networks' coverage by demanding the footage even when no pool arrangement had been made. It was Schonfeld's way of trying to get material without deploying his own personnel and equipment; and, some felt, that was one secret of how he had succeeded on the cheap.

Now the two men were on the same side, working at desks across the hall, and Schonfeld was boss. He saw Kitchell as a solid, methodical organizer, a facilities man who would make sure the equipment got to its location on time along with the manpower to run it. But he had come from NBC and that made all the difference. In Kitchell's world, there *always* had been plenty of money to do things *right*.

He was accustomed, for example, to planning for coverage of political conventions two or three years ahead of time, with budgets up to $15 million. For CNN, he had already gone to Detroit to make a presentation to the Republican National Committee for coverage of its convention in July 1980, but Schonfeld had scowled and said, "Don't worry about that! It's not until *next year!*"

In March the CNN president was still making faces at Kitchell and saying, "Look, Jim, the convention's not till *four months!* We'll *get* to it!"

"How will we do that," Kitchell asked, "if we're not prepared?"

"We'll cover it like a *news story*," Schonfeld exclaimed.

It drove Kitchell crazy and even made the placid Sam Zelman nervous. At CBS he, too, had been accustomed to the high-budget, plan-ahead style of the networks.

Jim Kitchell was used to working on a grand scale, but to Schonfeld that was like paying for a limousine when a subway ride would get you there just as well. (The story went that he and Reinhardt, in New York, had made a habit of giving their camera crews subway tokens and later demanding that the un-used ones be returned.) So when Kitchell asked for *seven* cameras for the headquarters when he really needed only *five*, and more than absolutely necessary for the bureaus, Schonfeld lost his patience.

"Why *that* many?" he hollered.

"Because some cameras at any given moment will need *down time*, for repairs."

"Don't tell me that!" Schonfeld screamed. "Don't tell me a third — or even a quarter! — of the equipment has to be down for maintenance! If a camera breaks down, we'll *fix* it. You don't *need* all that equipment! If we've gotta have twenty cameras for headquarters and bureaus, we'll get twenty-*one*! But dammitall, Kitchell, don't tell me we need twenty-*five* in case five are broken down!"

Of course, when it came to *studio* operations, Kitchell was speaking from experience. He knew how often equipment had to be repaired or replaced, while Schonfeld, who had never produced a live news program from a studio, did not know.

It was a curse on his back, this tug-of-war with Kitchell, and Schonfeld tried to be diplomatic: "Look, Jim, we can do it *better* than NBC, and *cheaper,* because *we know how.*" But there was seldom time for diplomacy and, inevitably, with a force equal to that of the buses passing by on West Peachtree Street, their shouting matches shook the walls of the old white house.

BUNKY HELFRICH

"We had set up a small architectural office on the first floor of the white house. Basically we were doing a fast-track construction project. We'd design one part of the headquarters building and give it to the contractor, Billy Wally, while we worked on the *next* part. We just kept trying to give him enough drawings so we could stay ahead of him.

"We worked closely with Gene Wright, coordinating all the engineering and hiring electrical staff to design the systems. Over at Techwood we had to do quite a lot of demolition to get through the old showers and locker rooms of the country club. The column spacing was relatively small, down there, so we took out a couple of structural columns to give 'em a little more studio space. And the ceiling height was low, so we broke out the existing slabs on the floor and excavated down to the top of the footings to get more height.

"The next problem was getting the air conditioning in there, because those facilities required enormous ducts where people could climb all the way through them. But then the sheet-metal union went on strike, just when we were putting these giant ducts in. We had to explain to the foreman that we had only three months to get on the air, that this strike could kill the whole deal. . . ."

TED KAVANAU

"There was a design for the newsroom that I vehemently opposed. They were gonna have these different sets against the wall, to go from one to another, and I said, 'Listen, we gotta show people this is not a place with two people working in a room reading copy. They'll think we're some little, tiny cable operator. We've gotta dazzle 'em with the size and extent of this operation. We've gotta look powerful! Bigger than anyone in the world!'

"So we had this meeting — Bunky and Reese were there — and we were all shouting and going crazy and screaming. I was shouting and saying, 'No, it's *not* gonna be done that way, it's wrong, dead wrong,' and Bunky said to me, 'Well, I think you should do it yourself. Go ahead. You show me where you want everything placed.' So I brought some drawings to him. I had a *total vision* of what it should look like, every part, down to every paper clip, like a huge machine with all the pieces fitting together. . . ."

Rick Brown got caught up in the frenzy right away. He had been hired to run the tape department; and, when Schonfeld told him CNN had ordered *seventy-two* videotape machines, he was amazed. Most of the incoming news feeds would be taken from Western Union satellites by the "farm" of receiving dishes outside the newsroom. Once the video and audio material was in-house, it could be run live or edited for airing. Having worked for Schonfeld, and knowing him as "Mr. We-Can-Do-It-Cheap" in the news business, Brown was startled to find himself in the presence of a man who was ready to spend money as if his very life depended on it.

The issue, of course, was *where* the money would go. To get CNN started, Schonfeld was going in two directions at once: eliminating all the costly things that engineers and technicians loved to have, while preparing himself to spend whatever it took to *get the news* physically. That, in the end, was all that counted. And videotape machines, without which no news material could be received and processed, were absolutely essential.

"The fact is," Schonfeld told him, "we're going whole hog here. At least for the first year, and maybe for the first *two* years, we'll have to spend like crazy! Because we have to get the coverage. We have to let 'em know we're here! We have to make sure that we *never miss* a story. If the other networks miss it, fine. If they get it, they get it. We not only have to do everything that everybody *else* is doing, but we have to *make* some stories *our own*. We're gonna *match* 'em and then we're gonna go *beyond* — to show ourselves to *be* something."

It was a powerful statement of what he saw as his mandate. While saving money in some areas, he had to put Ted Turner's news network on the map boldly and quickly.

When Brown discovered that Schonfeld still hadn't found someone to run the traffic department to handle the feeds from satellites (and from land lines running from the New York and Washington bureaus to Atlanta), he quickly asked for the job of setting up the whole operation. That, he felt, would be a real challenge.

Schonfeld, who had been annoyed that his original choice for the position had turned it down, hesitated; but then he shrugged and said, "Okay, Rick, the traffic department is yours."

"Uh, Reese —"

"Yes?"

"It's no longer the traffic department. From now on, we're gonna call it Satellites and Circuits."

Jane Maxwell stood in Burt Reinhardt's office.

"Oh, Jane," Reinhardt said, wearing his best salesman's smile, "you're just the person I want to see. Listen, we have this great deal we're offering to stations around the country. We're gonna make 'reciprocal agreements' with 'em!"

"What do you mean?"

"See, they'll give us *their* news and we'll give them *our* stuff." Maxwell tried to digest the idea. "The stations will feed their local stories to us," Reinhardt was saying, "and in return, we'll feed our full news coverage *back* to 'em."

But why, Maxwell wondered, would local TV stations want material from a network they knew nothing about? Why would they deal with a *cable* network? Aren't we the competition? Why would they want to help us get off the ground in the first place?

"Reciprocity," Reinhardt said.

"Yeah," Maxwell said, "but we're *paying* for their stuff, right?"

"No, no," Reinhardt said, elated. "We're *not* paying 'em!"

"We're *not buying* this material from them?"

"No, Jane, that's the beauty of it. We're not buying *anything*. They're just gonna *give* it to us."

"Burt, I don't believe that."

In New York, Maxwell had grown accustomed to the indignity of calling up TV stations and talking them into *selling* ITNA their material; but the idea of trying to get them to *give* stories to CNN, for something they may or may not want in return, seemed ludicrous and, from the outset, doomed.

"Look," Reinhardt said, "we've got something to give those stations that they're not getting now. The networks hold back until their evening shows, but we'll give 'em stuff *any* time, in the middle of the day! And you, Jane, are gonna help us *make* the agreements with 'em."

"To get their news for free?"

"Yes! For free!"

Maxwell went downstairs and found a table with a telephone. Alec Nagle and Peter Vesey were in the room along with Jim Rutledge, who would be on the assignment desk with her. She was miserable. With her husband she had moved into Sleazy Jim's, the efficiency-apartment building nearby, where Nagle and Kavanau and others were also living temporarily. It was drab and dusty and filled with roaches.

She hated Sleazy Jim's and hated being in the South and hated this old white house and, having been given the chore of calling TV stations to beg for their local news coverage, she already hated her job. She started to cry, head down on the desk, her shoulders shaking.

The idea for "reciprocal agreements" was one of the key inspirations behind the creation of Cable News Network. As Schonfeld and Reinhardt faced the task of covering the entire country without nearly enough CNN regional bureaus or reporters, they realized that it could be done only with the resources of local stations. If, in fact, they could make enough arrangements with far-flung stations in every state, suddenly they would have a powerful "network" of affiliates. Yes, giving away their own national and international news meant they would be turning CNN into a syndication service; but in return, they would get video and audio coverage of local events without spending a dime for it.

ED TURNER

"Just when we were starting up, there was an explosion of local news. Stations were going from half-an-hour to ninety minutes to two hours of news. They were doing news in the morning and at noon. And they desperately needed product. They needed video to fill the time. And along comes CNN offering plenty of product in exchange for their stuff.

"The big problem they had to get over was that they saw us as the enemy. Number one, we were cable; and second, we were doing news. We told them, 'Look, if you take our stuff you'll never have another slow news day. You won't have to worry about weekends anymore. Unlike your own networks, we won't hold anything back from you.' We'd ask them, 'Are you happy with the news service from your own networks?' Of course, they were not. 'By taking *our* news,' we'd say, 'you'll never have to wait for Cronkite to be finished before you can have the material. You'll get CNN's news just as soon as *we* get it on the air.'

"It was a tough sell, but we would say to them, 'How would you like to have your *competition* in town using CNN's stuff instead of *you*, pal?' And we started making deals with them. We could not afford to be in two hundred locations at once, any more than the big networks could. We had to go to the locals for spot news, the breaking stuff. The only way we could get there in time was by having them do it for us.

"Reese gave me the title of managing editor of the assignment desk, which was a job he had promised to Jane Maxwell. So it was my awkward task to explain to her that she was my deputy. I talked to Jane and said how much I was looking forward to working with her, and that as manager I would count on her to assume all responsibilities. 'I'm a great believer in hiring smart people,' I told her, 'because I'm dumb.'

"To this day, I don't know what she made of it. . . ."

The first people Maxwell called were news directors with whom she had dealt for years while at TVN and ITNA. In fact, the main reason Schonfeld had wanted her at CNN was that she could use her contacts; but after those calls, the going got tougher:

"Hi, my name is Jane Maxwell and I'm deputy managing editor for CNN . . . Well, we're an all-news cable network. . . . No, we haven't gone on the air yet, but see, we're going to be doing twenty-four hours of news and, uh, we'd like to give you our coverage in exchange for, uh, *your* coverage. . . ."

She spent her time on the phone, begging and cajoling and persuading and pleading. "Are you crazy?" the news directors would say. "Why should we give you our news?" So far, in the old white house, she had cried continuously for three weeks.

Then one morning, after Ed Turner thanked her for handling a call that he hadn't wanted to take, Maxwell replied with utter solemnity, "They always said I gave good phone."

Ed Turner, Alec Nagle, Peter Vesey and Jim Rutledge looked at each other and cracked up. And Maxwell, who had not intended to be funny, sat there as they rolled on the floor until she found herself blushing and smiling and, finally, giggling.

That was the turning point.

From then on, no matter how frustrated and miserable she became, Nagle and Vesey kept cheering her on. She'd been given a thankless task and the only relief they could offer was a sense of humor. So Nagle and Vesey began to deluge Maxwell with crazy, wonderful, merciless memos that would keep dissolving her tears into more laughter.

They joked about how Maxwell's knees were becoming raw from begging and addressed her as "Hane" as if she were Jane Curtin on *Saturday Night Live:* "Over to you, Hane!"

On March 6, 1980, Alec Nagle sent her the following memo:

HANE, INC., LIBRARY

TITLE: "Basic Begging" $9.75/10.75 Can.
     By Hane

A primer for phone begging, it includes instructions for pleading, begging, whining and supplication. A tape cassette of basic groans and moans accompanies the book. . . .

Nagle and Vesey sent her memos with little drawings of J-shaped telephones. They addressed her as "Our Lady of the Dial Tone." One memo, proclaiming that "only CNN has Hane," went on to ask: "What does this mean to the average cable system owner, lusting after Big Bucks? It means Big Bucks, because the HANE BEGGING SYSTEM has *never* failed to sway strong men to make decisions against their own self-interests."

When Maxwell revealed that she'd worn a bear costume during basketball games at Bedford Junior High in Connecticut, the memo writers lost no time:

The Cable News Network Question Of The Day: Which hard-working CNN staff member was actually, in a former life, THE

BEDFORD BEAR? That's right: in our very midst, there lives and breathes that American folk hero, the Bedford Bear! This staff member actually survived desertion in the middle of the basketball court before a crowd of "tens." The Bedford Bear led her team to an unbroken season. And now she works here! Even if you don't know who she is, remember to BLESS THE BEAR!

When Ed Turner asked her to help clean up his apartment and Maxwell threw a tantrum, Vesey promptly dispatched a "Tuesday Shopping List" to her desk and Nagle jotted down a dozen menial chores ("Vesey's socks . . . Nagle's rent-a-car . . . Vesey's underwear") on a memo concluding: "P.S. Do you do windows?"

As Maxwell kept pressing for the reciprocal agreements, Nagle sent her this memo:

Re: It's Gonna Work, It's Gonna Work, It's Gonna Work!

Chin up, you happy little malcontent — it's gonna work!

That's right, you delightful cloud of gloom, station managers all over the country are chomping at the bit to sign up for our fabulous CNN deal. And who can blame them? It's a great deal — they get to give us their stuff and we get to use it! Just because your batting average has hovered around .078 is no cause for alarm, you perky pessimist. They are just being coy! Sooner or later they'll see that CNN represents the future and *they*'ll come begging. That's when we want you to ask them to *pay*.

"There are no reasons for frowns, you charming little eighteen-hour-a-day gal," Alec Nagle wrote to her. "We're smart, we know what we're doing, we're *under way*. Once we get them to pay, we'll be able to buy a few more WATS lines so you can call longer and harder! Let's see that mouth perk up at the corners! Let's hear a big CNN cheer from the Bedford Bear! Let's *believe*, even if it seems to be screwed up! We're *smart*, Hane! It's gonna work!

"By the way," Nagle concluded, "have you done the laundry yet? Be a good little gal and get it done, please."

DON LENNOX

"I go up to meet Burt and he's sitting behind his desk in a dark suit, glaring at me, so I sit down. And the very first words out of his mouth are, 'You know, producers are a dime a dozen.' He tells me the salary and says, 'We have one position open. We have tons of people who want the job. For some reason, they want to hire you. So this is what we're gonna pay you. Take it or leave it.' I say, 'Well, Burt, I'm not here for the money. I'm here for the Experiment. I've *got* to be in on this because it's too exciting to miss. So I'll take it.' And he nearly falls out of his chair."

JEANEE VON ESSEN

"My husband and I were both journalists and lived in separate cities for a lot of our marriage. I'd just had a baby, so we were trying to get jobs in the same city. He'd taken a job in Mobile, but I had stayed behind in the Detroit area, and when he started discussing a job in Atlanta, we both said, 'Hey, that's where CNN's gonna be. . . .'

"Here was this beehive of activity, people just going nuts and running around, yelling, with ideas being splashed on the walls. When I asked where the bathroom was, they showed me and I went inside. As I shut the door, all these *bug wings* floated up from the bathtub. I thought they were alive! They were really termite wings piled in the tub, but every time you shut the door they floated up and flew around before settling back down. Then I saw there was no toilet seat, which is sort of critical for people of my gender, so I went back out and told somebody. They said, 'Oh, yeah,' and pointed — the graphics people were using the toilet seat to prop open their door, which otherwise would slam shut and make it too hot for them to work.

"So whenever you wanted to use the facilities, you had to go find the toilet seat and then carry it to the bathroom, where the bug wings floated up and down. . . .

"All of a sudden they figured somebody was gonna have to do something about international stuff. I was interested, so they asked me to start setting up a 'Foreign' Desk — this was before Ted Turner removed that word from our vocabulary, making it 'International' instead — but I had no experience in that. They had hired a fellow to be foreign editor, but he wouldn't be able to get down to Atlanta till a month after we were scheduled to go on the air. . . .

"They handed me an envelope with two résumés. That was it. Well, I wondered, how do you start a Foreign Desk? I decided I'd better get things categorized. Got a whole bunch of folders and made titles for them — countries, people, ideas — but there was no more room in the white house, so I took the folders out to my car and lined them up in the backseat, all in a row. From then on I carried 'em with me, drove 'em home, and in the morning I'd drive 'em back to work. So in those early months, the Foreign Desk of CNN was riding all around town, wherever I went. . . ."

In his quest for qualified people, Schonfeld worked up a system whereby Diane Durham called ABC bureaus asking for targeted staffers to call her back. Soon the name Diane Durham became a code word among ABC News people, signifying that CNN had struck again; and the raid was paying off.

Joining George Watson at the CNN Washington bureau was David Newman, senior producer of ABC's *World News Tonight*, and Bernard Shaw, the ABC Capitol Hill correspondent. Roone Arledge, president of ABC News, told Shaw he was making a serious mistake by joining a network that wasn't even on the air yet. "It won't be good for your career," said Arledge, who came up with more money as an inducement to stay. But Shaw figured it would be an opportunity to break new ground and make a name for himself. "If Edward R. Murrow represented the first 'new frontier' in television," he said, "then CNN will be the last."

With Sam Zelman's help, Schonfeld also got Don Farmer, another ABC reporter covering Capitol Hill (plus his wife, Chris Curle, from the ABC-owned station in Washington); and Bill Zimmerman, a veteran ABC correspondent. Ann Williams, a graphics expert, was lured from the ABC Washington bureau to set up CNN's department in Atlanta; and other defectors included Wendy Walker, starting as a secretary for CNN in Washington, and Christine Dolan. In all, fourteen people were jumping from that single network.

From *Broadcasting* magazine, March 17, 1980:

> Robert J. Wussler, president and owner of the Pyramid Enterprises production firm and former president of the CBS-TV network and CBS Sports, last week was named executive vice president of Turner Broadcasting System, R. E. (Ted) Turner's growing Atlanta-based empire. . . .
>
> By title he will be the second highest-ranking executive in TBS, but the chain of command was not immediately clear. Reese

Schonfeld, president of CNN, said that he had been told by Turner that he will continue to report directly to Turner.

Bobby Wussler was a big name from the world of network television and news. It would turn out that he would not have a direct hand in CNN operations, but behind the scenes he would have enormous influence on TBS policy and programming. Equally important was Wussler's inside track, through his contacts, on what the Big Three networks were thinking and doing at any given moment. He could be Turner's tipster on the maneuverings of the competition; he could act as a go-between to set up private meetings between Turner and top network executives; and, in general, he would be on hand to lend smoothness as well as advice.

BOB WUSSLER

"I was a corporate guy who'd spent twenty-one years understanding what was maybe the most complex, sophisticated corporation in the history of media — CBS under William S. Paley and Frank Stanton. . . .

"Ted was totally unstructured. He had three hundred people working for him. I said, 'Where's the table of organization?' He said, 'I don't have one. They all report to me.' And he believed that. He believed that everybody in the place reported directly to him. He might say that yeah, some people report to so-and-so, but he'd add, 'They really report to me. I tell them all what to do.'

"He's a great executive officer. He's got a great mind for the present and the future. He has a couple of basic tenets, like, 'Keep it simple. Don't make it complicated.' He also operates with twenty or thirty rules that he learned from his father while driving from Savannah to Chattanooga to Atlanta to Macon. . . .

"Ted's also a great salesman. He will go after and woo anybody. Then once he gets them and puts them on his side, he goes off to the next project. The reason he needed me there was because he was going to be off defending the America's Cup and wasn't going to be around much. And while he had no intention of letting me run the business or anything like that, he could tell the banks or anyone, 'Oh, yeah, call my guy Wussler. Send a letter to Wussler.' And when he was away, we would go over things every morning and night. . . .

"The people at CNN never quite knew what my role was, but they knew that I was number two to Turner and that he asked me about various matters all the time. . . ."

To fill positions in the Atlanta headquarters, Schonfeld had thrown out all the rules. His producers and directors were in their twenties and thirties — young, eager, in transition, looking for ways of getting ahead, coming out of the hinterlands where they had gained some initial experience, willing to work for almost nothing — and they were ready to pick up roots and transplant themselves to a strange city for the chance to be part of something "exciting" and "significant" even though it might go bust overnight.

Many were in flux, having bounced from one TV station to another. They were not models of stability. Among them were workaholics who partied and drank with gusto — once in Atlanta, they were drawn to Harrison's on Peachtree as if its bar were an oasis for wandering misfits. A good number were going through separations and divorces; others were on the verge of getting married or had wed in the last year or two and were now having babies.

So one trend that emerged was a new form of nepotism: the hiring of couples who would work at CNN together. It had started with Schonfeld and his wife, Pat O'Gorman, a film editor who had become CNN's videotape supervisor, and soon extended to several other couples who were coming aboard. Like Rick Brown and Jane Maxwell. Like Don Farmer and his wife, Chris Curle, a popular anchor for the ABC affiliate in Washington. Like Dave Walker and Lois Hart, who had been married in California less than a year before and would become another husband-wife anchor team. Like Lou Waters and his wife, Mardy, who became Ann Williams's assistant in graphics. Like Bill Zimmerman and his wife, Dini Diskin, a director; and like Paul and Danielle Amos, who had been producers at different stations in New Orleans. (At the station where Danielle worked, employees who got married were forced to decide which one would leave; so when CNN invited both her and Paul into the fold, they were astounded.) The list would grow and grow, shattering the myth that it was a conflict of interest for family members to work at the same news outfit.

TED KAVANAU

"I talked to Paul Amos and then I realized that his wife, Danielle, was a crackerjack producer. So when he came I got the two of them, which was lucky. I was always in favor of husbands and wives working together, anyway, because they'd have a lot to talk about. So we encouraged it. But the *main* reason it happened that way, to tell the truth, was that we couldn't *afford* a policy against couples. We needed people to work for us! We were so desperate that we couldn't make rules about what you *couldn't* do. Our rules were: 'Can you breathe and walk? Can you help us in any way?' And we did happen to get some very good people who came as couples. I mean, when we got Farmer and Curle, it wasn't a case of being desperate. Farmer was already a heavyweight, but we got *him* as part of a couple, too. . . ."

It was necessary to hire professional anchors. It was also clear that CNN needed producers, directors and senior writers with some experience. You didn't start the world's first twenty-four-hour news network without such people, not if you had any sanity — but then you needed rewrite people, lots of them, along with staffers to run cameras and work with videotape editing machines and computers. And it became apparent that the budget for all *those* bodies had been woefully small.

Jim Kitchell had been faced with the job of hiring on the technical end, while Ted Kavanau had been in charge of finding editorial people. They had been pulling against each other, from both sides of the budget, until they realized that the lack of union restrictions meant they could "combine categories" to create a new breed of television worker, a hybrid form of electronic news creature:

The video journalist!

It was Kavanau who came up with the term, although no one a day later could remember exactly when or how. The best guess is that Mad Dog had been sputtering in frustration at a million words per minute, spitting out various combinations of those words, when "video" and "journalist" came out one after the other. The VJ had been born.

JIM KITCHELL

"I think Reese's original projection was that all of the technical manpower for production — camera people, switchers, tape operators, tape editors, floor people, graphic artists and so forth, who would run the whole operation 168 hours a week — came to eighty-six people. And when he first told me that, I said it's not possible. No way! He said, 'Well, we've only got so many dollars.' So then Kavanau and I discussed the whole scheme of VJs and how we could go out to colleges and journalism schools and recruit young people. We could hire them for minimum wage and give them the opportunity to do *everything.*"

TED KAVANAU

"I was hiring all the producers and writers while Kitchell was in charge of the semitechnical areas. He would tell Gene Wright, 'I want this equipment,' and, 'I want this person to operate it.' But then I realized that he was gonna hire all these professional cameramen and videotape editors at about $21,000 a year and a crisis developed — because it was suddenly clear that we needed *twice* the number of people we were budgeted for. . . .

"I said, 'Look, here's what we'll do. We *won't* hire these professional people. We'll use the same budget, but instead of paying them $20,000–$22,000 apiece, we'll go around the country to colleges. We'll hire the best kids coming out of those schools, pay them *half the money* and get *twice the number.'*

"Reese's wife, Pat O'Gorman, and others went scouring the country for video journalists. We began recruiting and bringing in kids who had no experience whatsoever. We were confronted with the whole world waiting for us to die, with the networks waiting for this new experiment to fail — and yet the truth, what nobody knew, was that we had only a few seasoned professionals leading an army of neophytes!

"So we brought in this massive bunch of raw kids and tried to house them. We threw them into boardinghouses and they lived together — these hordes of kids descending upon Atlanta. The building at Techwood wasn't even complete. It was gutted and still under construction. And now all our computers and tape machines were starting to show up in crates, while we were faced with having to teach these kids how to *use* the equipment just so we could get on the air.

"That was the big untold story. While the world watched and waited, with less than two months to go, we started training an army of youth. What we had on our hands, at the final hour, was a children's crusade. . . ."

The next step was to find the cheapest motels in the surrounding area, for training and living space. They hired meeting halls at the Master Host motel and held classes at the white house, too. Rooms were booked at the Admiral Benbow Inn (the "Bimbo," they called it) and at the Rodeway, to supply temporary quarters until the young people could find apartments of their own. Collectively, the setup came to be known as the CNN College — there was even talk of building VJ dormitories. Their cramped meeting halls, now the classrooms, were filled with young video journalists listening to Professors Kavanau and Nagle, among others, speak about the need to "graduate" in time for May rehearsals at the Techwood newsroom.

The impossible had become the ridiculous.

FLIP SPICELAND

"With a month to go, we walked into the Techwood studio and the floor was still mud. One wall had all the windows knocked out, so it was open to the elements, and the cameras were over in the corner covered with tarps and sheets of plastic. We would be in there trying to do something and someone would come in and say, 'The fire marshal is coming by. We've all gotta get out of the building right now.'

"And we had no bathrooms. We had portable johns out in the back. I said to Rob Barnes, 'Where's the men's room?' And he said, 'You see that tree out there?'

"In rehearsals we were working literally from six in the morning till midnight, trying to figure out how to do it. To make my job even worse, we had not one shred of weather equipment. We had no weather wire, no map machines, nothing. I'm in there reading weather off the national wire, standing in front of a plywood board, with guys on ladders hammering over me and stuff falling down on my head. I was the only weatherman — they had hired Dallas Raines out of New Orleans, but he couldn't start until June 1, our sign-on date, so I was doing all the rehearsals with the different producers and anchors, twelve shows a day, and just going nuts, going crazy, and getting so tired and, I mean, I couldn't do it. . . ."

"Ted Kavanau did as much as anyone to mold our product on the air. He was a yeller and a screamer. He had this feeling that he wanted everybody upset, everybody right on edge, because he felt he got a better newscast that way. People were so tired that maybe he was right — without someone to get us mad, maybe people just would have given up.

"Alec Nagle was funny and bright and humorous. While Kavanau could make you mad, Alec could make you laugh. And God, you really needed to laugh. Someone said it was like the six weeks of boot camp, where every day goes really slow but, looking back, it went by very fast."

The CNN College was organized primarily by a pair of directors, Guy Pepper and Jim Schoonmaker, who made up schedules for classes. Few of the newcomers at these indoctrination sessions saw anything of Ted Turner, who had a myriad of problems of his own to solve. But once in a while he appeared with the suddenness of a passing tornado. During a lecture by Rob Barnes on computers, Pepper saw Turner standing in the back of the room and invited him up to say a few words to the group.

"I just want to welcome y'all to CNN and wish you the best of luck," Turner said. "See, we're gonna take the news and put it on the satellite, and then we're gonna beam it down into Russia, and we're gonna bring world peace, and we're all gonna get rich in the process! Thank you very much! Good luck!"

Even before Turner abruptly walked out, Schoonmaker and others at the session started having second thoughts about the seriousness of this endeavor. *Russia? World peace? Get rich? Is he kidding? We gave up good jobs to come here?* Some even considered leaving before the scheduled launch.

During an early rehearsal in the newsroom, Jim Shepherd was seated next to director Erik Shepherd (no relation) when he heard some commotion and yelled, "Quiet, goddammit!"

There was silence.

Jim Shepherd looked up and saw Ted Turner staring at him.

"Oh," the producer said. "Hi, Ted."

Erik Shepherd stood up. "That's *Jim* Shepherd," he told Turner. "I'm *Erik* Shepherd."

Jim Shepherd put his head down. A few minutes later he looked up and saw Turner gesturing for him. He got up and walked over.

"Hi, Jim," Turner said. "I like what you did. You're doing great. You're taking charge and keeping things quiet around here. That's the way it should be."

"Thank you," Shepherd said.

"But you know, Jim, you surprised me."

"Sorry about that."

"Oh, that's okay," Turner said. "By the way, Jim, you're fired." Shepherd's mouth fell open.

Turner smiled. "Now we're even," he said. "We've *both* been surprised today, haven't we?" When Shepherd nodded, Turner added, "Get back to work."

DAVE WALKER

"We rehearsed for about a month, just learning how to do it right or wrong or at least differently. In the newsroom, hammers were pounding left and right. The place was leaking. We kept saying, 'How in the hell are we gonna get on the air in two weeks?' The place was a shambles! Reese would stroll around, calm as he could be, saying, 'Oh, no, don't worry, it'll be ready.' And meanwhile, we were literally walking into holes in the ground!"

RICK BROWN

"When we first got over there, Techwood had this new-machine smell. The cameras and switchers were covered, in hopes that the dust wouldn't destroy them right away. It was cold, since the studio lights weren't all installed — but the building was churning out air conditioning anyway. One day we had to stay out of the newsroom, as it was enveloped in one big plastic sheet while they sprayed this clunky brown soundproofing on the ceiling, something they had to do before they could put in the lights. . . .

"As launch day approached, we were finding out that the BASYS guys, toiling away on the overnight shift, were not even close to having the computer system ready. Kavanau went into his crisis mode and got everyone together in what he called Paper Chase meetings. We had to unlearn everything we knew about doing things in the computer and learn how to do it the old way. Noisy old wire machines were ordered, along with papers and ribbons, and copy kids were hired to tend to them. Regular old typewriters were ordered for the writers, along with multicarbon script books. We had to order a regular mechanical TelePrompTer system, a conveyor belt on which the pages would be placed neatly end to end and run in front of a cheap camera that would send the image to the monitor mounted on the front of the studio camera. . . ."

During some of the dry runs, Kavanau pretended to be the weatherman (even though he thought television's use of weathercasters was distracting) and, standing in front of the weatherboard, he made up some great stories about "highs" and "lows" headed this way and that across the country. There were no actual feeds coming in, from the bureaus or otherwise, so Jane Maxwell assigned a crew to do a story on the training of attack dogs; and in place of real commercials, they used a public-service announcement about water conservation showing a wooden toy duck that dunked in a glass. Day after day, the newsroom was filled with the sounds of barking dogs, dunking ducks, clattering typewriters and buzzing wire machines, not to mention the sounds of construction workers and newspeople. . . .

JIM SHEPHERD

"Rehearsals? It was more like a plane crash. I don't think *anything* went right. We were doing dry runs and I'd have to say, 'Can you turn off the jackhammer a minute? I can't hear!' We were hauling cables right up to the night before launch. We had this wonderful state-of-the-art control room and all this glass behind us, but if you went behind that there was nothing! No power in half the building, no walls, no toilets except for the portable ones outside. . . ."

PAUL AMOS

"During the rehearsal time I started having nightmares. In my sleep I'd be back-timing my show and I'd wake up screaming, '*I'm ten minutes short,*' because that was one of the great fears. I mean, *no way* were we going to be able to gather enough material to fill all that time. And literally I had nightmares. I'd wake up in a sweat. I'd see numbers running through my head. It was just crazy, knowing there was a good chance that it wouldn't work, and yet we had to *make* it work.

"Ted Kavanau drove all of us like madmen. We had rehearsal after rehearsal after rehearsal. On and on! The basic rule for producers was to assume the assignment desk would provide us with absolutely nothing — and how in the hell are you going to fill your show? So here we were, feeling that what we were doing would make a mark on our business, that it would change everything, and meanwhile the opening day was approaching and I was waking up screaming. . . ."

Ted Kavanau, who wore his beeper even while jogging, wanted to *live* in the newsroom.

He had asked Bunky Helfrich to design a little "apartment" for him, right at the headquarters, with a cot. He wanted to eat, sleep and breathe it all.

Ted Turner vetoed his request. "People would think we're running a sweatshop," he said.

Kavanau could see the twenty-four-hour cycle of all-news television spinning in his head; he could picture it flashing by as if it were some gaudy, high-speed merry-go-round whose colorful horses each represented a different segment. When the time came to hop aboard, he would be *on* the spinning merry-go-round for the ride of his life.

The question was whether he and the others would be ready.

Everything had to fall into place. In rehearsals, he had been driving the herd faster and faster. He was a shouter, a screamer; he was extremely demanding and difficult to work with, especially when he "knew" what he was doing and someone got in his way.

"The Day of the Long Knives is approaching," he said.

The idea of the dry runs was to try rolling through four hours of programming at a clip. Work four hours, then stop and build on that. The system was set up, but so far it was all theoretical. Kavanau had no idea if anything would work in practice. During the dry runs he rushed around to keep things going, but the shows kept falling apart. Timings were off, anchors were flustered, tapes weren't matching stories and everything was breaking down. . . .

On a sultry night in May with about a week to go, Kavanau had no more desire to stay in the newsroom. He walked across the highway to Sleazy Jim's apartment building, slipped inside his tiny rented room and lay down on the bed. He couldn't sleep. Whenever he closed his eyes, he saw visions of himself in flames.

The whole world is watching and I have created a total disaster.

All night long, he lay awake staring at the ceiling and plotting his escape from Atlanta. He would pack his bags and slip away, just disappear and never return.

As the dawn came, however, he began to see the reasons behind the flaws and how he could fix them — as if he'd been struck by fresh inspiration.

Kavanau's image of the network was that the shows would constantly turn over, almost in a blur. Anchors would keep changing all the time, shifting in and out, giving an endless *drive* to the whole operation. Yes, he had wanted an *impossible* pace, he now realized. To come up with totally new stories every hour would *never* work.

During the dry runs so far, the shows had fallen behind because the writers had been unable to turn out new, finished scripts to fill each hour. But if each producer could throw, say, thirty percent of the previous news hour's stories to a *retyping pool*, indicating what changes were to be made, then the regular writers would be free to concentrate on completely new stuff — and most important, they'd have time to finish before the hour was up!

That morning, he walked back to Techwood with new vigor and determination. He called for a meeting with his producers, who were aware of the trouble they were in. Outside the building, which was surrounded by piles of dirt and wood, he grabbed some crates.

In a room with only three walls yet built, Kavanau stood on the crates to face this group of young people whom he had brought to Atlanta from all over. They were people who were counting on him, he knew, so he raised his voice and beat his breast as he made the speech of his life:

"I've been hearing that some of you have been saying among yourselves that this thing is not gonna work! That we're not gonna get on the air! That we're not gonna be a success! Well, that may be true for everybody else, but not for you!

"*I didn't bring you here to fail,*" he screamed. "You will *not* fail! You will not fail because I will not *let* you fail! If any of you cannot work under those terms, leave the room! Right now!"

No one moved.

The producers — Kathy Pepino, Paul Amos, Danielle Amos, Jim Shepherd, Tom Purdy, John Hillis, Don Lennox, Andrea Baer,

Susan Reed, Sarah Scott and Mark Aldrin — sat frozen as Kavanau continued, thumping his chest and jabbing his finger at them as he described his new system. . . .

JOHN HILLIS

"Everyone was scared to get up. There were eight or nine of us and Kavanau was our father. We had all come from different places. I don't think any of us knew each other at the time, but we had pretty much the same background, meaning that we'd worked in the fortieth market or below. Because that's what CNN could afford.

"So we didn't have an enormous amount of confidence in ourselves. And Kavanau was very imposing to a bunch of kids who'd come out of places like Louisville and Raleigh-Durham. He was from New York, with the gun strapped to his ankle, and having been Ted Kavanau, and looking and sounding like he did, beating his breast, yelling, '*I will not let you fail*' — well, nobody left the room."

Kavanau had reinvented the wheel . . . for television.

It was the same wheel that had been used by all-news radio since the 1960s. For listeners of WINS in New York, it had meant the constant refrain, "Give us twenty-two minutes and we'll give you the world." Round and round the wheel would go, with a good number of stories remaining virtually the same except for slight changes, while others dropped away to make room for new ones.

At CNN there would be much more than a simple news wheel, allowing for sports and weather coverage, financial news, commentaries and all the other things that Schonfeld had been planning, not to mention interruptions for live coverage of breaking events.

To what extent they would "go live" on any given day was the unknown factor. That was the wild card in the deck.

But underneath the chaos, spinning around, was the wheel of hard news that Ted Kavanau would make sure to keep filled with updated stories.

The biggest wild card of all, in terms of potential live coverage, was the hostage story. The U.S. embassy in Teheran had been seized by Iranian revolutionaries back in November of 1979. Some of the hostages had been released, but about fifty still remained; and by now they had been held captive nearly seven months. All during the planning and building of CNN, this story had threatened to break loose with the release or rescue of the hostages; and that could become the supreme test of the network's ability to go live and stay live. In fact, some eager staff members had been pressing Schonfeld to get on the air even sooner than June, to take advantage of the hostage story per se, arguing that by its very *ongoing* nature it was one of the longest-running live events ever.

During the technical rehearsals and dry runs, someone wrapped a little yellow ribbon around the pillar behind the anchor desk. That was the nation's symbolic reminder of the hostages. It was also CNN's way of never losing sight of the story; although some producers, like Jim Shepherd, were offended by the tackiness of the display and removed the ribbon for their run-throughs. It would remain as part of the newsroom's decoration, however, well after sign-on.

In the late hours at Harrison's, there was always talk about the hostages. Wouldn't it be great if they were released just as we went on the air? Wouldn't that be an absolute mindblower? If it happened, we would *murder* the other networks; we'd *commit murder* against the Big Three, they agreed as the booze flowed; and Alec Nagle went further by coining a phrase: "We'd *commit television.*"

Ted Turner and Bunky Helfrich were practicing for the America's Cup when CNN was preparing to go on the air. While Helfrich was in Newport, he was being accused by the Techwood news staff of having forgotten the bathrooms. (The sight of anchor people trotting out to use the Porta-Johns had been humorous only up to a point.) Helfrich was planning to put up a so-called South Addition to the headquarters building where the bathrooms would be, but this wing hadn't been completed and CNN's launch date was unmovable, whether such amenities were ready or not. For every other aspect of the venture, the same rule applied. It was all *happening,* one way or another. Turner had resolved to go on the air no matter what. From the bathrooms to the RCA satellite, from the newsroom's computer system to the sale of the Charlotte station, from the building of the bureau facilities to the advertising sales, and so on down the line, progress was *at whatever stage it had reached.*

Despite the six-month temporary transponder on SATCOM I, the troubles were hardly over. Turner's attorney in Washington, Bill Henry, a former chairman of the FCC, had drafted a memo to Turner about petitioning the commission for final resolution of the issue. "CNN will have an uphill fight at FCC," he concluded, referring to the fact that other programmers were also demanding to be included on the primary cable satellite.

Variety noted that "clearly the FCC is in a pickle" over having to decide whom RCA should favor in the matter. "The June 1st startup date, crucial for sales and contractual purposes, is rapidly approaching," the trade paper added, "and chances for settlement among the parties appear dim."

Bill Henry was quoted as "lamenting" that "CNN is beyond the point of return."

In April the FCC had agreed that CNN was entitled to use a transponder on SATCOM I until December only. The situation remained hardly comfortable.

Crucial to CNN was the sale of Turner's Charlotte television station. Bob Schuessler at WRET had played a key role in getting Westinghouse to bid $20 million, the only price Turner said he would accept; but then a coalition of local black groups contested the license on grounds that not enough minorities had been hired. Schuessler argued that the percentage of black employees had dropped below government quotas primarily because WRET was five miles from the nearest bus line, making it difficult for people without cars to commute. In any event, Turner went to the Charlotte Coalition with Henry Aaron, who was directing the Braves' farm teams, and met directly with the group's lawyers. In exchange for concessions costing Turner up to half-a-million dollars, the coalition dropped its complaint; and only a few weeks before CNN's debut, the FCC approved the sale of WRET to Westinghouse.

To keep going before he could get his hands on the money from the sale, Turner had obtained a $20 million credit line with First

National Bank of Chicago. The interest rate alone was twenty-five percent, or $5 million a year, which meant payments of over $400,000 per month.

"I'm just about flat broke," Turner had exclaimed back in April, when the Charlotte sale was being blocked. "The bank notes are due and I've got three hundred people on the payroll with no money coming in to pay them."

GERRY HOGAN

"In those early days we often knew we wouldn't be able to make the payroll. We'd be sitting there at night, trying to figure ways of coming up with the cash. I would fly up to New York and go around asking our advertisers to give us 'prepays' so we could cover things. 'We appreciate your support,' I'd tell them, 'but we've got a problem. The problem is that we don't have any more money. . . .'

"On Wednesday nights I'd literally be flying back from New York, carrying the checks, to put them in the bank on Thursday so we could pay our people on Friday. . . .

"One customer said he couldn't pay me, but he knew some guys in New York who might be able to help us. I said, 'We've got to bring Ted.' These guys had some off-shore money, I was told. So Ted and I went to see them. We were given the address of a townhouse on the upper East Side of Manhattan. We go up there and see a sign saying 'Acme Trucking' or something like that, and this big guy looking like a gorilla comes to the door. He takes us upstairs to the penthouse and we go into a conference room. Five other guys come in and now it's obvious that we're meeting, you know, with the 'boys.' . . .

"The leader said, 'No problem. We can do this. You just gotta do a few things for *us.*'

"Ted and I weren't ten minutes into it before we were looking at each other like, you know, *How do we get out of here?*

"We finally said, 'Let us think about it. We've really got to talk about it. We'll get in touch with you tonight.'

"We got out of there and never looked back."

Turner's financial strategist, Bill Bevins, along with his accountant, Paul Beckham, had some hairy moments in the early days of CNN's economic history. Placed as security for corporate debt was an undisclosed amount of Turner's one-ounce solid-gold coins from South Africa, called Krugerrands. (He had bought $2 million worth at $275 an ounce and, within a year, gold had hit $800 an ounce.) The Krugerrands were placed in a bank vault; but later, after refinancing, no one could remember the combination to the vault's door, so it had to be drilled open.

Bevins developed a reputation for ingenious methods of financing, to the point where it was believed that he was using money from the sale of beer and popcorn at Braves games to meet the CNN payroll. That story was apocryphal, but it expressed the very real fear that Turner was on the verge of economic collapse.

By May 1980, there were 16 million homes across the country wired for cable. While budget projections for the new network had kept rising to $2.5 million per month, the tally on how many households would be able to watch CNN's debut had been spiraling downward: first from earlier projections of 5 million to 3 million, then from 2.2 million to a pitiful 1.7 million.

Uncertainty over the satellite had caused a good deal of the setback, but otherwise the dominant cable operators were still taking a wait-and-see attitude. Terry McGuirk had been luring Teleprompter, the country's largest multisystem operator, but so far just a few franchises had been committed — in New York, Los Angeles and other cities — with only 169,000 subscribing households. Of nearly five thousand different cable systems in the United States, a total of 172 had signed up, provoking wry comments that CNN's debut might be seen by "three traveling salesmen in west Arkansas" or by "one little old lady in Iowa."

Turner was always anxious to see how cable sales were going. Whenever he saw Frank Beatty he would ask about the latest subscriber figures; and if they bumped into each other less than twenty-four hours later, Turner acted as if they hadn't spoken for a week: "Frank! Tell me how many more subs we got!"

FRANK BEATTY

"For the longest while we'd been selling just the *concept* of it. We'd been selling blue smoke, because we really couldn't show 'em what CNN was going to look like. When the cable people asked, we said, 'Watch the *CBS Evening News*. It's gonna be like that, only better.' Another problem was that most systems didn't have the capacity to carry another channel, anyway. There were still a lot of twelve-channel systems, then, and they'd say, 'Well, we have no place to put you.'"

The latest cable systems were carrying thirty-five channels or more; and while most new applications had included CNN in their bids, many operations were three years away from start-up. The struggle at this point was for the existing twelve-channel systems, a more difficult battleground because of the need for expensive modifications or adapters. The operators were also bound by the FCC's "must-carry" rules requiring carriage of local stations and leaving no way for CNN to be included.

Making matters worse was the fact that no cable system was available in Washington, D.C., preventing major newsmakers in the capital from watching at all. Turner already had plans for offering free satellite dishes to the U.S. Congress and the National Press Club. He had even installed a $10,000 dish on the lawn of Dan Schorr's home, so the Washington correspondent's children could see what their dad was doing.

Cable News Network was being offered to subscribers as part of a system's basic package. The charge to operators of the systems, fifteen to twenty cents per month per home, was not nearly enough to support the network. To provide just *half* of its operating budget, CNN would need at least 7.5 million subscribing households; and the other half would have to come from advertisers. By now, however, as the sign-on approached, there were only seventeen sponsors. (Time-Life and Sears were among them, but only Bristol-Myers had made a major commitment.) The prospect of Turner losing all of the $100 million he had committed to CNN had become more likely than ever.

To potential advertisers, the sales force was saying that people interested in news were "upscale" — richer, better educated, more active as consumers — and that because sponsors would be paying only for the people they reached, CNN was cheaper per thousand than they would pay for conventional network time. While the advertising community showed interest, there was still no generally accepted measurement of the cable audience. Companies such as A. C. Nielsen and Arbitron were gearing up for one, but meanwhile Turner's people would have to pioneer their own audience surveys. The *Wall Street Journal* summed up the issue by observing, "CNN is putting the whole issue of advertising and cable TV to the test well before anyone expected it."

Saturday, May 31.

Five of the six bureau chiefs, known as the "Gang of Six," had flown uninvited to Atlanta to express their fears that they would not be ready to go on line. But Rick Brown told them, "All you need is a camera and a mike, with a wire running to an up-link."

Now, ready or not, the bureaus were in place.

In New York, bureau chief Mary Alice Williams was preparing with Myron ("Mike") Kandel, financial editor, and Richard Roth on the assignment desk. A few months previously Williams had been told to "order ten miles" of cable for the hundred and ten stories of 1 World Trade Center, where the bureau was on the lobby floor. She had become, in effect, a construction foreman; and she had dealt with unions that had "tried to shake us down and threatened to pour acid in my face."

Cindy Druss was bureau chief in Chicago, with producer Linda Ringe, in Suite 409 of Merchandise Mart Plaza.

Peter Vesey was the only member of the "Gang of Six" who had not gone to the meeting in Atlanta. Managing editor George Watson of the Washington bureau was huddling with chief Vesey and his assistant, Jim Schultz, as well as producer Dave Newman, in the office at 2133 Wisconsin Avenue in Georgetown.

The San Francisco bureau chief, Donna Sykes, was being assisted by Tammi Weine at 50 California Avenue; in Dallas, chief Larry LaMotte and his assistant, Sandee Myers, got set at 1 Main Plaza; and Peter Spear headed up the Los Angeles bureau, with Scott Barer assisting, at 6920 Sunset Boulevard. The latter office was plagued by equipment problems: its microwave-satellite link had not been patched together yet; and on Thursday night, two cameras had been stolen from the bureau. Replacements had arrived from Atlanta, but they still wouldn't work, so Pete Spear borrowed a camera from an independent producer.

The London bureau chief, Françoise Husson, was operating from 31 Foley Street; and in Rome, Mark Leff and Dennis Troute waited at Via dei Robilant 1B. . . .

With about thirty hours to go before launch, how could anyone in the Techwood newsroom predict what story would break in time to be carried *live* in the first hour?

Civil rights leader Vernon Jordan had been shot and taken to a hospital in Fort Wayne, Indiana. There had been rumors that President Carter would leave Washington and fly there to pay a visit to Jordan at his bedside. All response from the White House had been negative; official denials were still being issued, but Jane Maxwell was running on instinct. If she were the president, *she* would go.

She called the local station in Fort Wayne, an NBC affiliate. By now she had completed about thirty-five "reciprocal agreements" with stations, but no exchange deal had been made with this one. She spoke to the production manager and said, "I understand that the president may be going there tomorrow. I don't have much of his schedule, but what are your plans for coverage?"

"Where did you say you're from?"

"CNN."

"CNN?"

"Cable News Network. We'd like to buy your live coverage of that event."

"I don't get it."

"I know you've never heard of us," Maxwell said, "but we're a network signing on tomorrow, and I just want to know if we can buy your material."

"We're affiliated with NBC. We have to sell it to *them.*"

"You can also sell it to *us.* We'll pay the same price."

"Well, I don't know if —"

"You *can.* Believe me."

It was perfectly legal for the station to sell its coverage. Maxwell waited. At last the word came back: "Okay, you've got it."

Now she left the assignment desk and went over to Satellites and Circuits, in a corner of Master Control, where her husband was working with colleagues Bill Papa and Ken Dickman. She could have picked up the phone, but this order seemed to require a personal delivery.

"I want you to book a feed," she told Rick Brown, "from ten A.M. to ten P.M. tomorrow." She gave him the name of the NBC affiliate in Fort Wayne, Indiana, as the origination point.

"Twelve hours? Are you sure?"

"Book it," she said, covering any of her doubts with an air of confidence. They discussed which direction to run the feed. It could come directly down to Atlanta by "telco" land line, but that was very expensive, or it could go by land line to Chicago for up-link to a Western Union satellite, which was cheaper.

"I'll book the AT&T line to Chicago," Brown said.

By evening it was confirmed that at some point the next day, on Sunday, President Carter would visit Vernon Jordan at the hospital.

Early Sunday, June 1.

Rick Brown took a call from AT&T about his twelve-hour line order from Fort Wayne to Chicago. "You've got no problem on it," he was told, "with one exception. From 5:30 P.M. to 6:30 P.M. Eastern Time, you're blocked by NBC."

"Why?"

"They previously booked the only video line coming out of Fort Wayne."

"Coming from *where* in Fort Wayne?" Brown asked.

"From their affiliate."

"I see. Any idea where NBC is taking it to?"

"To New York," the AT&T engineer said.

"By any chance," Brown said, "do you see any orders there for ABC or CBS?"

"Not possible. As I say, NBC's got the only line that goes out. No, wait a minute — I see here that NBC has given ABC and CBS permission to receive the feed in New York."

Bingo, Brown thought. *We can receive it in New York, too!*

"Okay," he said, "please keep my booking for 10 A.M. to 5:30 P.M. going from Fort Wayne to Chicago, and also for 6:30 P.M. to 10 P.M. And thank you very much. I really appreciate your help on this."

Brown told his wife that the AT&T booking would be fine except from 5:30 to 6:30 P.M. "We're blocked out of Fort Wayne during that hour by NBC, which has the only line out of town. They're taking it to New York. But who do you think they're *sharing* it with? I'll give you two guesses — and both of them are right!"

"Where are they originating from?" she asked.

"From the same station we are."

"Shit!" Maxwell said.

NBC, ABC and CBS would have any video material out of Fort Wayne from 5:30 to 6:30 P.M., to use on tape for their evening newscasts. They would share the line and its cost. And it was becoming clear that President Carter would probably make his public appearance during that same hour — out of the twelve that Maxwell had booked. Unless CNN could add on to the feed in New York, it would be blocked by all three of its competitors, the broadcast networks, from the moment it went on the air at six o'clock.

"Shit!" Maxwell repeated.

She called Alan Statsky at the NBC weekend assignment desk in New York. "Hi, Alan, this is Jane Maxwell — at CNN in Atlanta? We're calling because we want to join your five-thirty feed from Fort Wayne."

"Well, Jane, that's just not possible."

"I don't understand. I hear that ABC and CBS are joining your feed."

"Yes," Statsky said, "and that's because this feed is a *network* feed."

"Well, we're a network, too, Alan. If you're letting the other networks join the feed, you can't tell us we can't join it."

"That's not my understanding, Jane. But besides, the feed is coming from the NBC affiliate. It's coming from our station's live transmission truck at the hospital. It's *our* station, which means it's *our* material, which means that CNN does not have access."

"Oh, really?" Maxwell said. "By any chance are the other networks picking up that same live shot?"

"Yes, Jane, they're sharing on the feed. And yes, they're getting access to our station's live shot. But you are *not* allowed to join. And we are *not* giving you access to our live shot."

"Wait one second, Alan. It is *not* your live shot. It's the *station's* live shot. The station can sell it to whomever it wants to. And, in fact, the station has agreed to sell the material to us."

"Jane, it's coming from an NBC affiliate. You *cannot* have access."

"I beg to differ!" Maxwell said. "If the other networks have access to that material, then we do too!"

"Jane, once again — this is an NBC affiliate, so you can't have access!"

"Alan, once again — I beg to differ. We are buying the coverage from the station, just as *you* are buying the coverage from the station."

"Jane," Statsky said, "you cannot buy an NBC affiliate's material!"

Maxwell's voice grew deeper. "I really hope, for *your* sake, Alan, that you have *not* told the station we can't buy their material."

There was silence at both ends. Implicit in Maxwell's statement was that NBC could be at the receiving end of a lawsuit, but she had no desire to put such a threat into words and embroil CNN in a legal battle on its opening day.

"I've got to go," Statsky said, hanging up.

Maxwell stood at her desk and looked around the newsroom; all around her was a buzz of activity as if a storm were building. The noise came in waves of intensity. People were in motion — but you couldn't really talk to them until things settled down, if they ever would. She took other calls, becoming part of the racket again. When Alec Nagle came by to check on her progress with NBC, she said, "I haven't heard back from them. I've been working on other things, but I'll try to call in a minute," and he moved on.

When she finally did call, a different NBC desk person answered. "Alan Statsky, please."

"I'm sorry, but Alan's knee-deep in executives right now. Can I take a message and have him call you back?"

"Please tell him Jane Maxwell at CNN in Atlanta called. Thank you," she said, suddenly smiling. She could picture the NBC newsroom in New York, where this junior deskman was surrounded by frowning news managers as they muttered about Reese Schonfeld being up to his old tricks. The fact was, however, that CNN had the law on its side.

A short while later, Statsky got back to her. "Okay," he said, "you can join the feed."

"Alan," Maxwell said without a pause, "please have your people tell AT&T that we want to have the line fed into our New York bureau. I will tell my people here. Thank you," she added, abruptly hanging up. She stood quickly and shouted over the din to Nagle across the room. "Alec! We got Fort Wayne!"

As she was running back to Master Control to tell Brown, who would make the land-line arrangements from New York, Nagle smiled broadly and puffed up like a kid.

*   *   *

By late afternoon of Sunday, June 1, 1980, more than three hundred guests were gathering under two huge tents on the grounds of the former Progressive Club. There were dignitaries and politicians, cable operators and advertisers, employees of Turner Broadcasting and their relatives; R. T. Williams was producing WTBS coverage of the party, with Bill Tush hosting; and it seemed that reporters on hand for CNN's inauguration nearly outnumbered the new network's own staff members, who were about to try to cover the world.

Suffering from a hernia, Reese Schonfeld limped around outside as he waited to make one of the speeches at the ceremony leading into the sign-on. He would have preferred being inside the mansion, down in the basement, where his nervous colleagues were keeping an eye on the clock while scrambling to get ready.

He had put everything into motion to make the biggest possible splash as a live network. The news departments of ABC, CBS and NBC normally relied on their affiliates to go live with local, breaking stories; networks did not usually go live, their stations did, and networks hardly ever used domestic satellites for news feeds. But Schonfeld, ingeniously, had placed the Chicago, Dallas, San Francisco and Los Angeles bureaus in the same buildings where the up-link control rooms were located; and now, down in the basement of Ted Turner's Tara on Techwood, for the first time in history, a *network* was about to receive direct, live coverage from its overseas *and* domestic bureaus, routinely using a mixture of satellites and phone-company lines.

Once the faucet was turned on, it would never be shut off.

Schonfeld had sent Mike Boettcher down to Key West, Florida, to cover the Cuban boat people's arrival — whether any Cubans arrived on schedule or not. He had ordered a satellite truck to accompany Boettcher. The main point was to demonstrate CNN's technological flexibility and, in effect, to say to the world: "See? *This* is what we do! This is what we're all *about*. We are different! And we're *magic!*"

The trouble was, over the past few days all the news had died down. CNN could have access to a local station's live coverage of Mount St. Helens — but the volcano, refusing to cooperate, had gone back to sleep. The rioting in Miami was over. There were no hurricanes in sight. It was past 5:30 P.M., Sunday, and not a political creature in Washington, D.C., was stirring.

To impress the audience with overseas coverage, Schonfeld had enlisted Jay Bushinsky, a *Chicago Sun Times* correspondent in Jerusalem, to give a live satellite report in the first hour. But today even the Israelis and the Arabs were peaceful.

Wasn't *any* news happening *anywhere?*

In the basement newsroom, at the satellite desk in a corner of Master Control, one of the monitors was showing the live feed from Indiana. Jimmy Carter had gone to the hospital by now.

Rick Brown and his colleagues watched the monitor. All they saw was the closed door of Jordan's hospital room. Occasionally a nurse walked by. They'd been paying for the land line from Fort Wayne to Chicago since ten o'clock that morning. CNN had been getting the feed via satellite, from the Chicago bureau's up-link dish, until 5:30 P.M., when they'd been forced off the bird as expected. Now they were on the AT&T land line, having joined the NBC pool feed from Fort Wayne to New York.

The broadcast networks were taking the feed to use a bit later, for video reports on their evening news shows. Only CNN was poised to carry President Carter live.

But a snag had developed. From the New York bureau, there were *two* land lines down to the Atlanta newsroom: one was feeding the video and audio material from Fort Wayne, so the second line would be needed to bring home the Jerusalem feed after it was down-linked in New York. At the last moment, however, AT&T had reported to Brown that the second land line could not be connected.

"We can't find the *loop* for that line," an AT&T engineer had said.

"What do you mean?" Brown had yelled into the phone.

"We've tried and tried, but it's not here."

"Well, you'd *better* find it."

One small wire, needed to make the second land line functional, was missing. "So," the engineer said, "you're gonna be blocked."

"Blocked by what?"

"By your *own feed* from Jerusalem. There's gonna be a hot switch in New York, taking place at six-thirty. You'll be cut off from Fort Wayne, automatically, to pick up the Mideast satellite feed."

So only *one* line was available and, because Jay Bushinsky's live feed from Jerusalem would be taken at six-thirty, the "hot switch" would be thrown at precisely that moment. In a split second, the Jerusalem feed would take over the New York–Atlanta transmission line while the coverage from Fort Wayne would disappear. If President Carter failed to emerge from Vernon Jordan's hospital room by 6:30 P.M., the story could no longer be carried live — unless, beforehand, they canceled Bushinsky's satellite feed altogether and lost the money they'd paid for it.

They did not cancel the Jerusalem feed. All of Jane Maxwell's efforts with the local Fort Wayne station and NBC could wind up with no payoff in terms of live coverage.

At 5:40 P.M., the crowd outside gathered on the lawn to face a reviewing stand in front of the four pillars of the new TBS headquarters. It was still a bright, hot day as Ted Turner stood facing his guests amid the presence of four combined military bands.

"I'd like to call our ceremonies to order," Turner said. "We should be on the air at six o'clock, as predicted. We have a few statements from some visitors and some people who are with us. . . ."

First up was Tom Wheeler, president of the National Cable Television Association, who called the birth of CNN a "telepublishing event marking a watershed in providing information." Next was Bob Wussler, who remarked that CNN "will provide, for the first time in history, an electronic record of each day's events." Wussler introduced Schonfeld, who said it had been "one year, twenty-two days and seven hours" since Turner had called upon him to join "his voyage over unchartered waters." Then came a benediction by the Reverend William Borders, pastor of the Wheat Street Baptist Church in Atlanta. Then Turner again.

"You'll notice that we've raised three flags," he said at 5:59 P.M. as a live CNN camera was focused on him, "One, the state of —"

Six o'clock. The News Channel flickered to life. On the viewers' screen was Turner, live, at the podium.

"— Georgia, where we're located; second, the United States flag, of course, which represents our country and the way we intend to serve it with the Cable News Network; and over on the other side, we have the flag of the United Nations, because we hope that CNN's international coverage and greater-depth coverage will bring, both in the country and in the world, a better understanding of how people from different nations live and work, and hopefully bring together, in brotherhood and kindness and friendship and in peace, the people of this nation and this world."

Turner lifted a piece of paper and read some words of dedication:

To act upon one's convictions while others wait,
To create a positive force in a world where cynics abound,
To provide information to people when it wasn't available before,
To offer those who want it a choice;
For the American people, whose thirst for understanding and a better life has made this venture possible;
For the cable industry, whose pioneering spirit caused this great step forward in communication;
And for those employees of Turner Broadcasting, whose total commitment to their company has brought us together today,
I dedicate the News Channel for America —
The Cable News Network.

Turner stood with his hand over his heart as the five members of the color guard marched in front of the podium. The drums rolled. The military band played the national anthem as CNN's first viewers saw the American flag and then the crowd alongside the circular pool in front of the building. As the last notes faded, Turner whooped out a lusty "Awwriiight!"

It was 6:04 P.M.

In the newsroom, at the anchor desk, Dave Walker and Lois Hart got set. They were trying to remain calm, as if this were just a normal newscast. Just a few feet away in the pit, shouting at each other, were Ted Kavanau and Sam Zelman and John Baker. While the clock was running out, they were arguing over how Walker and Hart should introduce themselves and the new network.

"They gotta make an opening statement!"

"No, no, no!"

"How about something like, you know, that our *mission* is —"

"No!"

"They should at least say that this is CNN and we're here to —"

"No, they shouldn't say anything like that! Just let 'em open with the news!"

"We gotta have a *statement!*"

"How about, 'Welcome to your window to the world'?"

"No!"

Ten seconds to go. . . .

The three producers kept screaming at each other. Zelman, exasperated, turned off his hearing aid.

The producers quieted down.

Walker and Hart faced the camera.

Guy Pepper's voice came over the intercom for a final, send-off message to the crew: "Just remember, shit flows downhill."

Amid another drum roll, the CNN camera was zooming in on the six satellite dishes in back; and now viewers heard voices announcing cities and countries around the world, as if the earth stations were being bombarded with urgent reports from beyond the blue sky. The screen was filled with a closeup of one of the white receiving dishes, but suddenly the scene shifted to the inside of the new CNN headquarters, with live shots of staffers in the all-electronic newsroom. A graphics title ("CNN") appeared and then rolled over. It was replaced by another legend ("THE NEWS CHANNEL") before Dave Walker and Lois Hart were revealed at the anchor desk.

"Good evening. I'm David Walker."

"And I'm Lois Hart. Now here's the news."

They were off and running until the end of the world.

"President Carter has arrived in Fort Wayne, Indiana, for a brief visit with civil rights leader Vernon Jordan," Lois Hart continued. "Jordan is in serious but stable condition now at Parkview Hospital. He is recuperating from the gunshot wound suffered early Thursday morning. . . ."

In Master Control, Rick Brown and Jim Shepherd watched the monitor showing the closed door of Jordan's hospital room. "Come on outa there," they whispered.

"We'll have more on the president's visit later on in the hour," Lois Hart was saying, "but first Richard Blome takes a look at how this small town in Indiana is handling the shooting of a prominent black leader."

It was an edited, videotape report on the situation in Fort Wayne, while the monitor showing Vernon Jordan's hospital door revealed no activity. . . .

Dave Walker gave a quick follow-up on investigations of the shooting and moved into the second story of the hour:

"In New London, Connecticut, police say a man apparently upset over a family problem went on a shooting spree aboard an Amtrak train en route from Washington to Boston . . ."

Hart picked up the next report: "New York Yankee slugger Reggie Jackson had a close call. A man fired a gunshot at the baseball player, over an argument over a parking space . . ." She tossed the Jackson story to the New York bureau, where Mary Alice Williams continued with videotape coverage. Williams gave a detailed description of how the Yankee hero, having slugged an eleventh-inning homer against the Toronto Blue Jays, had gone out "partying to some of his favorite bars" in Manhattan when the incident occurred. "Three shots zinged past Jackson," Williams reported, adding that each had missed its mark, but an investigation would continue —

Thud.

The transmission from New York suddenly died and CNN suffered its first "glitch" of many to come.

"Cut away!" someone in Atlanta yelled. "Get outa there!"

Back to the anchor desk, where Walker and Hart had been listening to more heated arguments from a few feet away, this time over which story should come next.

"We're apparently having a little problem in New York," Hart told the camera with utter calm. "We'll go on with the news now," she added, as if sending a message to the frantic producers that *she* was in control. "Tomorrow would have been the last day in the life of mass murderer John Gesey, but instead the man convicted of more murders than any other person in American history will spend his execution day inside prison . . ."

Walker took the next one: "Meanwhile, Mount St. Helens has its first quiet Sunday . . ."

It was, in the absence of any more volcanic activity, a news report without news. Walker did mention that when the mountain had exploded two Sundays ago, it had killed at least thirty-three persons and had caused a billion dollars' worth of damage.

The gang in Master Control kept pleading with President Carter:

"Get outa the room!"

"Get outa the room!"

That was the refrain as Shepherd, Brown and others watched the live feed from Fort Wayne on the monitor. It was 6:14 P.M. as Walker led into another news item: a "filler" about airline safety from CNN Washington correspondent Joe Pennington, six minutes long.

"Let's go, Jimmy! Outa the room!"

At the anchor desk, Walker looked at the camera and said, "California's final run at the primaries this Tuesday. We'll look at the story, and much more, when the News Channel continues." It was 6:21 P.M. when CNN cut to a shot of the newsroom, with background sound of a news-wire machine, before going to its first commercial.

It featured actor E. G. Marshall:

There are many medications for acid indigestion or heartburn relief. Which one is right for you? For years, Maalox has been recommended most by doctors . . . There were titters in the newsroom. The product was particularly appropriate.

The second commercial, for Nestea, came up. On the monitor, the hospital door opened. The president of the United States appeared. He walked right up to the waiting microphones and began to speak. . . .

The group in Master Control was stunned. "Take it!" Ted Kavanau yelled. "Take it, take it! Get out, get out, get out! Forget the commercial! Take-it-take-it-take-it! Wipe out and go live! TAKE IT!"

They took it. It was 6:22 P.M.

The president was now on screen. "— and with, uh, surely," he said, caught in midsentence. But he was cut off and the screen went blank.

Kavanau was gesturing toward the anchor desk. Dave Walker got the cue and started speaking. Now *he* appeared on screen, also in midsentence:

"— Fort Wayne, Indiana, and is now meeting with reporters. We now *switch live* to Fort Wayne, Indiana."

Back to Carter again. "— for today. Again, I've been given a very accurate report from his own physicians that he's recovering well. . . ."

It had happened. Carter was right there, live, with CNN receiving and transmitting the story *as it unfolded* before any other TV network had it in any form at all.

"Goddammit, that shows 'em!" Ed Turner shouted with pride and glee. "We interrupted our first commercial break to bring 'em a news story!"

The president was answering questions and, after more than seven minutes, at 6:29 P.M., with less than a minute to go before the hot switch, the group in Master Control was now praying that Carter would *stop* speaking in time.

"Wrap it up," they said.

"End it," they pleaded.

As if he could hear them, Carter paused. "Thank you very much," he said. The news conference was over.

The clock hit six-thirty and the hot switch was thrown and there, on the monitor, was Jay Bushinsky in Jerusalem! The group in Master Control broke into cheering.

"God has looked down on CNN," Rick Brown yelled, "and said He likes us!"

CNN viewers, however, had no idea of the real drama that had taken place in Master Control. They had seen the commercial wiped away, abruptly, followed by the president's live appearance. They had seen the news conference up until about 6:29 P.M., but then, *before* Carter had finished, CNN had cut back to Dave Walker at the anchor desk.

Ted Kavanau had known about the hot switch coming and had waited until the last moment before deciding to drop out of the Fort Wayne feed. In about twenty seconds, the news conference would be cut off and the screen would turn to color bars.

Kavanau boiled over with frustration, but he needed CNN to keep control of its own format.

"What should I tell them?" Walker asked. "What do you want me to do? Where should I go next? What do you want me to say?"

"Tell 'em the *networks* are *screwing* us!" Kavanau shouted back as he stomped off. The suggestion was not intended to be taken seriously, but it did have a therapeutic effect.

Zelman tried to make a suggestion and so did John Baker, but they were talking at once and suddenly CNN cut away from President Carter — seconds before the news conference was ending — and Dave Walker found himself on camera again.

"There you saw the president speaking moments ago, live from Fort Wayne, Indiana," he ad-libbed. "We had to interrupt that, so that we can take a feed live from the Mideast momentarily."

Now Walker saw hands waving at him. No, no, the producers were saying. Even though the Jerusalem feed was ready, they weren't going directly to Bushinsky. So Walker abruptly switched gears: "Two days from today, the nation's presidential primary season comes to an end, on June the third . . ."

It was "quick and dirty" all the way.

Cable News Network, which the *Boston Globe* that week called "the most audacious challenge to TV network news in the history of American broadcasting," jolted into the second half of its first hour.

At 6:30 P.M. Eastern Daylight Time, Jay Bushinsky waited in Jerusalem and Mike Boettcher stood on a dock in Key West, Florida, both ready to go live. Their reports would be up-linked to different satellites and fed to the Atlanta headquarters; and if all went well, the live video and sound would be beamed instantly up to SATCOM I and back down to the cable audience. A diagram of how the signals were supposed to work in one-sixth of a second would show a series of jagged lines over part of the planet — from "point to point," as they called the relays — and right now, both Bushinsky and Boettcher could be seen on separate monitors.

The live feeds were in place.

"For Cable News Network's inaugural broadcast," Lois Hart was saying to the camera, "President Carter was earlier interviewed by CNN's senior Washington correspondent, Daniel Schorr, and our managing editor, George Watson. . . ."

What followed was an excerpt from their interview at the White House, taped the day before; then came Bernie Shaw, live at the Washington anchor desk, with a rundown of national headlines. Finally Atlanta was set to take the feed from Bushinsky five thousand miles away.

"Cue him," Ted Kavanau yelled. "Come on!"

Bushinsky appeared on the main screen. "It's 12:35 A.M. here

The old white house, first home of CNN

◁ Ted Turner, at the satellite farm

The new home of CNN

Courtesy Cotten Alston

Reese Schonfeld,
the founding president

Courtesy Cotten Alston

Burt Reinhardt,
the first active employee

Courtesy Cotten Alston

Schonfeld (right) and Reinhardt,
as CNN goes on the air

Dan Schorr,
the senior correspondent

Terry McGuirk,
who helped convince cable systems

Alec Nagle, the "sparkplug"

Ted Kavanau, the Drill Sergeant

Gerry Hogan,
who went after advertisers

Sam Zelman,
the old pro on a last fling

Jim Kitchell,
who worried about operations

Ed Turner,
who signs his memos "ET"

Rick Brown,
who ran the satellite desk

Jane Maxwell,
also known as The Hane

Frank Beatty (left) and Roy Mehlman, who helped sell CNN

Bernie Shaw and Mary Alice Williams, anchors

in Jerusalem," he said, "and we've been following the fast-moving Israeli political crisis throughout the day for this first live satellite transmission to the Cable News Network. . . ."

As it was all coming together, Reese Schonfeld finally admitted to colleagues that he'd been plagued by a hernia for three months. He stood bent over at his desk, grimacing, and decided to get himself to the hospital for an operation — not right now, of course, but as soon as he could break away.

Schonfeld looked up and saw Turner wandering through the newsroom. "Ted," he said, elated, "how did you like the way we cut away from our first commercial to go to Carter? It couldn't have been better if God had written it."

"Yeah," Turner said, grinning. "That'll show 'em we'll never bow down to the advertisers. You can always run the ads later. Who cares about ads anyhow? It's a *news* operation."

A moment later, Turner made his way into Sam Zelman's office and found a TV set so he could watch the Braves game on his SuperStation. Zelman's office wasn't wired for cable, but Turner found WTBS on the UHF dial in time to see his team finish playing the Los Angeles Dodgers.

The Braves won, nine to five.

"Awwright!" Turner said, strolling back into the activity of the newsroom.

In Florida, standing on the dock at the Key West Naval Air Station, reporter Mike Boettcher was accompanied by a camera person, a sound person and a "mobile earth station" leased for his live reports on the flotilla of Cuban refugees. But the flotilla, mainly because of heavy seas, had suddenly stopped arriving. The sight of hundreds of boats carrying refugees to the Florida beaches would not provide a background. Instead, for his interviews, Boettcher had rounded up a member of the Cuban Volunteer Force along with a doctor working with refugees.

Without any reliable system for knowing exactly when he would go live on the air, Boettcher and his tiny crew had enlisted the help of a young Cuban refugee, who had disembarked from a boat earlier in the week, telling him to go stand at a distant pay phone. The young man, who barely understood English, waited with the phone to his ear until he heard Rick Brown in Atlanta suddenly shouting, "Cue him! Cue him!"

"Cue?"

"Shout!" Brown explained. "Yell!"

The young man turned from the phone and screamed, "Ahhhhhh!"

This signal was relayed to Dean Vallas, the producer on the scene who, according to plan, blew a police whistle.

But the relay team was seven seconds late.

While all the crew's makeshift signals were being passed down the line to him, Mike Boettcher was *already* live on camera with the microphone in his hand and . . . picking his nose.

"Stay with us," Lois Hart told viewers at the end of the first hour. "We're going to have all kinds of news, sports, weather and special features, *from now on and forever.*" At last, she had made the "statement" that her producers had been demanding. Hart and Walker, who would celebrate their first wedding anniversary at midnight, were being relieved of anchor duties.

Jane Maxwell had gone into Master Control a few minutes before Hart's sign-off; and now Alec Nagle came roaring and laughing through the glass doors. He grabbed Maxwell and hugged her, spinning her around and shouting, "And that's why we call her" — he paused for emphasis, as if he were Ed McMahon introducing Johnny Carson — "*Maaaagic Haner!*"

RICK BROWN

"I still believe that CNN's first hour was its best hour. As if we were the 1980 inheritors of the Charles Lindbergh legacy, we proved that all those experts, who said we didn't know what we were doing, didn't themselves know what they were talking about. Most of the experts, of course, were too dumb to know that they had now been disproved, but we at the very least proved our own abilities to ourselves. I loved hearing about unhappy network crews zooming into Key West, saying their weekend had been cut short because of the press that CNN was getting for covering the refugee story live. From then on, it was never *our* responsibility to prove anything to anyone. It was only *their* responsibility to find out, for themselves, that CNN 'finally arrived' in its first shining hour on the air, on Sunday evening, June 1, 1980!"

The second hour of CNN's existence was filled almost entirely by Bill MacPhail's sports department with an assortment of stories anchored by Bob Kurtz and Nick Charles. It was the slickest show of the evening. Then because it was Sunday night, the two-hour *Prime News* show at eight o'clock on weeknights would have to wait; so Lou Waters and Reynalda Muse did the anchor chores for another hour of news. After giving a sports rundown as part of the newscast, Fred Hickman said, "And now back to Reynalda at the anchor desk," but instead of the woman appearing on camera it was the man. Waters, looking bemused, decided to smile and say, "I'm definitely not Reynalda at the anchor desk."

The Schorr-Watson interview of President Carter filled most of the block from 9 P.M. to 10 P.M., followed by more news for an hour with Kathleen Sullivan and Don Miller. Sullivan would be described by one writer as "pretty but credible — just what every news director looks for," and her voice would be said to be "able to cut glass." Miller, a dashing figure who was half English and half Canadian Ojibway Indian, would be described as having "the rumbling pipes of a bass calliope."

For all of its sporadic mishaps, the new network had opened with the kind of splash its creators had envisioned. Columnist Dick Williams of the *Atlanta Constitution* wrote that it had been the "start of a revolution in which Ted Turner made good a boast, Reese Schonfeld realized a dream and a group of news people started a process that may not stop in our lifetime."

Until tonight, Williams wrote, the question had been "Will Turner pull it off?" Now, he added, it was "How long do you think it will last?"

The answer in the minds of many was "Not very long."

Rumblings of competition had begun, but for now, while Turner was out on the edge by himself, his potential rivals were simply waiting to see him twist in the wind.

Broadcasting magazine did some calculations: "The mathematics say that in the first months of operation, CNN will lose about $2.2 million per month. If all goes well, the gap between expenditures and revenues will steadily decrease and within three or four years CNN will hit the break-even point. . . ."

Three or four years!

To make matters more precarious, those projections were based only on the premise that Turner could continue *alone* in the all-news TV cable field. And the competition, while laying low, was coming.

"I'm scared all the time," Turner confided to *Panorama* magazine, which observed the rumblings from other media groups and concluded:

> After two or three years, these companies will have the option of conceding the field to CNN, of going into competition with it, or of making an offer to buy it out — backed by the threat of high-powered competition.
>
> That is why CNN needs economic success almost from the first. The boss may be a rich man in his circles, but $100 million is less than one-sixth of what The Washington Post Company took in last year and there are several other huge vultures circling in the sky. No wonder Ted Turner is scared.

Fred Friendly, former CBS News president, while conceding that Turner's creation of CNN already meant that "he will be the link to TV's future," nevertheless predicted his demise: "He's the first man on the beach; unfortunately, the first man on the beach rarely stays around to develop the colony."

The fact was, invading forces were headed for the same shore. Two of the nation's most powerful broadcasting corporations, ABC and Westinghouse, were joining forces to create a cable news network with the facilities, personnel and financial resources able to bury Ted Turner and CNN.

FOUR

"It was a gamble. Everything's a gamble. You know, the sun could fall out of the sky tomorrow. The plane could crash. The lights could go out. You know, life is a gamble."

AT TECHWOOD they had created a video-gameroom for news junkies addicted to the never-ending quality of it all. The newsroom had a life of its own. There in the basement of the mansion, always beckoning, were those enticing thrills and surprises. At its heart was the clock and the wheel, the news wheel spinning round and round according to its schedules and rundowns, its cut-ins and cutaways, its dull times and frenzied times — you went downstairs and jumped aboard, blood churning as you hit the ground running, and no day or night was ever quite the same as the one before. They were workaholics and insomniacs and zombies and crazies, all jostling together in an underground world.

The so-called open newsroom had been created by placing Control A, informally known as the Pit, right next to the anchor desk. Jim Kitchell had built this "control room" inside four posts so he could throw up glass walls in case it got too noisy. Producers and directors in the Pit had to learn to modify their yelling by what they called the "Shout-A-Com" method; in other words, they tried to shout carefully. The setup worked well enough so that Kitchell never had to put up the glass walls; but once in a while CNN viewers were privy to the offstage commotion, such as the time a female director was heard, without explanation, declaring from offstage, "I'm gonna kill him! I am going to *kill* him."

If a producer ran out of news, the director might cut to a public-service announcement. Otherwise they often cut to a full-screen billboard with the words CABLE NEWS NETWORK; and playing in the background was a loop of electronic musical sounds that seemed to be made by a pencil hitting a Coke bottle while someone hummed on a kazoo. It came to be known as the Queer

Beat Music. During some of the crises, they interrupted by cutting to Camera Five — an unmanned camera focused on the Pit itself, as the Queer Beat Music played over the bumper shot. Viewers at home would see a pantomimic version of the director arguing with the producer, accompanied by the weird electronic music. When the argument ended, the anchors reappeared and the news resumed.

The show that started at 11:30 P.M. Eastern Time was geared to Californians tuning in at 8:30 P.M. in their time zone. The audience on the West Coast was deemed to be "less serious" than other groups, so the news was "softer" and presented at a faster pace. Don Lennox, who had come from California, produced this "Rock 'n' Roll" version of CNN from the Pit as if he were a disc jockey.

Ted Kavanau prowled the newsroom day and night, often taunting those who suffered from exhaustion. (When producer Jim Shepherd had worked forty-eight hours straight and tried to leave, Kavanau snapped at him, "What are you, a *woman!*"). Burt Reinhardt was always looking for ways to cut down costs. ("What's the difference," Alec Nagle asked, "between Burt and a phone booth?" Answer: "The phone booth will give your dime back.")

When Reese Schonfeld wasn't there he watched from home, often calling in the early morning hours to complain or make suggestions. His crews out in the field were operated by producers called "one-man bands," who combined the functions of cameraman, soundman, editor, and even reporter. This "bottom-line" method of coverage inspired a field producer from one of the commercial networks to wisecrack that CNN stood for "Chicken Noodle News" — but Schonfeld knew that impressing the other network people was not his mission.

He was torn between *spending* and *saving,* at the same time, to keep the wheel moving; and here on the ride with him were his children, the producers and directors and anchor talent, along with all the others in support, who scurried around to push the never-ending wheel. As one female video journalist told her male counterpart: "Sure, I'll sleep with you — when the show is over."

They were beginning to realize the implications of the fact that the show would *never* be over. An anchorperson could say, for example, "We now interrupt the news — to bring you the news!" Breaking stories could be told in bits and pieces, in fragments of information as they were received, so that viewers who stayed tuned could share in the evolution of a story from the first bulletin all the way to completion. "It's like going to someone's house for dinner," Sam Zelman exclaimed, "but instead of sitting in the living room waiting to be served, you're joining the host in the kitchen where all the work is being done."

"Wait a minute!" Ted Turner told an interviewer from *Home Video* magazine, who mentioned some criticism that CNN seemed to lack focus. "Wait just a goddamned minute! You think it lacks focus — what is focus, anyway? If you're live all the time, how can you have focus? Focus means that you know where you're going! You can't focus in on somethin' unless you know what it is you're focusing on! Focus is something a newspaper has, because there's a day to think about it. Or with a magazine, there's a month. Whoever said that was a yo-yo!"

So much for focus. Instead there were the ragged edges — often more ragged than anyone at CNN intended. In the days after going on air, electricians and painters and carpenters were still hanging from rafters to complete their work. At the Washington bureau Bernie Shaw was reading copy live when two painters came on screen behind him. They were outside the window, carrying a ladder and holding their paint cans. They stopped to chat with each other. Shaw looked into his monitor and saw them, but he didn't blink. He kept speaking to the camera with a straight face while the painters, as if performing a vaudeville routine for the CNN audience, finished their conversation and walked off.

Then there was the cleaning woman who walked up to Shaw's desk while he was on the air. Unaware of her CNN audience, she reached down and grabbed his wastebasket, then calmly dumped the contents of the basket into a large bin before replacing it and moving on. And once Shaw himself was caught on air, as he waited to go on, doing a song-and-dance act by humming and tapping his pen on the desk.

"Here is news, alive with all its wonderful technical warts and missed cues," *Variety* observed a few days after the opening, "and it all worked."

It even worked when the revolving panels of the weather map nearly swallowed Stu Siroka, on his first day of work, as he stepped toward the wall. "I suppose I'm lucky I'm still alive," he said, but then the panels spun around and hit him. "Help!" Siroka shouted to Dave Walker at the anchor desk. And it worked, too, when the same weatherman's body got "lost" in the Chromakey, a process used to put one picture behind another. All the CNN viewers could see was Siroka's bald head, from the neck up, suspended in front of the weather map.

It worked, also, when CNN rolled a list of temperatures around the country in front of pictures from the Atlanta zoo that showed a monkey climbing a tree and, quite calmly, masturbating; when a reporter said that "Mary Ass Williams" was standing by; when another correspondent announced that scientists were trying to grow "genetically engineered orgasms" in the lab; and when Dan Schorr, reporting from the Washington bureau, found his clothes on fire after a light bulb had exploded. When CNN cut away and returned to him, Schorr gave viewers a summary of the "small mishap" that they had witnessed.

When John Holliman reported on the National Spelling Bee in Washington and concluded that the word *glitch* had made the final difference between first and second place, Lois Hart, in Atlanta, was laughing as she came back on air. "We know how to spell *that* word *here*," she said.

On Monday, June 2, the results of all that "noodling" with daily formats by Alec Nagle and others in the old white house began to unfold. From 2:30 A.M. until 6 A.M. Eastern Daylight Time, CNN replayed the best of the previous reports and features, maintaining the ability to go live but otherwise rolling tape until the sun began to rise.

The network had never run through a complete, twenty-four-hour rehearsal; and now, twelve hours after going on air, there was still no way of predicting how the full cycle would go. On paper the weekday schedule looked like this:

6:00 A.M. THE AM NEWSWATCH — Two Hours
  National and international news, weather, sports and farm reports by John Holliman along with business news from New York with Stuart Varney, all fast-paced, interspersed with commentaries and vignettes ranging from "Staying Fit" to "Home Handyman" to "Your Astrological Day."

8:00 A.M. THE CNN MORNING REPORT — Four Hours
News and features, with cut-ins from the bureaus, presenting
the total mix with more commentaries and topics from gyne-
cology to auto mechanics.

12:00 P.M. TAKE TWO — Two Hours
Don Farmer and Chris Curle, the other husband-wife anchor
team, presenting "news, reviews and interviews," plus reports
on Hollywood, pets, cooking, gardening, fashion and so on.

2:00 P.M. CNN AFTERNOON — Four Hours
Pairs of anchors taking up the desk for each hour of news mixed
with sports and Wall Street reports, along with health tips, gos-
sip, movie criticism and light features.

6:00 P.M. SPORTS AND NEWS WORLD — One Hour
Highlights of both.

7:00 P.M. MONEYLINE — Half Hour
Lou Dobbs anchoring the nightly live show from New York
with Myron Kandel, financial editor, with emphasis on Wall
Street and business news.

7:30 P.M. CNN SPORTS — Twenty Minutes

7:50 P.M. TELEVISION TONIGHT — Ten Minutes
Kevin Sanders, media critic, previews the best bets on TV for
the rest of the night.

8:00 P.M. CNN PRIME TIME NEWSCAST — Two Hours
No holds barred. Counterprogramming with news against what-
ever the Big Three networks are doing in any given Time Zone.
Alec Nagle's show.

10:00 P.M. FREEMAN REPORTS — One Hour
Sandi Freeman, 36, formerly hostess of *A.M. Chicago* on
WLS-TV, presenting a national call-in show with a live
studio audience. Interviews with newsmakers on the set or via
satellite.

11:00 P.M. SPORTS TONIGHT — Half Hour
Highlights with Charles and Kurtz, who don't mind sharing
their opinions.

11:30 P.M. NEWSDESK — Hour and a Half
More, more, more, more . . .

1:00 A.M. PEOPLE TONIGHT — One Hour
Lee Leonard, interviewing showbiz personalities, hosts from
Los Angeles, where it's still only 10 P.M.

2:00 A.M. SPORTS UPDATE — Half Hour
   Latest results, especially for the 11 o'clock crowd on the West
   Coast.
2:30 A.M. OVERNIGHT DESK — Until 6 A.M.

And so it went, round and round. . . .

Sandi Freeman's talk show, beginning at 10 o'clock that Monday
night, included a taped interview with Senator Edward Kennedy,
who had been scheduled to appear live. Schonfeld had given
Freeman the flexibility of conducting her interviews at the CNN
bureaus in Atlanta, Washington, New York, Chicago, and Los
Angeles, wherever the day's top newsmakers happened to be.
The sessions would be live, so cable viewers could call with
questions.

   At the last minute, however, Kennedy canceled his live appearance. Well, Schonfeld said, we'll shoot it on videotape, then
edit the piece in time. But Kennedy suddenly changed the venue
from Los Angeles to New York, because he had been offered a
chance to appear on NBC's *Today* show. Okay, Schonfeld said,
we'll go there. Then Kennedy switched the arrangements twice
more: first to Newark and then, finally, to the airplane en route
to Cleveland. That was the only way he would allow CNN to
interview him; and Schonfeld, more determined than ever, ordered two camera crews to board the plane with Freeman.

   The interview on the plane proceeded, but Kennedy wound up
granting only half of the full hour he had promised. In the end,
Schonfeld ordered Dan Schorr to fly to Atlanta, where he and
Freeman appeared together on the set to fill out the time. The
whole thing was a disaster.

   "We should have walked away from it," the CNN president
finally admitted. He was exasperated and, even more, disgusted
by Kennedy's contemptuous treatment of the new network.

   Schonfeld's vision of Freeman's talk show was that "it's gonna
be today's news and we'll go with whatever that is." That, he
felt, was the ideal approach. He aptly called his style "working
on the edge" — as his hostess flew all over the country to con-
duct her show live and, eventually, became so tense that she
developed hives.

*   *   *

In the first weeks and months they went on the air *knowing* they didn't have enough material to fill the time. On one occasion Jim Shepherd came running up to Don Miller, who was anchoring, and realized that his feet were flying from underneath him. The count was coming down to *three, two, one, live,* so Shepherd spun around and sat down behind the anchor desk. He handed the copy up to Miller and then lay on his back underneath the set while the show continued.

JIM SHEPHERD

"Then there was John Hillis standing up in the middle of the newsroom, and we were all pretty busy in our own little head trips at the time, working to prepare our shows, and John was having one of those days where everything that *could* go wrong *did* go wrong. You could count on the live shot *not* being there, on the tape *not* rolling, and he had twenty more minutes to go without anything to put on the air!

"So John stood up in the Control Room and shouted, 'Goddammit, I'm *dying* down here! Doesn't anybody *care?*'

"We all looked up and shouted, '*No!*'

"But then, of course, we helped him."

There was always a real sense of urgency to get material on the air. Paul Amos was doing a three o'clock show and itching to get video on a story that was breaking. In the middle of it, the video was still unavailable but a wire photo cleared, so he ran out to get it.

PAUL AMOS

"I raced back into the Control Room and said, 'Listen, this story is coming up, but when we get to it we won't have time to load the graphics systems, so here's what we'll do. I'll take this photo and put it in front of the camera that's shooting the anchor who's *not* reading the story. Then you just take that camera and I'll hold the photo for you as still as I can. Then go back to the *other* anchor again.

"So I ran out to the Pit, rushing to put it on, and I stuck the photo right in front of the anchor who *was* reading on the air. So now the anchor's voice is coming from behind the photograph. . . ."

*   *   *

They were *throwing* new copy at the anchors. The producers threw it up on the desk and the anchors grabbed scripts as they were reading. Sometimes the anchors were lucky to get copy *at all*. Before their shows began, they would go to the wire machines and rip off stacks of copy — for security.

LOIS HART

"We'd get to forty minutes and start screaming: 'What do we do *now?*' Somebody would say, 'Where is that package we had two hours ago?' They'd run and get the video and put it on the air again. Then the schedule for the anchors kept changing. It was a big issue. Should we put on two people for an hour and then alternate with another team every hour? Should we do half hours? Should the anchors change *positions* when one team came on and one came off? These great discussions went on endlessly, but it felt like they were rearranging deck chairs on the *Titanic*."

DAVE WALKER

"Reese knew everybody was looking in. He saw the guys at CBS and the other networks laughing at Ted Turner, for two basic reasons — one, he wouldn't have a legitimate news organization, and two, he was gonna spend himself into the ground. So Reese and Kavanau desperately wanted to prove 'em wrong. If we said we were going to Jerusalem or Washington, then by God we were gonna *be* there. And at the same time Reese was always fighting the money battle — so if we *lost* a feed, that's five thousand bucks he's just spent for nothing!"

JEANEE VON ESSEN

"I was getting to the newsroom at five every morning and leaving past nine at night. A week after we went on the air, I got home and put my head against the tile in my kitchen and the phone rang. It was Jane Maxwell, saying the leader of Japan had died, so I went right back to work.

"We hadn't done anything about covering Japan, but I got on the phone and called the Japanese networks to try to get some videotape. First I had to explain what CNN was. Luckily there was a man at a Japanese station, NHK, who agreed to give me videotape. By now it was eleven-thirty and I knew I wasn't going home. I'd be there all night.

"I started calling around, looking for free-lance reporters in Japan. Everybody was busy, but I thought, *Jeanee, you're gonna do this. You're gonna figure this out. Where to call? Where to get the name of a reporter to do this piece for the videotape?*

"I got information over there and a number for the Tokyo Press Club. I called and said, 'Do you have a bar?' They did. I said, 'Could I speak to the bartender?' They put me through and I said, 'Do you know a good free-lance reporter who speaks English?' The Japanese bartender said he knew a guy named John Lewis and gave me his number.

"I called Lewis in Tokyo and explained. He says, 'You're a *what?* A twenty-four-hour *what?* From *where?'*

"I said, 'We're a twenty-four-hour news network in Atlanta, Georgia. We have some videotape over at NHK. Can you do a package for us?'

"He got the videotape and edited the piece and put on a voice track. They drew a rising sun in crayon and wrote CNN TOKYO.

"We added on to the networks' satellite feed. I got on a pool call and they were going, 'Okay, here's the CBS feed,' and then 'All right, NBC's turn,' and, 'Is ABC here yet?' I heard a voice say, 'No, but CNN is here.' They said, 'CNN? You gotta be kidding.' The network guys laughed and wouldn't let us get in there until the end of the line. But finally, on our monitor, here comes the video feed with the hand-drawn sign and everybody in the newsroom goes, 'My God! CNN TOKYO!'

"John Lewis was reporting for *us,* from *Japan.* We were clapping and cheering and yelling. I'm screaming and jumping and there it was, a package out of Japan, when only a few hours ago we hadn't known there *was* a Far East."

Don Farmer and Chris Curle made an attractive, articulate couple. Their midday show, *Take Two,* was a CNN centerpiece from the beginning and gave them a certain stature.

But the young producers who dealt with Farmer and Curle often felt that Farmer, the veteran, wanted to run things *his* way. Few news producers handling updated stories lasted more than a week with *Take Two,* because Farmer would insist on going through scripts to see which reports he wanted to read. If he disliked some of the copy, he tossed it overboard. The news producers began calling Farmer and Curle "Ham and Cheese" and "Attila and Hun."

Over drinks at Harrison's one night, Jim Shepherd told a group of listeners, "Hey, remember I went up to Farmer during one of the breaks? Wanna know what I said to him?" The others never knew when a Shepherd story was truthful or fabricated. What counted was that his stories were uproariously funny and, even better, that they took on the proportions of useful myths. "Tell us!" they roared.

Farmer was at the anchor desk, going through the script and discarding pages. Right on the air, he was skipping certain stories. Finally, during a commercial break, a furious Jim Shepherd walked up to the desk, calmly put his elbows on the table and said: "Hi, Don. Let's just smile like we're having a good time, okay? Like two good ol' boys. Like we're not having an argument, which is what we're about to have. Now, you're gonna read that story because I *told* you to read that story. I'm the producer. You will read that story because, if you *don't*, we're just gonna leave the camera on you. We won't go to breaks or anything. When you get up and walk away from the desk, we'll follow you with Camera Five. We'll go down the hallway to the john and follow you into the stall. And we ain't gonna leave, while you're sitting there, until you read that story. Okay, Don, keep smiling. Break's over."

Whether it actually happened that way would be impossible to tell without polygraph tests for both Shepherd and Farmer, but that's the way it was told at Harrison's — the way the other producers *wanted* it to go.

From *Newsweek* magazine, June 16, 1980:

> Much like Muhammad Ali, Ted Turner has enlivened and enriched all the games he has entered. Though he may occasionally mistake himself for one of his military heroes, his sheer exuberance is always infectious; the relish makes up for the hot-dogging. More important, in an age of play-it-safe corporate bureaucracy, bold spirits like Turner have become precious commodities. . . .
>
> Whether 24-hour news is an idea whose time has come is considerably less clear. Aside from the question of viewer receptivity, and the problem of cable's limited market penetration, there loom

serious doubts about Turner's financial staying power. Some experts are convinced that CNN will eventually be forced to surrender the all-news cable field to journalistic organizations with deeper monetary resources. . . .

Maybe so, but consider what Turner is achieving right now. He is pushing television news to its farthest frontiers. He is providing viewers with an important new option. He may even galvanize the networks into expanding their own newscasts beyond what many critics dismiss as a superficial headline service. As for CNN's chances for survival, the fact that it is Ted Turner's current crusade may be reason enough to anticipate success.

George Babick, head of CNN's New York sales office, offers perhaps the wisest advice about how to regard anything his boss touches: "If Ted predicted the sun will come up in the west tomorrow morning, you'd laugh and say he's full of it. But you'd still set the alarm. You wouldn't want to miss the miracle."

Turner's latest "miracle" rose last week. It will be worth watching.

To All Concerned [June 16, 1980]
Cable News Network is just a few weeks old and even though I am in Newport I have watched the broadcasts much of the time. I just want to tell you how pleased I am with what you have accomplished so far. CNN is absolutely terrific! Keep up the great work.

Ted

There was no smoking allowed in the newsroom. Those who did smoke were warned by the phrase "Burt Alert!" whenever Reinhardt appeared. The policy had come from Turner himself.

To All Employees of Turner Broadcasting, Inc. and Cable News Network [later in 1980]
I have just finished a tour of our beautiful headquarters. Everywhere I went I saw discarded soft-drink cans, candy wrappers, cigarette butts and assorted trash. There may be some slight excuse for this because there are not enough trash containers and ashtrays around the building. I am making sure that adequate trash containers and ashtrays are placed at various places in the building. After this is done I do not want to see one speck of trash on our grounds anywhere.

If you intend to litter on our premises please do us both a favor and resign now.

I hope this is all that ever needs to be said about this subject. We have beautiful facilities and we have visitors from all over the nation and the world. *I want the building and grounds to sparkle!* Thank you in advance for your support.

Ted Turner

Because the faces at the anchor desk kept changing around the clock, the network was in the process of "demystifying" the role of on-air talent; the real star of CNN, from the beginning, was the news itself. At the same time, it was impossible to ignore Kathleen Sullivan's personal qualities. Without apparent effort, she was a combination of contradictory extremes: shy but sexy, insecure yet confident, serious about her work yet able to laugh at herself. Sullivan was every man's vision of the damsel in distress; and once, Reese Schonfeld even wistfully mused about how great a boost for CNN it would be if she were sent to Northern Ireland on a story and kidnapped by the IRA in Belfast.

In fact, Schonfeld had sent Sullivan to Nicaragua before the network's launch. She had gone to cover the political upheavals in that country, but the excursion had resulted neither in a kidnapping nor in a brilliant series of videotape reports to be used when CNN was on the air. Schonfeld had assigned Dean Vallas, a field producer, to go with her.

REESE SCHONFELD

"We got good stories, but it was not a success. I had totally misread her. Dean Vallas was this very handsome Greek guy. I thought they would really hit it off, but she hated him. I had totally misread her. Unfortunately, I didn't realize that Kathleen's taste in men was for Waspy intellectuals. So it didn't work at all and they hated each other. It was the first time she had covered a world-class news story, though, and she did fine. She gave us a presence in Nicaragua and gained some credentials for herself. But her agent did call to complain about how she and Vallas weren't getting along. I learned that she was a woman who liked things very, very well-regulated and organized. She was not the kind of reporter who liked to rough it in the field."

* * *

During the rehearsals before airtime, Schonfeld had assigned Alec Nagle to what was called "the care and feeding of Kathleen Sullivan."

JIM SHEPHERD

I love Kathleen to death and I hate Kathleen. It was that kind of relationship, back and forth, depending on the mood. Kathleen Sullivan is the only person I ever saw who 'killed' a sweater. She came off the set one night, angry about something. Bill Zimmerman and I were standing there as she started swinging this expensive sweater down from a box of script paper. It got hung on one of the clasps and she just ripped that sweater to pieces. Zimmerman looked at me and said, 'Well, I certainly think *that* made her feel better, don't you?' I mean, she was just that kind of person. She got sick one night and it was like a major process to get her to the doctor. It took four producers to get her to the hospital — one to hold her hands, another to mop her forehead, and so forth. Four producers to get somebody like that to calm down.

"One time Alec left me a note to 'congratulate' me on being assigned to her temporarily. 'Proceed carefully,' he wrote, because she was a delicate filly. But Kathleen was the one who had 'star' written all over her. She couldn't hide it, although God knows she tried. She fumbled when she read and she'd make up ad-libs that would drive you crazy. She liked you or hated you and changed her opinion a couple of times a day. She was the best of times and the worst of times, with no middle ground."

Dallas Raines, the handsome weathercaster nicknamed "the Reverend" because of his strong religious views, sometimes seemed to be delivering his report to Sullivan instead of to the audience. When Raines pointed to the weather map and saw that a huge picture of an insect had been superimposed over Texas, he turned to Sullivan at the anchor desk and said, "I tell ya, the mosquitoes are *awful* down in Texas, Kathleen. They're just about that big down there, too." And Sullivan, with a reputation for enjoying the attentions of men, flirted right back.

JIM SHEPHERD

"Alec Nagle was everything in the world I had ever wanted to be. He had breeding and a track record, yet he was the nuttiest man I ever knew. He was also the best producer I knew. He could take chicken feathers and make steak out of 'em. He could take a story and give it a twist and style that was his own, and he was just wonderful to work with. He taught me so many things. He'd tell us that the lead story of a newscast was what you *said* it was, not what everybody assumed. . . .

"We'd rock and roll and change things around to be different. We were creative and our juices were all flowing. We were at that point in the stages of drunkenness that Dan Jenkins wrote about: fourteen feet tall and bulletproof. You know how bumblebees theoretically can't fly, but they *don't know* that and do it anyway? Well, we were bumblebees who *knew* we couldn't fly and yet we were off the ground."

"All right, campers!"
   "It's a giant!"
   "You were great!"
Nagle would dash into the newsroom, leaving no doubt among the floor people that their efforts were appreciated. He was their supervising producer, reporting to Ted Kavanau but taking on the role of cheerleader. He put the machinery into motion, sent the spirits soaring. He was doing the *national-local* news; this was showbiz, folks, and it *meant* something to the man on the street. During Nagle's airtime there would be no dry-formal-pompous stuff if he could avoid it. He was the heart of these early days, bringing it all together with his energy. When he looked at the bank of monitors and raised his fists in the air, proclaiming victory, the others followed suit; and as their enthusiasm swelled into a wave, Nagle himself became the peak that hit the wind.

And oh, the merciless humor. One target was a young correspondent whose faux pas would cause Nagle to shout, "Wing Commander Stupid! There he goes!" During one report the correspondent said, "As any fatal car-accident victim will tell you," and Nagle, roaring with laughter, yelled, "Wait! Did you hear what he just *said?* I *want* that *interview!* Wing Commander Stupid does it again! He's so *stupid!*"

In Nagle's view, each CNN bureau had its own style. He loved the scrappy Dallas office, where just a few reporters under bureau chief Larry LaMotte were digging up four or five stories a day. And he hated the Washington bureau, which tended to deliver the standard government stuff as if from an ivory tower. Nagle made these comparisons in order to mold his producers' approach toward news. He wanted CNN's reports to be "real" and down-to-earth and, above all, related to the viewers' lives. He had written as much in the introductory manual:

"We all must resist the temptation to take the easy route and merely interview the company presidents, who seem to have all the answers. Actually, most stories are far removed from the corporate world, down there where the folks are living. People power is very basic to television news. We have to do it better than anyone else. It will make us special."

Nagle's own life was a paradox. Despite his energy and the impression he gave of being a tireless worker, he kept fairly regular hours. He came into the newsroom and gave himself entirely to the experience of building that particular show. He would tell his producers, primarily Paul Amos and Jim Shepherd, "No, look, do it *this* way," and they would try to grasp his meaning and deliver the goods for him. When he was *on* the clock, he was on it fully. He went to work and *lived* it, with gusto; and after each exuberant effort, Nagle tried to put the show behind him as he walked out. His second wife, Dial, who played no role at CNN, was trying to get him to stop smoking cigarettes and to stop drinking. But he was so consumed by his job that those addictions seemed to fill a void as soon as he was away from the newsroom.

He took pills for a weak heart. He had suffered at least one attack before turning thirty-six. Dial would yell at him to take better care of his health and he would feel that she was nagging him. He called her "She Who Must Be Obeyed."

JIM SHEPHERD

"Alec would tell wonderful stories about Roger Grimsby at WABC in New York. He would tell us the guts-and-orgasm stories about KGO in San Francisco: 'The night we led our show with the penis on the railroad track!' He was a teacher and friend and drinking buddy and everything in the world you'd want to work with, all in one package. I knew he was the funniest guy I'd ever met in my life, and I wanted to drink with him and hear every story he told. . . .

"We were cocky and arrogant and overbearing, and we drank too hard and we worked too hard, and the place was full of all these relationships and affairs that were hotter than the surface of the sun for thirty days before they burned out.

"We were intense. One-dimensional. Driven. And we were nuts, for doing what we were doing. We used to work seventy or eighty hours a week and still go out and drink all night. We were bad for that. We unwound the only way we could. Because we had a crazy man named Schonfeld, who would come downstairs and go wacko at a moment's notice, and another crazy man in residence named Kavanau, and then all the rest of us who were selectively nuts anyway.

"I mean, we were the dissidents. We were the people who would have never succeeded at traditional places because we were too hard to control. We were headstrong and impetuous. But because of that, we were perfect for CNN. We were perfect for guerrilla warfare, because you could never teach us to march in step. It was like taking the Dirty Dozen and putting them together until they become a unit. . . ."

In mid-July, when the Republican National Convention opened at the Joe Louis Arena in Detroit, there were seventy CNN staff members on hand. From correspondents to technicians, they had been drawn from all the bureaus in support of anchors Bernard Shaw, Mary Alice Williams, Dan Schorr and Bill Zimmerman. Compared to the facilities and manpower of the other networks, it was a small and even makeshift operation; but "the new kid on the block" made use of its unlimited airtime. With the kind of flexibility that underdogs are often forced to achieve, CNN regularly switched to Atlanta for the rest of the world's news; and the convention itself became, in effect, a breaking story among many others within the all-news format.

MARY ALICE WILLIAMS

"We had a trailer, but the networks had trailer *parks,* and we had this little, teeny skybox with no glass. You couldn't hear yourself think. Whenever the band struck up, it was so loud that we had to go to a commercial. . . .

"It was gonna be Reagan's convention. He was gonna get nominated there. So the big story, the *only* story, was who his vice-president was gonna be.

"By the second day, it got down to a clear choice between former president Gerald Ford and George Bush. So we had the thing knocked: 'We're reporters, we know how to cover this.' We had staked out a reporter at the hotel where Reagan was, so when Ford came out of the room our reporter could shove a mike in Gerald Ford's face and we'd get the beat live. Was he taking this job as Reagan's vice-president or not?

"So we ordered the video lines. That was cool. And then the deal went down. Former president Ford comes out of the room and he walks right up to our reporter. The mike with the CNN flag on it goes right up to Ford's mouth and he speaks — and there's no sound!

"That's when I learned that for television you have to order a video line *and* an audio line. . . ."

As the Democrats were gathering in New York, Hurricane Allen was paying a visit to the Gulf states. When the storm watch had begun, Dallas Raines and Flip Spiceland had started placing calls to weather bureaus in Jamaica, Puerto Rico, Cuba, Haiti and Miami. Allen was being billed as potentially the worst hurricane in recent history, stirring up winds as high as 170 miles an hour. Over nine days, Raines and Spiceland would deliver 755 reports as they tracked the storm's progress toward the Texas coast.

FLIP SPICELAND

"It was the first big thing that people really watched us for. I think those were our highest ratings for a while. Dallas and I stayed there in the studio, but of course we did send reporters to the site. I'd work all day and go home to sleep for about four hours, then come back and work midnight to six. It was the middle of the night when Marvin Scott and I were at the anchor desk and the hurricane was gonna move in. Our reporters in Texas were sleeping and we had no feed coming in, so Marvin called a *cab stand* in Galveston. We talked on the air with taxi drivers about how the weather was."

MARY ALICE WILLIAMS

"By the time we got to New York, we had this convention thing figured out. No problem. We'd made all the mistakes. Now we knew about audio lines. We had two little trailers and, again, our teeny skybox with no glass. This time I would be anchoring from nine in the morning until seven-thirty at night, when they'd bring in Bernie Shaw and Dan Schorr for prime time while I'd go down and be a floor correspondent until midnight or whenever it finished.

"So the first day everything was cool. We got up there and I anchor from 9 A.M. to 7:30 P.M. Bernie and Dan walk in. I turn over the reins. I walk down to be a floor correspondent. Only I don't have the credentials! We weren't a big-enough network. We had what was called *peripheral* credentials, which meant we couldn't actually be on the floor.

"So I race over to the perimeter and hook into the feed. I look up at our skybox. And *sparks* are showering down. Jesus has just arrived in the CNN booth! The sparks fly and the power goes. No power in our booth. I realize that they have just blown every-thing up there. And we're on the air!

"Beth Gralnick gets in my ear and says, 'Babe, you're carrying the network. Talk!'

"I'm down there without credentials, without a clipboard, without notes, without a field producer, without anything, and I'm going, 'Blabbedy-blabbedy-blabbedy,' and, 'We're here on the convention floor,' and, 'Here's what's happening,' and just going, 'Blabbedy-blabbedy,' until this young guy comes over to help me.

"Without asking, he went out on the floor to be my field pro-ducer! He pulled every major Democrat over to where I was, on the sidelines, so I could interview them. The big story was the Kennedy-Carter split. And everybody involved in that story was brought over to me by this young guy, whom I had never met, who was acting as my field producer.

"His name was Jesse Jackson.

"I will never forget that. I think he saw me in trouble. He knew we were a new network, or *maybe* he knew, but he did it and we never talked about it. Once our booth went back on the air, I didn't see him again — except for many years later, in the 1988 campaign, when we ran into each other. I said, 'Jesse, I never thanked you for saving my ass in 1980.'

"He said, 'Well, I've always felt it was one worth saving.'"

With eight years of special-events coverage at CBS behind her, Beth Gralnick was picking up some of the slack in CNN's ex-perience by acting as free-lance convention producer at Madison Square Garden. To her, it was a "luxury" to be able to switch away from long, boring stretches of the convention to CNN's coverage of other stories — a luxury not enjoyed by conventional networks.

Bill Zimmerman, accustomed to ABC's facilities, told a reporter in New York, "We don't have enough money, we don't have enough cameras, we don't have enough equipment. We're stretched pretty thin, like a rubber band that would break if you twanged it. If somebody got sick, we'd be in bad shape. The three networks have about 650 people apiece and all the goddamn equipment in the world. Our situation is the opposite. We're stretching some people beyond their capabilities. And we're doing a better job than we had any right to expect."

In late August a memo to CNN employees was issued by Burt Reinhardt: "John Baker has been appointed Vice President of Cable News Network in charge of Production and Operations. This appointment is effective immediately." It meant that Baker had been named to replace Jim Kitchell, who had moved into a corporate position at Turner Broadcasting System. Kitchell's office would be right there in the Techwood building, of course, but he was no longer on the CNN payroll; and his clashes with Schonfeld were henceforth, supposedly, over.

"My major criticism of Reese is that he doesn't know how to deal with people," Kitchell would say. "He rips into them when they make mistakes and it creates serious problems in morale."

"Kitchell's talent is to know how to give concessions to unions," Schonfeld would retort. "That's why the networks are in the kind of shape they're in — because they don't stand up and fight."

The schism grew wider after opening day and boiled up again in July. At one point Kitchell confronted Schonfeld and said, "Reese, you want me out of here, don't you?"

"Well," Schonfeld said, "I guess so."

"All you've got to do is say I'm fired," Kitchell said, "and I'll go away. It doesn't bother me. I've got a contract. But if you want me out of here, say so, because we're going downhill."

Soon afterward Kitchell got a call from Reinhardt, who invited him to dinner. At a local restaurant, the two men exchanged pleasantries until Kitchell said, "Burt, we both know why we're here. You're here to try to make a deal with me." In Kitchell's view, Reinhardt was acting as the hatchet man for Schonfeld with the intention of buying out his contract for much less than it stipulated. "There are no deals," Kitchell continued. "I'll go away, but the contract gets settled penny for penny, dollar for dollar, and that's that. Now let's enjoy our dinner."

At the same time Turner was up in Newport for the America's Cup trials, racing *Courageous* and losing to a new, faster yacht named *Freedom*, with Dennis Conner at the helm. When he heard about the news network's problems, Turner asked Kitchell to stay until he returned from Rhode Island and could deal with it himself.

John Holliman delivered his daily agriculture report from the Washington bureau, but he also made weekly trips down to Atlanta. Holliman, a farmer's son, had planted a garden in the dirt that now filled the swimming pool outside the newsroom window. Each Monday he would come to Techwood and go outside, while the camera followed him, to show viewers how the plants were growing.

"That's the national news," an anchor would say, "and now let's go to John Holliman and the garden."

But from one week to the next, there was no visible progress. Not a blade of grass had sprouted from the dirt.

After two months of telling the nation how to grow flowers and vegetables without any tangible evidence that he knew what he was talking about, Holliman finally brought in the state agriculture department to take a look at the soil. It turned out that when the swimming pool had been filled, the dirt had been treated with chemicals so the growth of weeds would be retarded.

The mystery of Farmer John's garden had been solved.

By fall a rich harvest of squash, tomatoes, beans and other vegetables began appearing on the CNN anchor desk.

Over the summer of 1980, the network had found a number of opportunities for demonstrating its abilities. In July, when the Shah of Iran had died, CNN took a live satellite feed of the funeral. That same month, investigative reporter Jean Carper broke the story of an epidemic of brain cancer at a Texas chemical plant, for which she would win an ACE award. At the Republican Convention, CNN had given the first report that George Bush would be Reagan's running mate; and after the

Democrats had nominated Jimmy Carter to run for reelection, Richard Nixon had given CNN his first public assessment of the upcoming campaign.

But getting a chance to latch onto a small story that would grow bigger over time was more difficult to come by. One way was to get to the scene *before* an event took place; and so, when Ted Kavanau heard a prediction pinpointing the exact day that an earthquake would devastate southern California, he dispatched reporter Liz Anderson from the L.A. bureau to cover it with a crew.

"Okay," Dave Walker in Atlanta said, "now let's go live to Elizabeth Anderson and check on that earthquake."

"Nothing to report yet," came the report.

The fact that there wasn't the slightest rumbling did not dissuade Kavanau from ordering new, live feeds on a regular basis: "Go to the earthquake again! Take it!"

Kavanau, now nicknamed "Take-It Ted," was convinced that all of America would be swept up by the suspense.

"Anything shaking out there?" another anchor asked Anderson, again live via satellite.

"No, nothin' shakin'."

So it went, in feed after feed, until Cable News Network had scooped the world's media with the story that Los Angeles had not, repeat not, slid into the sea.

In September, however, a story allowing CNN to "go live, *stay* with it and *make* it important" suddenly occurred. At a missile site near Damascus, Arkansas, an explosion killed an air force employee and injured twenty-one others. The blast left a crater 250 feet wide, forcing the evacuation of fourteen hundred people for twelve hours.

One piece of debris had been hurled across the landscape, coming to rest a few hundred yards from where the Titan II missile had exploded in its silo. Was it a nuclear warhead? The air force was denying it, but local people were obviously upset over the thought of a military convoy trucking out anything so dangerous over their country roads. Reporters were being kept out of the base while men labored inside, so the correspondents for networks and newspapers had little news to relay back.

Schonfeld was sure that the piece of debris in that field was a five-megaton thermonuclear warhead. It was Kavanau who came down on the side of caution, and the two friends found themselves in escalating verbal combat until Mad Dog shook his finger, trembling with fury, and blurted, "Don't you tell *me* what to say on the air, you . . . you . . . you *distortionist!*"

While a local Arkansas station was providing CNN with coverage, the reporter went on air to say that the air force public information office at the base *denied* that there had been a warhead on the missile; but Bernie Shaw, from Washington, broke in to say that he had an unimpeachable source at the Pentagon who *confirmed* it was a nuclear device.

"I am told," Shaw said, "that workers on the base are searching for it right now."

The national wire services picked up his story and ran it, crediting the new network with having broken the news.

But for CNN the story had much greater ramifications, as reporter James Alan Miklaszewski arrived on the scene with a transportable up-link. Here, suddenly, was a news event that was ongoing and unfolding, without any predictable end, amid the most dangerous and suspenseful kind of circumstances. His raw pictures, and interviews with local officials, were being transmitted without interruption or qualification; and when the government tried to block the media's view of the search area, Miklaszewski hired a truck with a cherry-picking crane, so his cameraman could continue shooting from its elevated platform.

As the story unfolded over the next three days, Miklaszewski stayed with it, sending back live reports every half hour until the warhead was removed from the site. To Schonfeld's delight, the "process" of newsgathering became part of the experience: "By the way," Miklaszewski told viewers, "these pictures are being brought to you by CNN cameraman Ron Dean, who is perched in the cherry-picker fifty feet above the ground. That was the only way we could bring you these live pictures of the apparent removal of what is said to be . . ."

The camera atop its cherry-picker truck kept silent vigil over the next three days. Even while other CNN programming continued, Schonfeld and his producers ran the pictures inside a small box at the corner of the TV screen — until the air force announced that indeed there had been a nuclear warhead. The coverage marked a high point in the network's short history.

Bill Zimmerman was normally calm and unruffled, but one day in the fall he leaped from the anchor desk and chased "Take-It

Ted" Kavanau clear out of the newsroom. It happened when the Iran-Iraq war was heating up and Kavanau was pushing the assignment desk to get live phone calls from Baghdad and Basrah, where Iranian bombs were dropping. Just as soon as they had a witness on the line, Kavanau would yell, "*Take it,*" meaning that the anchor should pick up the phone and start interviewing — even before the call had been screened.

Bill Zimmerman, on camera, said into the phone, "Hello, sir, what is the situation there right now?"

The reply, heard by CNN's audience, was in Japanese.

While folks in the newsroom were giggling, Zimmerman asked a few more questions; but the Japanese businessman in Iraq could neither understand nor speak English. After fumbling his way off the phone, Zimmerman got through the rest of the newscast. His adrenaline was pumping and he yelled at Kavanau, "If you ever do that to me again, you son of a bitch, I'll kill ya!" Kavanau yelled back. Zimmerman jumped off the anchor desk and went for him. Kavanau ran. Zimmerman ran after him. Both men were still shouting at each other as they disappeared through a door into the back offices, on their way out of the building.

In October, Westinghouse Electric announced its intention to buy Teleprompter and combine its operations with Westinghouse Broadcasting. The deal, put at $646 million, would be the largest in the history of the electronic media, catapulting Westinghouse into a dominant role in the cable industry.

The corporation already held licenses to six television stations and owned Group W Productions. Now it was getting Teleprompter's cable systems representing more than 1.2 million subscribers. Under its new president, Daniel L. Ritchie, Westinghouse Broadcasting was planning to move into the cable-television field with highly competitive programming. The attack was coming.

Stuart Loory arrived for work at the CNN bureau in Washington on October 6, 1980, to replace George Watson as vice-president and managing editor. Watson, having left ABC News in the spring to play a major role in creating the bureau, had developed second thoughts about his new professional home. He had been upset over attempts by Schonfeld, Kavanau, Nagle & Company to "control" the Washington bureau. Atlanta wanted more lively, feature-type material out of the capital.

After resigning, Watson said of CNN in an interview, "I felt that the quality and quantity of news could have been better and higher." He had wanted to do more in-depth pieces, he continued, but the new network had evolved into a cross between local TV news and all-news radio. It assumed, Watson said, that the viewer has a "gnatlike" attention span.

As one colleague put it, however, "George can't come to grips with CNN's inexpensive way of doing things. He'd rather go back to spend, spend, spend."

Stu Loory, with the notable exception of his four years as a highly respected White House correspondent for the *Los Angeles Times*, had been accustomed to working for the "underdog." He had been a reporter for the *New York Herald-Tribune*, in competition with the mighty *New York Times*; and he'd worked at the *Chicago Sun Times*, underdog to the *Chicago Tribune*.

For the *Sun Times*, Loory had led a reporting team that produced a spectacular series of investigative stories. The paper had gone out and bought a bar, the Mirage, and then waited for city officials and union leaders to come in and "hang themselves" by trying to solicit bribe offers. In another investigation, the team exposed auto-insurance frauds after posing as accident victims. The paper was making waves and taking heat.

"It turned out that with every new prize we won," Loory said later, "I was getting into deeper and deeper trouble."

When his boss took him out to dinner, Loory was expecting a raise. He was fired.

So after twenty-five years of newspaper reporting, Loory went to the CNN Washington bureau to start again. In his first few days he reported, three hours ahead of anyone else, that President Carter would debate Ronald Reagan at Convention Hall in Cleveland.

The League of Women Voters, sponsoring the debate, had decided to exclude independent candidate John Anderson. It would be a two-man confrontation, to be carried from Cleveland by the three major TV networks. Why, Schonfeld wondered, couldn't we find some way of turning it into a *three*-man debate? He called Loory in Washington.

"Listen, Stu, what do you think of the possibility of including John Anderson?"

Loory had been on the job for only a week. "What do you have in mind?"

"Well," Schonfeld said, "we can start with the *real* debate, in Cleveland. Let 'em answer the first question and then, at some other location, you can have Dan Schorr put the *same* question to John Anderson."

"I see. . . ."

"We let *him* answer it, *live*, while we're now *taping* the debate in Cleveland."

"I see. . . ."

"When Anderson is finished, you roll the *tape* showing the *next* question to Carter and Reagan, with their answers. Then go back to Anderson, live again, for *his* answer. And so forth!"

"I see," Loory repeated, although he didn't. Unaware of the immense technical challenge involved, he added, "Gee, Reese, that's a tremendous idea. Let's do it."

He negotiated with Anderson's people, who went along because, otherwise, their man was being excluded altogether.

STU LOORY

"We went and hired Constitution Hall in Washington. I walked out on the stage, when it was empty, and it was an awesome sight. Reese said, 'Don't worry. We'll get a remote truck down here with all the necessary equipment and we'll do a good job.'

"Reese got a bus down from New Jersey and they parked it out in front of Constitution Hall. I had been expecting some huge, gleaming van, the kind that has ABC SPORTS painted on it, but instead I saw this little, beat-up, old school bus converted into a remote truck. It was either gray or dirty white and hadn't been washed in years.

"When we got on the air that night, it was like simultaneously composing and playing a symphony, for the first time, live, without rehearsing."

"Good evening from the Cable News Network and welcome to the presidential debate. I'm Daniel Schorr, speaking from Constitution Hall in Washington. So that you can understand what's about to happen, what you'll be seeing is an expanded version of the debate that's sponsored by the League of Women Voters. In Cleveland, President Carter and Governor Reagan will be responding to questions by a panel of journalists, and at certain points will engage each other directly in rebuttal. Here in Constitution Hall, which has been leased by CNN for this purpose, John Anderson will respond to the same questions, and he will engage in the rebuttals before an audience invited by the Anderson campaign organization."

Schorr jumped into a dense thicket of words to explain what he just said.

"CNN will carry the start of the Cleveland debate live, until Reagan and Carter have replied to the first question. Then, Congressman Anderson will reply to that question. And we will then resume the proceedings in Cleveland, but from tape. So, in effect, Congressman Anderson will be 'inserted' into this debate, at every logical point. He will thus become a full participant in CNN's presidential debate, the great debate that has become a greater debate. . . ."

One effect was that CNN's debate kept running farther and farther behind the Cleveland one. Producers and assistants outside Constitution Hall used videotape recorders to capture the statements made by Carter and Reagan, while CNN was airing Anderson's live answers. Then someone played the next Cleveland tape, while another person kept recording the current debate there. In addition, a stenographer was listening to the live event and writing down the questions, which were hand-carried to Schorr so he could put them to Anderson.

Then it got complicated.

In the truck, people on the recorders were getting hopelessly confused. They were playing tapes out of sequence and even, in one case, forgetting to press the record button. There were awkward moments as the audio failed, as Carter was shown talking out of sync, as Reagan was seen answering a question that CNN viewers hadn't heard, as the screeching sound of tapes being rolled backward could be heard while the candidates spoke . . .

"We're learning as we go along," Schorr quipped.

Finally, about forty-five minutes into it, the young people in the truck were able to get things under control; and from then on, the "three-way" debate went along without a hitch and became part of television history.

A few days later John J. O'Connor of the *New York Times* wrote that CNN had "cleverly and deservedly garnered national attention" for its experiment, adding that despite the mishaps it had offered "an intriguing glimpse of a possible future when, armed with the multi-channel capacities of constantly expanding cable, all third-party candidates will have access to a national forum that has proved impossible on limited, over-the-air network television."

Reacting to some in-house criticism, Loory sent a memo to the staff: "The dust has cleared and in retrospect I think we can all congratulate ourselves on blazing a new trail in American journalism. . . . I think some of you were wondering whether Cable News Network should have gotten involved in this adventure at all. Let me share my own thinking on that with you. The League of Women Voters acted irresponsibly in excluding a man who is on the ballot in fifty states. . . . The American people were entitled to hear his views. . . . We saw that we had an opportunity to right a wrong, a time-honored function of American journalism, and we did it. None of us should feel ashamed of what we did. Indeed, we should all feel damn proud. . . ."

The whole production later ran on public television, with the errors corrected. Schonfeld, who had disappeared from Constitution Hall when the technical foul-ups had seemed hopelessly out of control, would be quoted by friends as saying he thought Anderson's presence in the debate had won the election for Reagan.

Ted Turner and Reese Schonfeld shared a birthday dinner in November.

"Suppose, Reese," Turner said, "that some people are going to compete with us. What's that competition likely going to be? How would they do it?"

Well, Schonfeld said, they would probably come up with a "headline" news service. They would deliver brief, fast-paced stories that would be repeated or updated every twenty or thirty minutes. It would *not* be varied and flexible, the way CNN was designed, but the main advantage would be its appeal to busy viewers or those with short attention spans.

The year before, Turner and Schonfeld had decided against such a headline service because it wasn't in their interest to have audiences watch CNN only for a short time. "There's no reason to let people think they can get all the news in half an hour," Schonfeld had said, "when you want them to watch you for two or three hours!"

"But if someone does come up with a headline service,"

Schonfeld now warned, "it could be very popular and really give us competition."

"Why don't you draw up a format for me," Turner said, "and a budget. If we're going to have competition, it's best to be our *own* competition."

Soon afterward, Schonfeld walked into Turner's office at Techwood and gave him a format with a budget. It was outlined in just a few pages, sketching the basics of a round-the-clock, headline news service for cable television.

Turner slipped it into his desk.

By the time CNN was covering its first national election on November 4, 1980, it was still not taken too seriously by the other networks — especially in Washington, where most of the national news stories originated and where the networks traditionally sank the largest chunk of their resources and expertise. Turner's network was clearly an unequal combatant in the capital, with only about half the number of correspondents and camera crews as CBS or NBC or ABC — even though it had to fill up more airtime than all three put together.

Dan Schorr and Bernie Shaw were two exceptions to the inexperience at the CNN bureau in Georgetown. While neither man would have turned down more back-up support and status, they seemed to relish their underdog role the way Stu Loory did.

For Schonfeld in Atlanta, battling the networks meant reaching for new schemes at every turn. He considered hiring a TV critic to "preview" the Big Three evening newscasts for CNN's audience on the West Coast. The critic would watch the network newscasts in the East, a few hours beforehand, and then perhaps say, "Watch ABC for the first three minutes, because they've got some good film from Iran, but then switch to CBS for the best report on the president's trip."

The idea made Schonfeld chuckle with glee.

Now in the fall of 1980, the CNN president was setting forth to improve weekend programming, beef up the quality of news writing and keep increasing editorial staff. And of necessity, he was spending money. As if coverage of the conventions and campaigns hadn't been expensive enough, there were rumors that the American hostages in Iran would be released just before or after the election. Their homecoming would be an emotional story and Schonfeld could not let CNN miss it.

So while the U.S. election returns were coming in, Dan Schorr was dispatched to Frankfurt, West Germany, with Jane Maxwell and a crew to wait for the hostages before their transfer to an American military hospital in Wiesbaden. They weren't alone in the effort: "Never," someone said, "have the networks traveled so far and spent so much to cover a story no one is sure will ever happen."

By making sure that CNN would be there if something did happen, Schonfeld was paying the price of keeping pace with the Big Three. The hostage story didn't break then, but that was beside the point.

What did happen in November was the MGM Grand fire in Las Vegas, with a death toll of eighty-three. The disaster was covered, at first, through one of CNN's reciprocal agreements with local stations. By now there were nearly fifty such deals for exchange of material, and when the hotel caught fire, KLAS was the local broadcasting partner at the scene.

The staff in Atlanta pleaded with KLAS to go live and stay live. The station did so. When the pictures were carried simultaneously by CNN to an audience nationwide, they showed the burning building with helicopter-rescue teams hovering above as people tried to escape the flames and heat. There were dramatic scenes, of personal heroism and of tragedy, unfolding moment by moment. Watching the coverage, Burt Reinhardt felt he was seeing for the first time what CNN could do best. And he was convinced, at last, that the all-news network would succeed.

LOU WATERS

"I was anchoring when it came on the air. The hotel was burning and we didn't have anything written, so I had to ad-lib. I did that for about three minutes, looked up, and Kavanau stepped into the Pit. 'Keep talking,' he said. So I kept talking. They got raw videos by satellite and threw 'em on the air, and Kavanau just repeated to me, 'Keep talking!' That was a challenge for me. It was an *hour and a half* later when I stopped talking.

"Alec Nagle was watching from the back of the newsroom. I was about an hour into it when he walked up during a break and just tapped me on the shoulder and said, 'I believe it. You *made* me believe it.' Then he walked off. That was his way. He was just really satisfied that CNN was doing something it was designed to do.

"If I had thought about it, I would have said, 'No, I can't do that.' But when you just *don't think* and go ahead and *do* it, then you find out that you *can*. And all of a sudden you get past that barrier — which is what CNN was like in a *lot* of ways."

Danielle Amos was producing her last show before taking maternity leave at five o'clock on a Friday in November, with Lou Dobbs anchoring. As usual there was chaos in the newsroom, and Dobbs watched in horror as his nine-months-pregnant producer ran around the place, jumping over cables, right to the closing moments when it was time for an "assignment desk update."

The update was a simple device to move from one hour of programming to another. At the assignment desk on this occasion was Ed Turner, facing a camera, ready to give a live wrap-up of major stories covered and reports coming up later. He was reading over the script, aloud, waiting for a cue.

"Let's check in with Ed Turner," Dobbs told the viewers, "for a summary of what's coming up next on the News Channel."

The director cued the camera person, a female video journalist. She waved to Ed Turner. But he ignored her.

On the desk facing Turner was a small monitor where he could see when his own image came on. But the monitor's switch had been thrown the wrong way; he was watching a different channel. He was on the air but didn't know it.

The video journalist waved at him. "You're on! *Go*," she said, making faces and jumping like a monkey. So Ed Turner, a clown at heart, went into an act of his own. He slammed his hand to his chest. He clutched his neck as if in sudden pain. He held up his tie as if hanging himself with it. He went through the excruciating motions of a man having a heart attack, all for the live CNN audience across North America to Hawaii, until Master Control could cut away.

The incident was Danielle Amos's send-off from the newsroom to the maternity ward. She went into labor two nights later and little Robbie Amos was born the next morning. Ted

Kavanau sent a camera crew to the hospital to cover the earliest gurgles of the first CNN baby.

Thanksgiving . . .

During live coverage of the New York parade, CNN went to a commercial. Ted Kavanau checked the monitor and saw the Mickey Mouse float. He jumped up and down, screaming, "Producers! Take the air! It's Mickey! You have to show Mickey! You're gonna miss him!" There was silence, followed by an explosion of laughter. Kavanau broke into a sheepish grin.

Christmas . . .

Don Miller and Kathleen Sullivan were anchoring. Before their newscast, they decided to close the hour with Miller holding a little piece of mistletoe over Sullivan's head and saying, "Kiss me." She would smile, and perhaps even blush, as he gave her a delicate peck on the cheek.

At the end of the show, Miller held up the tiny piece of mistletoe and they went through the routine. What Sullivan didn't know was that in Miller's other hand was a very large *branch* of mistletoe. After kissing her cheek, he swung the whole bough onto the anchor desk in front of her.

"*Now*, Kathleen," he said, "let's get down to business."

Sullivan did, in fact, blush; but then she cracked up and replied, "Do I have to get out the whips and the reindeer again?"

The figures were in.

By the end of 1980, CNN had signed on 663 cable systems reaching 4.3 million homes. The expectation for 1981 was that up to 400,000 new subscribers would be gained each month, for a total of eight million.

The network currently needed $2.1 million per month, or more than $25 million a year, to operate. Eight million subscribers at an average of seventeen cents a month would mean only $16 million for the year. Advertising dollars still couldn't come close to covering the rest. At the end of 1980 there were seventy-eight sponsors. The revenue from commercials for the first seven months was less than $3.9 million.

Turner was losing an average of $2 million a month. And he was adding new bureaus — in Detroit, Miami and even Tokyo. He was pouring money back into his product; and at this rate,

CNN would have more than seven hundred employees by the end of 1981. If news costs didn't rise and if CNN could gain in all areas, it was possible to start breaking even in a year.

But there were reports that ABC was planning to invade CNN's turf in 1982 with its own cable news service. There were no leaks yet that ABC and Westinghouse would join forces. But Turner knew he would not have the field to himself for much longer. Ironically, the more CNN proved its worth, the greater the threat of high-powered competition; the closer he came to success, the sooner Ted Turner was bringing his challengers out of hiding.

While Ronald Reagan was being sworn in as the fortieth president on January 20, 1981, word came that the hostages in Iran were being released. CNN viewers were informed by a flashing bulletin; and then a split screen carried both stories live. The network also switched back and forth, from the White House to Algiers and West Germany, as the hostages made stops.

In Atlanta there was pandemonium.

DAVE WALKER

"Marcia Landendorff was on the desk, setting up a live beeper with a long introduction. She was about to talk on the phone with the mother of one of the hostages: 'I have Gary Smith's mother on the line. She must feel a great deal of warmth and relief today, knowing her beloved son is coming home.' On and on she goes, finally saying into the phone, 'Mrs. Smith, how do you feel now that your son has finally been released and is coming home?' The woman answers, 'Well, he's not my *son*, he's my *cousin*, and I really don't know him that well. . . .'

"Then I'm on the air and Kavanau says, 'Take it!' So I pick up the phone and it's some guy at the embassy in Iran.

"I say, 'Can you tell me what's going on?' The guy tells me no, he can't. I say, 'Thank you,' and hang up. So we go on to another story, but about a minute later here comes Ted again.

"'I got a guy on the phone,' he says. 'Take-it-take-it-take-it!'

"So I pick it up and it's the *same guy.* He says, 'This is *you* again?'

"'Yes. Have you heard anything more?'

"'No.'

"'Thank you,' I say, putting down the phone and staring into the camera. . . ."

*   *   *

Paul Amos had picked up a day on weekends as supervising producer, so he was on hand to help follow the hostages as they headed home. Amos came in to take over from Tom Purdy, who explained that they'd be bringing in live coverage of Irish television when the hostages made a stopover at Shannon Airport. There was a certain amount of risk involved, because you could never predict what a local station — in this case, an Irish one — would do.

Finally, word came that the hostages had landed in Shannon, where the plane was being refueled for the rest of their journey to the United States. They had come out of the plane and waved while walking down the ramp. The scene had been recorded by the Irish station, which was about to use the tape in its 6 P.M. newscast. It was near 1 P.M. in Atlanta; CNN was monitoring the broadcast and getting set to go live with it as soon as the hostage segment appeared. No other American television would be carrying it.

Rick Brown, in Master Control, saw on the monitor that Irish TV was in a commercial for Weetabix, a version of shredded wheat. Bob Cain and Reynalda Muse were at the anchor desk. Ted Kavanau was in the Pit. Ken Dickman in the satellite department relayed word to him: "We're watching Irish TV and they're in a commercial right now. We expect that they will come out of it at the top of the hour to open their show."

The Pit told the Master Control engineer to go into a two-minute break. "But be prepared to drop out of it early."

CNN would break out of its own commercial after just one minute, if need be, giving Cain and Muse time to set things up quickly by saying, "Okay, we're going to take you now to Irish television, which is showing a videotape of the hostages taken just a few minutes ago." Then the switch would be thrown to the Irish feed.

Schonfeld was wandering around the newsroom to keep an eye on events, as he normally did during big stories, and now he walked into Master Control to watch the monitor.

"What's this?" he said. "What are we looking at?"

"It's Irish TV," Brown said, noticing that Schonfeld was trembling. "They're in a commercial."

Why, Schonfeld wondered, *was CNN still in its* own *commercial?* He hadn't been told that the network was about to switch. All he knew was that CNN was running an advertisement while, at any moment, Irish television would be showing its tape of the hostages. Schonfeld didn't want to miss it; he wanted CNN to punch up the Irish programming, Weetabix and all, to be ready.

"*Goddammit!*" he said, lumbering out of Master Control. Just then CNN broke from its commercial and returned to Cain and Muse, who were about to lead into the hostage tape. Schonfeld did not know his anchors were back on camera.

"Reese, wait!" Brown said. "Wait a minute!"

But he was on his way, a massive figure whose upper body was leaning forward at such a precarious angle that his feet had to move faster and faster to keep up. Kavanau rushed toward his boss to stop him. Schonfeld continued toward the rear of the anchor desk, heading for the Pit in the belief that CNN was still in its own commercial. Suddenly he shouted:

"YOU PRIME ASSHOLES, GET THAT OFF THE AIR!"

No drill instructor ever yelled louder. The sound and fury blasted through the newsroom. The anchors dropped their heads. The audio man in the Pit cautiously turned off the microphones, then turned them on again just in time to catch Cain saying, "Oh, my goodness."

Schonfeld's directive had gone up to the satellite and down to cable systems, all live, and could not be reversed.

Stunned by the sound, Cain and Muse were still facing the live camera as the raging CNN president crossed directly behind them in full view of CNN's audience. The two anchors waited for the storm to pass, not daring to move a muscle, although Muse visibly tensed up.

Then, dead silence.

Cain calmly said, "Now, to Irish television. . . ."

MARY ALICE WILLIAMS

"The day the American hostages came home, they stayed on the campus of West Point at the Thayer Hotel. We had gone up there and staked out this place on the roof of an insurance company building, right across from the Thayer gates, so that we could see them. Obviously, we were not going to have access to these people. We got there first and everybody else wanted our space. CBS was down on the ground. And we had all these cameras along the parade route as the buses came with the hostages in them, but we didn't have a switcher. I mean, what's the good of having multicameras if you can't switch between them? But we had this guy holding the wires. I don't know how he did it, but every time the director wanted to switch cameras, this guy would take the wires and change them, and it worked. Meanwhile, our people, Gerry Koch and Dave Silver, figured how to put our little microwave van at the absolutely quintessential spot where it had to be to send a live signal back to the bureau. So even though NBC and ABC and CBS had all this expensive equipment, nobody could get out except us!

"I'm standing up there in a long coat, with this blond hair and everything, with lights on me, and I'm about to go on the air, and some father walks by with his four-year-old daughter and she sees me and says, 'Daddy! Look! Dan Rather!'"

The first months of 1981 marked a period of escalating activity: gavel-to-gavel coverage of hearings on Alexander Haig's nomination as secretary of state; and live courtroom coverage of two trials, one pitting Creationism against Darwinism and the other involving Carol Burnett's lawsuit against the *National Enquirer.*

The coverage was costing money. Turner was thinking about raising much-needed capital by selling a million new shares of company stock; and meanwhile, he was making appearances on WTBS to hawk bumper stickers ("I LOVE CNN") for five dollars apiece.

He was also toying with the idea of letting one of the "biggies" join him as a partner, as another way to get an infusion of cash. In the corporate game, one rule was that you jumped into bed with the enemy if survival was at stake.

By this time, also, he had begun making moves toward *selling* CNN's coverage to broadcast stations — even to affiliates of the Big Three networks, who might be willing to pay for the availability of a twenty-four-hour news service.

Bill Leonard, former president of CBS News, recalled in his memoir, *A Lifetime at CBS,* that by the spring of 1981, the long-range implications of a twenty-four-hour news service available to CBS affiliates "made us wonder whether we should not take steps of our own to offer viewers the same service or something close to it."

After commissioning a study and finding out how costly such a venture would be, Leonard made an offhand remark that "it might be a hell of a lot cheaper just to buy CNN," to which Gene Jankowski, president of the CBS Broadcast Group, replied, "Do you think we could?"

Leonard got on the phone to Bob Wussler, suggesting an "ultrasecret" rendezvous between Turner and Jankowski. Here was one kind of situation for which Turner had hired Wussler in the first place; and sure enough, Jankowski and Leonard flew to the old Hartsfield Airport in Atlanta, where Turner and Wussler were waiting for them at Hangar One.

Turner was delighted. At the very time that he was calling CBS programming a disgrace to America, here was the head of CBS flying down to see him about buying Cable News Network.

"I'll sell you CNN," he said, *"forty-nine percent* of it." Or less. That would give him plenty of new cash reserves. Well, they said, we need fifty-one percent.

"You CBS guys are something," Turner said, laughing as he chewed a wad of tobacco and spit the juice on the ground. "Someday I'm going to own you. You bet I am. Remember I told you." The meeting ended with Turner inspecting the CBS plane and offering to buy it, then abruptly changing his mind. "What's the difference?" he quipped. "I'll own it anyway, one of these days."

On Monday, March 30, 1981, John Hillis was producing the two o'clock show from Atlanta. Bob Cain was at the anchor desk. It was a dull newsday and Hillis was having trouble filling the hour. President Reagan had given a speech to the AFL-CIO at the Washington Hilton and CNN had carried it live, with Bob Berkowitz on the scene. But the speech was over and Hillis threw in a four-minute piece about sewing in China, from an ITN feed.

In the Washington bureau, Cissy Baker (the twenty-two-year-old daughter of Senator Howard Baker of Tennessee) was running the assignment desk. She rummaged through the papers, searching for inspiration, then sat back and pounded her hands on the table.

"What we need around here is a good *fire* or something," she said. "We need some action! A good *shooting!*"

It was an offhand remark whose timing was the stuff of fiction. But that's what she said.

"Shots fired," a voice on the police radio reported. "Hilton Hotel."

Baker turned to Vito Magiola, who was in charge of the Washington bureau's field crews, and said, "Gosh, Vito, don't we have a crew over at the Hilton?" Before he could reply she looked down at a schedule sheet and exclaimed, "Holy shit! President Reagan's at the Hilton!"

CISSY BAKER

"We just scrambled. The radios were clogged and we couldn't get through to anybody. We kept homing in on the police scanner. We'd heard 'Shots fired' and then Reagan's code word, but we didn't know if the president had been hit. Nobody knew.

"Reporters all over town were flying over to the Hilton, but Vito and I waited to send ours. We knew the streets of Washington like the back of our hand, and we figured it would take Reagan's motorcade about seven and a half minutes to get from the Hilton back to the White House. So we gave him up to ten minutes to get there. If he was okay, our White House people would tell us by then that he had gone through the gate.

"But then we heard Nancy Reagan's code name, Big Red, on the scanner. When the Secret Service said, 'Big Red to GW,' Vito and I looked at each other. We knew what it meant: Nancy Reagan's motorcade had been dispatched to George Washington Hospital.

"Vito called our microwave van and said, 'Mini-Seven, drop everything and get to GW Hospital. Get your mast up and get a crew at the emergency entrance.'"

John Hillis in Atlanta took a call from Jeff Roth, the Washington producer.

"Reagan's been shot at," Roth said.

"Say what?"

"Reagan's been shot at."

"Get Bernie in the chair and get him there fast," Hillis said. "We're gonna break out of this China piece and take him."

"Wait a minute," Roth said. "I gotta get him to sit down, first! I gotta get him to put some information together!"

"Get him down and get ready!" Hillis said. "I'm breaking *out* of this."

JOHN HILLIS

"Within thirty seconds of the phone ringing, we cut out of the China piece and Bob Cain was on the air doing whatever he could do, with my frenzied prompting in his ear.

"He told the viewers, 'Now, for more information on this, we go to Bernard Shaw in Washington.'

"Bernie had sat down so fast that he hadn't put on his mike yet. He started talking and then, after fifteen seconds, he suddenly reached over and picked up his mike. Then he started talking again. It would be a minute or two before the radio networks would break the story.

"Bernie did that for about forty seconds, with whatever material he had, and then threw it back to us. Bob Cain started faking it: 'We'll keep you up to date as soon as we have any more information.'

"Burt comes walking in and he leans over the edge of the monitor bank. 'Go to Washington again and don't come back here.'

"So I picked up the phone and said, 'Jeff, I got an order from Reinhardt to go to you and stay with you.'

"Jeff said, 'I can't do that! We don't have any information! We don't know anything!'

"I said, 'Jeff, I don't think it makes any difference. Get Bernie in the chair and get ready to go. . . .'"

It was 2:32 P.M. Eastern Standard Time when Shaw reported that shots had been fired at Reagan, leading the other TV networks by four minutes. Then Shaw was first to report that the president might have been hit by a bullet. Because the microwave van had been sent to the hospital, CNN had the only shot of Reagan walking into the emergency room with his arm over a Secret Serviceman's shoulder. From the scene, Scott Barrett had relayed word on his two-way radio.

But Shaw steadfastly refused to go with unconfirmed reports that Reagan's press secretary, James Brady, had been killed. As so-called reliable sources were calling the Washington bureau to say that Brady was dead, and as those all around him urged an immediate airing of that report, Shaw kept shaking his head.

"I can't," he said.

"He's *dead*," the others kept saying. "Bernie, please, you *gotta* go with it!"

"No," Shaw replied, "not until you know for sure! Not till it's been announced by the White House!"

When official word came that Brady was alive, staff members marveled at how Shaw had maintained his own standards of journalism despite their frantic pleas for haste.

With Dan Schorr's help, he would stay at the anchor desk for more than seven hours, until ten o'clock that night; and CNN would continue virtually nonstop with the story for a total of twenty-nine hours. Bill Zimmerman and Don Farmer flew up from Atlanta, taking over as Washington anchors later in the night.

Meanwhile, fourteen reporters from the bureau scrambled around the city to keep picking up bits and pieces of information; and Reynalda Muse took off for Denver to cover the family of John Hinckley, who had been held in the assassination attempt.

During the night, when the other networks signed off, local stations across the country picked up CNN's coverage.

When it was all over, the ten-month-old news network would claim a number of other victories: First with tape of Hinckley's home in Colorado, delivered by satellite. First with coverage of the Dallas pawnshop where the gun was believed to have been purchased. First with coverage of a grim-faced Vice-President Bush in Forth Worth, Texas, as he departed for the capital.

Stu Loory scored a beat at 5:40 P.M. by breaking the story of Hinckley's motive in the shooting — related to his desire to impress actress Jodie Foster, who had appeared in the movie *Taxi Driver*, about a man who threatens to assassinate the president after being spurned by the woman he loves.

Such details were hitting the air in no particular sequence. CNN's viewers got the story in the jumbled way that a journalist receives fragments of information before transforming them into an orderly, polished report. The "process" of gathering news determined the form in which that news was delivered. With CNN's unlimited time, the story could unfold at its own pace. With all those "ragged edges" exposed.

By 10 P.M., Sandi Freeman had two of Hinckley's former Texas schoolmates as her guests on *Freeman Reports*.

Stationed outside the hospital to give live updates, Scott Barrett suddenly appeared on CNN's air without knowing it, shouting, "Goddammit! Which network's catering service is that?" Complaining that ABC's people were eating better, Barrett was cut off in midsentence by the Washington bureau, where an anchor said, "We seem to be having technical difficulties." In the background, Jim Rutledge could be seen repeatedly slamming his head against the wall.

For Ted Turner and Reese Schonfeld, CNN's reporting of the assassination attempt led directly to their biggest confrontation yet with the other networks. The fight, over being able to share in "pool" coverage of the president, had been coming for months; and in fact, Turner's lawyers had been on the brink of filing suit against the White House and the networks on the very day of the shooting. Steve Korn, a young attorney working with Tench Coxe, was about to board a plane to Washington when he was paged at the Atlanta airport and told, "You'd better turn around, because two of our defendants have just been shot — President Reagan and Jim Brady."

Pooling, begun in the Kennedy administration, was a practice whereby all the news organizations were represented by a small group (or even just one reporter) designated to cover certain presidential or White House events. In the case of television news, any video material was made available by the pooler to all the others.

But the three traditional networks had taken over *exclusive* operation of TV pool coverage, with the full sanction of the White House. The deal was that each network would provide coverage on a rotating schedule; and although allowed access to material by subscription, Cable News Network had been excluded.

On the day of the assassination attempt, neither Schonfeld nor anyone else at Cable News Network knew where to turn for video of the actual shooting. They knew that ABC was responsible for pool coverage of Reagan's speech, but were unaware that the "traveling pool" job had been given to an NBC cameraman.

Schonfeld called Stu Loory and Jim Rutledge in Washington. "Who was pool on this?"

"ABC," they said. But no pool video was available.

Ordinarily Schonfeld would have waited for it to be delivered, but this situation was not ordinary. So when ABC televised its footage of the shooting, CNN recorded it and immediately threw it on the air. Angry ABC executives charged that CNN had stolen their material, which had *not* been part of pool coverage.

Why hadn't Schonfeld been informed about the change in pool responsibility from ABC to NBC? Why didn't NBC's video of the shooting become available to CNN until nearly five o'clock?

It was time for a new offensive against the traditional networks.

REESE SCHONFELD

"We had relied on the fact that there was a pool cameraman with the president, to cover the traveling shots. When I called to complain, there was no concession by the networks. I figured this would be happening from there on. There had been a series of small issues, on other presidential trips, and now it was clear that we just had to try and formalize our relationship with 'em."

Before getting CNN on the air, Schonfeld had met with lawyers from all three networks, telling them that he wanted CNN treated as an equal in coverage of the president and the White House. "We want to be a full member of the pool," he said, "and to use our own guys to shoot."

The lawyers acknowledged that "some kind of compromise" was in order, but failed to get their own news departments to agree. One reason was simply tradition; also the unions representing network employees would not accept material shot by CNN's nonunion crews; and the networks shared a dislike of Schonfeld, whom they had accused of "cheating" at ITNA after he'd taken pool video, even though he'd had a right to.

TENCH COXE

"It had always amazed me, not just as a lawyer but as a citizen, that the Justice Department had never challenged the networks' monopolistic position. The world was really afraid of them. We had arguments with the networks over what we could and couldn't use. They regarded broadcast news as *their turf*. They resented the new kid on the block, so it was clear that until we got into the pool, CNN would never be recognized as anything but a minor force."

REESE SCHONFELD

"I had been fighting this battle for fifteen years. The networks maintained absolute control of television news in three ways: by control of communication, through AT&T lines; by their unions, whose high rates prevented new services from coming into the market; and by joining in pools to their own advantage, while keeping others out or charging absurdly high rates for material.

"But pooling, by its very nature, is illegal! It goes against the Fair Trade Act. It *can* be done, if all the competitors are permitted to share equally and aren't disadvantaged, but they were disadvantaging me from the very beginning!"

Over the years, Schonfeld had wanted to sue the networks for using "pools of convenience" — by which, instead of competing with each other, they combined their resources to cover some expensive events. For the material, other competitors were billed for twenty-five percent of the cost; but at ITNA Schonfeld had refused to pay those prices, arguing that the whole practice was illegal. In fact, the networks' own lawyers agreed with him; but the news departments of ABC, CBS and NBC refused to admit that they "covered their asses" by sharing material.

In cases where Schonfeld thought he had caught one network giving tape to another network, he would cry foul and shout, "*A pool to one is a pool to all.*" It was an illegal game with limited players, Schonfeld felt, and his vigilance had angered the networks well before he took over CNN's helm.

TENCH COXE

"When we demanded to get into the pool, the networks called us 'Chicken Noodle News' and said we wouldn't be able to carry such a heavy responsibility of presidential coverage. They said, 'You guys don't know what you're doing,' and, 'You're underfinanced.' We said, 'We *can* do it and we *will* do it and we want in!' After the Reagan shooting, we talked to people at the White House. It was clear that *they* didn't want to disturb the status quo. Jim Baker, the White House Chief of Staff, told us, 'No, we can't do that. You'll have to sue us.'"

*   *   *

When Bill Bevins complained to Turner about the money a lawsuit would cost, Turner talked with Schonfeld and said he wasn't going to back down no matter what. He felt he had to sue.

"Let's go for it," Turner said. "Let's get 'em."

On Monday, May 11, 1981, Turner and Schonfeld stood together at a morning press conference in Washington, D.C. There was no need for Turner to raise his voice. Instead, he read from a statement: "Cable News Network today files suit against the American Broadcasting Company Incorporated, CBS Incorporated, and the National Broadcasting Company Incorporated, seeking damages and declaratory and injunctive relief for violations of the antitrust laws of the United States, resulting from their practice of pooling news coverage and from various other predatory and illegal practices directed at Cable News Network.

"Also named in the suit are President Ronald Reagan, White House Chief of Staff James A. Baker and Deputy Press Secretary Larry Speakes, for violation of Cable News Network's right to equal access to cover presidential news conferences, trips and other presidential activities and White House events, as guaranteed by the Constitution of the United States."

Later, when Secretary of State Alexander Haig was flying to China and CNN was bumped from the list of those who would be on his plane, Turner's attorneys worked straight through a weekend to get a hearing. The attempt failed and Haig flew without CNN aboard, so the original complaint was amended to include him as a defendant.

Another target of the suit, which had been filed that morning in the U.S. District Court for Atlanta, was the National Association of Broadcast Engineers and Technicians, the labor union representing crews employed by ABC and NBC. Both networks had been voting against including CNN in rotations for "tight" pools permitting only one TV camera. Their contracts with NABET prevented them from taking pool feeds from any source except the two other unionized networks.

ED TURNER

"By suing the president and the networks, we got everybody's attention. We had to establish parity, because that was critical to being acknowledged as serious. The White House is what gives you access to the daily doings of the president, whether he's in Washington or somewhere else in the United States or traveling abroad. The suit became a symbol that we were in earnest."

"The three major networks should not be able to dictate the terms of our coverage, limit its scope or combine their resources to effectively prevent CNN from competing with them," Turner said at the press conference. "And the president's staff should not be allowed to deny CNN equal access to cover presidential activities and White House events."

It was the White House itself that was granting only to ABC, NBC and CBS the right to participate in "expanded" pools, where more than one camera crew was allowed.

"If the White House has the right to name who is going to be a pool," Schonfeld said, "it becomes a fundamental question of freedom of speech. We believe the networks are pressuring the White House to keep us out."

"We can compete with any of the networks one-on-one," he said. "It's when the three of 'em gang up that we have problems."

Turner went on to call for a congressional investigation into the networks and the movie industry for "polluting the minds of our people" and "tearing down what was once the strongest, hardest-working country in the world." He called for "massive change in network programming and motion picture releases — change to glorification of the good guy instead of the bad guy, change from indecency to decency, from immorality to morality, change to programming that appeals to the best in people instead of the worst."

A reporter suggested that he was calling for a witch-hunt; he retorted that the networks were *worse* than witches and *needed* "to be hunted down and prosecuted."

Turner showed a one-hour documentary called "TV: The Moral Battleground." Aired over both CNN and WTBS, the program examined sex and violence in television. A special screening was being arranged for members of Congress, Turner said.

Late in May, Turner heard that Westinghouse Broadcasting Company, still in the process of buying Teleprompter, had confirmed plans for its own Group W cable news network.

There was more. He learned that Teleprompter's 115 cable systems, of which ninety were still not offering CNN, had been advised to "go slow" in deciding whether to take Turner's service — because Westinghouse would offer its new one at a price far below cost.

And still more. Schonfeld, at a seminar in Colorado, heard that Westinghouse was not making the challenge to Turner all alone. It was joining forces with one of the Big Three networks, ABC. Schonfeld called Turner; they knew they had to get ready for CNN's biggest battle yet.

A few weeks later, Turner made an opening move by petitioning the FCC to deny the Westinghouse-Teleprompter merger in order to prevent "a scheme by Group W to create a monopoly in the distribution of news programming by cable." He charged violations of the antitrust laws. And he revealed that, according to new information he'd received, Group W was going to offer its news network *free* to cable systems.

The bombshell about ABC's involvement was not yet public, but the war had begun.

Competing against ABC/Westinghouse would be costly, on top of the expensive White House pool suit and the financial drain of what had become a busy year for the news business.

In April, they had covered the first launch of Columbia I, the space shuttle, with Bill Zimmerman seated on the roof of a tiny trailer in a lawn chair. While ABC News had erected an entire building for its coverage, Zimmerman sat outside with an umbrella shielding him from the rain as he reported the space shot.

That month Zimmerman also conducted an interview with Georgi Arbatov, a leading Soviet expert on the United States; and then CNN had live coverage of the Cuban May Day Parade, along with Castro's speech, as Mike Boettcher simultaneously provided commentary. It was the first live broadcast from Cuba in twenty years.

The shooting of Pope John Paul II, in May, occurred during CNN's daily feed out of Rome. The valuable footage rolled in at 12:55 P.M. and was on by 12:58, a clear scoop. But three minutes later, ABC News broadcast the same pictures. Schonfeld and Reinhardt cried foul; the roles had been reversed, with CNN accusing a Big Three network of stealing its material.

"Obviously," John O'Connor of the *New York Times* observed, "the competition thickens."

*　　*　　*

In July at the Hyatt Hotel in Kansas City, about fifteen hundred guests were attending a tea dance when two indoor aerial walkways collapsed, killing one hundred eleven persons and injuring nearly two hundred more as the steel and concrete structures plunged to the floor. Jane Maxwell shouted at her husband on the satellite desk: "Book Kansas City!"

"From what time to what time?"

"From now until the end of the world!"

Oh, Rick Brown thought, *it's one of those. . . .*

But when he dealt with AT&T for a land line, he was told, "One of the networks may want it."

"That doesn't matter. I ordered it first."

"Yeah, but they're the networks. You're just CNN."

"No," Brown countered, "I'm CNN and *they're just the networks.*"

"Well . . ."

"Oh, *please* help us out. Listen, the fact is, we're going live with this and we have to get it up so we can see the pictures and feed some tape in."

"What's going on in Kansas City?" the AT&T engineer asked.

"Well, there's a hotel and a bunch of people were dancing on the catwalk and it collapsed. We don't even know yet how many people were killed."

"Oh, my God!" the AT&T man exclaimed; and because of his sudden, personal involvement in the story, he made sure that CNN got the first live video pictures. Later he told Brown that he had gone home and said to his wife, "Did you see that hotel thing on the air? I was the one who brought that stuff in for 'em!"

Cable News Network was gaining recognition and strength, with subscribers and advertisers coming aboard at a steadily climbing rate. And then, as reported in *Broadcasting* magazine on August 11, 1981, the enemy guns opened fire: "Westinghouse and ABC have combined forces in Satellite NewsChannels, a joint venture designed to produce two 24-hour channels of advertiser-supported cable news that will be beamed free to cable operators. . . . The Group W/ABC venture puts them in active competition with the Cable News Network of Ted Turner. . . . Bill Scott, the senior vice president of Group W's Radio Group, who is taking over as president of Satellite News-

Channels, said he'll use a paraphrase of the Group W all-news radio motto: 'Give us eighteen minutes and we'll give you the world.'"

The invading troops were landing on the beach in order to conquer Turner's developing colony. With Schonfeld sitting there, he reached into his desk and pulled out the eight-month-old format and budget for a round-the-clock headline news service.

"Here," Turner said. "Do it."

FIVE

"Think things through as much as you can. Then give it a hundred percent. Always be cheerful. Never get discouraged and never quit. Because if you never quit, you're never beaten."

ON A MONDAY MORNING in mid-August 1981, Ted Turner called a meeting in the Techwood conference room to inform the CNN staff of his response to the ABC-Westinghouse challenge. Ed Turner, knowing what was coming, experienced a terrible, sinking feeling as he thought, *Oh, my God, another network! We've just gotten the basics in place. The refinements, and the sophistication we must have to acquire journalistic credibility, don't come easily. They take years to acquire and we've barely got Journalism One behind us with CNN. Now it's back to summer school!*

Bunky Helfrich attended the staff meeting. When he had returned from the America's Cup trials the previous summer, he had continued with renovations at the former Progressive Club — starting with the bathrooms. The CNN headquarters in the basement had been completed — although its "rotating set" designed by Ron Baldwin had failed to rotate properly; the graphics area set up by Kitchell had been way too small for the volume of work being produced by Ann Williams, Fran Heany and the team; and overall, despite Schonfeld's early enthusiasm, the network had already outgrown its newsroom space — and Helfrich had set about completing the WTBS facilities on the ground-level and upper floors.

Now Turner held up his favorite sword again and announced a "preemptive first strike" against Westinghouse and ABC, whose first stage of Satellite NewsChannels was scheduled to appear in the spring or summer of 1982. The initial SNC offering would be a repeating headline service; it would be followed by a network with a more flexible format on the order of what CNN was already producing. To defend himself, Turner was launching a counterattack against SNC, comparing the move in his mind to President Franklin Delano Roosevelt's declaration of war against Japan immediately following Pearl Harbor. He was starting up a *second* round-the-clock, all-news service, to be called Cable News Network II, which would go on the air at midnight, December 31, 1981, just four months away.

This new "short form" network would use CNN's material for its news stories, but it would need its own building and newsroom with a separate staff of producers, directors, anchors and technicians. "We're gonna do our *own* headline service," he said, chewing on his cigar. "We're gonna offer everything they say *they're* gonna offer, except that ours will be on the air *first* and it'll be *better!* They have only money to lose, but we have *everything* to lose. We have to stake out this territory now or we'll lose it forever. This is the time in cable history where you either establish your bona fides or you don't."

His announcement was made following a few days of solitary contemplation on the grounds of his five-thousand-acre plantation in Jacksonboro, South Carolina. After that, Turner had returned to Atlanta to lead the charge. For staff members, it was an unforgettable moment as he issued his battle cry and declared that instead of retreating he was firing back.

"Ted's happy — we're at war again," a grinning Schonfeld said afterward, making it plain that he himself was not exactly miserable about it. "Ted's reaction to competition is to go on the offensive. He doesn't go into his shell and wait. When somebody aims a punch at *him*, he throws a punch at *them*."

I've got four months, Bunky Helfrich was thinking. *Four months to put up a whole new building for another cable news network! This is ridiculous!*

That day the architect called a contractor and said, "Look, I've got to have a building over here, next door to CNN headquarters. I want you to get here as soon as you can, with or without a permit, and let's put up a building with twenty thousand square feet of space. Just start with a shell, while we get rolling with the design for what goes inside. No, we don't have any idea what it's gonna be. I realize it's crazy, but you know Ted. We've got only a hundred twenty days until New Year's Eve. . . ."

The next morning a big orange bulldozer, looking very much

like a tank, came rolling and roaring onto the grounds of the former country club. The bulldozer started moving dirt to create a hole in the ground for the foundation of CNN2's headquarters — the Butler Building, staffers nicknamed it — and the sight of the earth-moving made such an impression that, years later, a number of people would swear that the bulldozer had appeared not the next day but that very afternoon.

What did happen, however, was that a CNN camera in the main newsroom swung away for a "bumper shot" of the earth-moving outside the window. When the bulldozer came into view, an Atlanta city official saw it on his television screen and checked to see if Turner had obtained a permit. When the answer came back negative, the building department issued orders for the dirt to be replaced until permission was granted.

TED TURNER

"It was basically a defense, but in defending you often attack. We were holding the ground. We had CNN already, and they were gonna attack with two channels.

"They wanted to get on the air in a hurry, so the short-form service was much easier for them to do first. We were gonna start even sooner. And I figured — knowing they were two big companies and that they were both public corporations, and how slow those kinds of operations usually run — that if their losses were bigger than anticipated, the people in charge of this project would come under criticism. . . .

"And I knew that if they ran into unanticipated difficulties, there would be friction between the two fifty-fifty partners. You're much better off competing against a split command than against a single command, because split commands spend a lot of time trying to figure out what to do and so it's easy for 'em to get into an argument. I find that partnerships work okay when things are going well, but they're put under a great deal of strain when things don't go as anticipated.

"So even though we were very, very strapped financially, and they knew it, I decided that we would beat them to the market. We would split the market for that service, so they would not be as viable. I didn't know exactly how long we could last. I think the two of them had resources a hundred times greater than mine. I did know that in a war of attrition we'd lose."

*　　*　　*

Eventually the new network would be renamed Headline News, but at first Turner called it CNN2 in order to "count on the good name of the first one." He had gotten the idea from the British Broadcasting Company's use of the names BBC1 and BBC2.

Schonfeld went to Ted Kavanau and said, "Do you want to have your own network?"

"Sure," Kavanau said.

Now came the supreme test of Kavanau's ability to work harder and longer than anyone else, while driving his team toward the goal. Four months! Just two years ago he had been broke and depressed in that Brooklyn brownstone; but now, after having played a key role in TV-news history with CNN itself, he had the burden of creating a whole new network.

And he loved it.

Turner went to the newsroom as a guest on *Take Two*. He sat next to the anchor desk with Chris Curle and Don Farmer, who asked him, "What was your first reaction when you heard that Westinghouse and ABC were going to start another cable news service?"

"Well, Don, it's real *interesting*," Turner said with sarcasm, "because all of the networks pooh-poohed the idea when we first announced we were going to do it. Now they're coming in because they can see that we're becoming tremendously successful."

Citing Westinghouse as "the largest group broadcaster in the nation outside of the three networks," Turner raised antitrust questions over its link-up with ABC. "But in Washington today, the Reagan administration is letting anything go." The FCC had approved the merger of Westinghouse and Teleprompter into a $3.2 billion company because it "would probably provide *competition* to the networks." Turner said, "but the day after, Westinghouse announced that they were going in *combination* with a network."

"Competition my foot!" he added.

With ABC's capitalization of $800 million, he said, smiling, "We now have a raid against us, committed to our destruction, of approximately $4 billion — versus our capitalization of $200 million!"

"You're in remarkable good humor today, Mr. Turner," Curle observed.

"They're fifty times bigger," he went on, "but with the Super-Station and the Cable News Network, we've always been the little guys fighting the big guys, and I really relish the fight."

"Can you keep going?" Farmer asked. "There are a lot of rumors around in financial circles that Ted Turner, no matter how good his intentions, no matter how good his product, is going to need the help of some *other* conglomerate to *fight* the conglomerates."

Turner replied that we would seek help from either of the other two networks against ABC if he had to: "I will do whatever is necessary to survive. *The only way they're gonna get rid of me is to put a bullet in me!*"

But, he said, becoming a partner of another network would be a "last resort" — indeed, the very thought of it seemed to make him squirm — "because I really like our company being independent, and I hope we can stay that way."

Farmer led into a QUBE poll of cable viewers in Columbus, Ohio. (The QUBE system had been a pioneer of two-way television, inviting people at home to punch a little hand-held keypad connected to a central computer. In this way viewers could give "answers" to questions.) When Farmer asked his audience in Ohio to "tell the truth" about their opinion of CNN, eighty-five percent punched out that they thought it was "excellent" rather than good or fair or poor.

"Holy smoke!" Turner cried out. "You know," he said, becoming emotional, "when we started this whole thing — because I knew we were walking in where, in fact, one of the articles said, angels fear to tread — I said it then and I say it now, that even if I knew we were going to fail when we started, I would've gone ahead and done it anyway, because even if we were only on for a short period of time" — his voice began to crack — "we would have shown what responsible journalism on television could do."

Then he addressed the newsroom staff: "I'm really proud of what we've done and I know everybody here is, too, and we've worked hard, haven't we? I mean, this has been the hardest-working group of people that the world has ever seen!" Facing the possibility of losing all that they had achieved, he wanted them to know he would not let them down. The fight was on, and they could count on him. "We're gonna keep in there swinging. You know, onward and upward. I don't know where we're goin', but we're goin' there in a hurry. Awwright!"

The next day Turner flew to Boston to meet with cable operators during a conference in the elegant Copley Plaza Hotel. A standing-room-only crowd, including reporters, gathered to hear his announcement. He strolled over to a piano at one side of the room and played a mournful dirge. "That's for Westinghouse," he exclaimed.

The cable people were on his side. They knew that subscription figures for CNN had grown to nearly eight million households and that Turner's prospects for breaking into the black were fairly good, so the Westinghouse announcement had been a shocker. They knew, also, that Satellite NewsChannels would be offered to them *free*. Their loyalty to Turner, rather than to a broadcast pair that had lobbied against cable for years, was being put to the test.

To warm them up, Turner played a videotape of his appearance on CNN with Farmer and Curle. Then he tossed away his microphone and yelled, "I don't know if these things are working, but I don't need one! I probably could holler to the whole country without a satellite, I've got such a loud voice!"

As they laughed he told them, "When I cast my lot with the cable industry ten years ago, I *dreamed* that all these things would happen . . . and it's not unexpected that the three guys, the second-wave companies, the three major networks, would be in a state of panic and try to figure out a way to cut themselves in and get control of the news on your cable systems, at a belated time, when they see what tremendous damage we are doing to them!"

Turner again announced his new headline-service plan. "We're gonna start exactly at midnight to ring in the New Year." Now reading from notes, he called CNN2 a "compact, hard-news summary of the day's events" offering a "continuously updated, thirty-minute wheel of hard news with a five-minute window for cable systems to insert local news."

Then he dropped his notes and grew intense. He was talking to the cable industry — he needed those system operators — and yet was speaking to his adversaries, too. ABC and Westinghouse were still one-move players, he felt, and they needed to see who they were up against: "You know, I've always been a fighter. And I remember when this industry was scrapping for survival. We've always been scrapping. We've had to fight for our right to live against these networks that are now standing in line to utilize your channels. We had to fight for our lives. You'll find that I've spent a great deal of my time and money in Washington, helping you fight these battles, because your battles have been my battles ever since I joined the industry. . . .

"We are going to commence immediately — we are going to spend, promoting Cable News Network in the advertising arena, during the next twelve months — write this one down — fifty million dollars. . . . The SuperStation is going to spend a minimum of thirty million dollars, too. Our company is going to spend eighty million dollars advertising our services nationally during the next twelve months. . . .

"Timing is everything and the Good Lord and Destiny are looking after both of us. If we had lost the retransmission-consent battle, we'd all be a lot poorer. But we've won every important battle we've needed to, against those no-good SOB's" — he had to stop while they roared with laughter — "that are trying to sneak in the door now."

He announced that he was also creating a twenty-four-hour CNN *radio* network.

Then came a bigger surprise: "Within the next sixty days we are going to announce a partial use of our footage, and compilation of our news, to compete directly with broadcast news!" CNN would be syndicated to TV stations, he said, "and we hope that ABC and CBS and NBC affiliates will preempt the network news to carry *our* news." More laughter and applause. "It's gonna be a lot more economically advisable for those affiliated stations, because of how the networks screw 'em — the way they'd like to do y'all!"

The cable people loved it.

He read a quote from a *Los Angeles Times* article the weekend before, in which a network executive had said, "The new Westinghouse-ABC joint venture marks a quantum leap in established television's commitment to the new media. These people are the big time. The big blow is to Turner. It's a little like General Motors coming in after Studebaker announces a new car."

"Well," Turner said, "I would say we're more like Toyota."

He held up a magazine. "Now, let me tell you, this is *Forbes* on the newsstand now, and the headline is 'Don't Count Ted Turner Out.' Pick one up." The story referred to Group W president Dan Ritchie. "Awwright, listen to this: 'Ritchie refuses to gloat, but his associates aren't as discreet,' and this is a quote here: 'The days of Mr. Turner's clear sailing are over.'

"*Clear sailing, my ass. I'm losing a million a month!*

"'Turner will have to sell out cheap,'" he read aloud, looking up. "Would you like me to sell to CBS? Instead of having an independent news network? If General Motors makes a mistake and puts out a bad car, we want to be able to come out and say it on the news! You'd never see that on ABC, CBS and NBC! Because they're concerned about the billions of dollars that the auto companies are spending on the Super Bowl and the World Series. . . ."

He moved in for the kill. "The most damning thing of all," he said, referring to the ABC-Westinghouse plans, "and I'm sure they're gonna retreat from this position, but they have forever lost credibility as a journalistic source. . . ."

He took his time. "The one thing is, you guys and girls and ladies in the cable industry, you are learning. A year ago, you knew very little about news, but you're learning a lot about it. I mean, *I* didn't know much about it, either" — the cable crowd laughed as he stretched it out — "but I knew enough to know that the broadcast-news approach was the wrong way to do it, because they panic everybody. Their approach has turned our young people against serving in the military, by showing nothing but Abscam and never showing congressmen and senators in a good light. They've turned our people against our wonderful government, and they've turned our people against business . . . they're anti-religion, anti-family, anti-American, you know all those things I've said, but they don't cover it, they only cover the stuff that's good for them, they manage the news, but *awwwright*, here it is . . ."

He held up some newspaper quotes from Roone Arledge, head of ABC News. "They put a *showman* in charge of the news to get the *ratings* up." But his point was that Arledge had said ABC would give its footage to Satellite NewsChannels *only under certain conditions*. Turner quoted Arledge: "ABC News will maintain someone in its own organization who will decide what can be released to SNC. The big stories are going to be held for the ABC Evening News."

"In the history of journalism," Turner exclaimed, "no one has ever started a journalistic endeavor admitting that, through a conflict of interest, they were going to withhold from the American people, from the people of any nation, major stories until it suited their major profit center! They have destroyed their credibility in this industry and with the American people!"

He quoted an ABC spokesman: "Our first priority remains our network news operation. Our facilities will just supply extra footage for the cable service that won't be in competition with broadcast news."

And another Arledge quote: "If Barbara Walters were to interview the Ayatollah Khomeini, obviously we would consider that an exclusive for *ABC World News Tonight.*"

"*Anybody who goes with them,*" Turner roared, "*is going with a second-rate, horseshit operation!*"

He paused. "Are there any questions?"

In September, several hundred broadcast journalists were converging on New Orleans for the thirty-sixth annual convention of the Radio-Television News Directors Association. The speeches and luncheons and conferences, amid nearly five hundred exhibits, would be held in the Marriott Hotel. The three-day convention was set to begin with a keynote address by Richard Wald of ABC News. Walter Cronkite was to receive the prestigious Paul White Memorial Award, the RTNDA's highest honor, named for the man credited with building the legendary CBS News team of the World War II era that included Edward R. Murrow and William L. Shirer.

Schonfeld had decided to send four delegates from CNN: Sam Zelman, Ted Kavanau, Alec Nagle and Jane Maxwell. Zelman and Kavanau were obvious choices because of the wide respect they commanded; and Kavanau would get a chance to talk to the news directors about syndication of CNN2. Maxwell hated conventions, but she knew the people from the stations; and Nagle was the spiritual leader of CNN's newsroom. Yet he was surprised to have been chosen. The RTND convention was a big deal, and this would be his first official trip for the network.

In April, Kavanau had replaced Ed Turner as CNN's managing editor, and Schonfeld had moved Nagle into Kavanau's job as senior producer. Now that Kavanau had been put in charge of CNN2, Jane Maxwell had taken over the assignment desk as managing editor. Ed Turner had been appointed executive producer and anchor in charge of a newly instituted *Two-Minute Newscast* at the end of each hour. Schonfeld, with the shifts, was reaching for more depth and flexibility.

The concept of giving two minutes of up-to-date headlines, along with a forecast of stories to come, had been Nagle's creation. Over the past months, his presence had grown even stronger — but he was clearly exhausted. One Sunday evening he had gone to the condominium where Brown and Maxwell now lived. They had sat together on the ground-floor terrace; Brown played the guitar, they sang and drank wine. At one point, Nagle stood and said, "Life is beautiful. I can't wait until I have an office where I can hear the clock ticking." He wanted to be out of the craziness, he said, away from the noise, in an executive position that would allow him to "put my feet up on the desk and, once in a while, go out to lunches and do things that executives do."

"You'd hate it," Brown said.

Nagle laughed. "I know. But I'd sure like to give it a try."

Zelman, Nagle and Maxwell flew to New Orleans on the same plane, with Kavanau scheduled to follow the next day. Nagle and Maxwell, who had come to regard each other as close friends, sat together. The night before, Nagle had ended a month-long period of not drinking. He had gone out to a restaurant, with Ann Williams and others, and gotten smashed. Now he fell asleep during the flight, and when he woke up he said, "I just dreamed that when I woke up the airline had changed the upholstery." Maxwell laughed, agreeing that the plane's seat coverings were indeed ugly.

In New Orleans, the three CNN representatives went straight to the Marriott. Nagle had reserved a room in another hotel, but he planned to check in there later. The first task was to open a hospitality suite on the twenty-seventh floor, where Maxwell had booked the adjoining bedroom for herself. In the empty suite, she and Nagle looked at each other. They were newspeople, with no clue about what to do at a convention.

"I've never opened a hospitality suite," Nagle said.

"Neither have I," Maxwell said.

"Well, Sam will know what to do. He's been to these things before. Thank God for Sam."

Sure enough, Zelman took charge. "We have to order liquor," he said, and they took care of that. "Now," he added, "go down to the management and get some easels and put up a few CNN signs. And pick up some programs and brochures."

After dinner they opened the CNN hospitality suite at seven o'clock. They sat there, waiting for visitors. It was still a fact of CNN life that relatively few people knew much about the all-news network, so they continued to wait in the empty suite with all of the unused liquor. At last, when one man wandered in, Nagle and Maxwell remained in their chairs as if to say What do we do now?

Nagle seemed shy and even depressed; gone was the gregarious personality; in this situation, calling for social niceties and inane chatter, he was lost. He lit another cigarette and poured himself another drink.

"Hi, there," Zelman was saying to the stranger. "I'm Sam Zelman. I'm vice-president and executive producer at CNN. What's *your* name?"

"Well, hello, Sam, I'm . . ."

Maxwell kept watching, to get the drill down, while Nagle smoked and drank and pulled into himself. After the third visitor arrived, she got up and said to him, "Hi, I'm Jane Maxwell and I'm the managing editor of CNN."

"Oh, yeah, Jane, we've talked on the phone. I'm . . ."

It was working, but Nagle still sat in the corner and quietly drank. Maxwell tried to prod him. "Hey, Alec, get up and *talk* to some people," she said, but he refused to move.

He's not able to do this, she thought, *and right now I can't sit and talk with him.*

As more news directors and station managers came into the suite, she and Zelman became busy making small talk and fixing drinks. Unlike the other networks' fancy hospitality suites, theirs had no bartenders or waiters.

"Let me see," Maxwell was saying as she held up a bottle. "I'm not quite sure how to make a vodka sour, but . . ."

Once in a while she glanced over at Nagle, but he never moved. At about eight-thirty, Zelman turned to her and said, "Well, Jane, I'm off. I'm leaving it in your capable hands." And he was gone.

The party continued. At last one of Nagle's old friends, Don Dunphy from WABC in New York, walked in. Nagle had been eager to see both Dunphy and Roger Grimsby, his idol; and now he stood, introducing Maxwell and Dunphy to each other, but the drinks had caught up and he didn't look well. Nagle sat back down, then sprang from the chair, ran to the bathroom and closed the door behind him.

Maxwell and Dunphy paid little attention. Both had seen Nagle drink before. But as ten, fifteen and then twenty minutes went by, they became concerned.

"He's been in there a long time," Maxwell said.

Dunphy went to the door and knocked. He knocked again. Then he opened the door and saw that Nagle had gotten sick. He helped him out, walked him into the adjacent bedroom, put him on the bed, undressed him, covered him and walked out, closing the door.

About a dozen visitors were still in the suite. If they had noticed anything, they gave little sign of it. Shortly after eleven o'clock Maxwell yelled, "Okay, one last drink for everyone!" When they all booed, she blushed and said, "Well, fellas . . ."

At last, near midnight, it was over. The place was littered with liquor bottles and glasses and beer cans. Maxwell stood there, wondering what to do next. Alec Nagle was in the other room, on her bed, not making a sound. She went inside, checked to make sure he was still covered, grabbed her suitcase and backed out. In the suite, she pulled down the Murphy bed and climbed in, quickly falling asleep.

In the morning there was still no sound from the other room. Maxwell hurriedly showered and dressed; she went out to the hall and down the elevator — the convention was starting up for real. She grabbed some coffee and walked into one of the ten o'clock seminars. She attended one conference after another, looking for Zelman or Nagle. She saw neither man and, finally, at about two in the afternoon, she went back up to change.

Standing outside the door of the suite were two New Orleans policemen. She walked up to them with a funny feeling in her stomach. The door was open. She went past the officers and inside. Sam Zelman came over to her.

"I'm really sorry," he said.

"What's going on?"

"I couldn't come down and find you, because I'd have to do it with a police escort."

"What is it?" Maxwell pressed him, but she didn't really want to know, and when she heard Sam's next words and saw his lips moving, saw the gentle expression in his eyes, somewhere the words of the song came to her, *the day the music died*; and Sam was still talking about how the hotel had no registration record for Alec and therefore his death was listed as "under suspicious circumstances," so Sam was under house arrest "and I thought the police would frighten you," he was saying . . .

A few hours earlier, Zelman had gone upstairs to the suite and knocked on the door. He had used his own key to let himself in, looked around, gone to the bedroom and found Alec Nagle's body on the bed. He called the hotel desk and told them. The police came as he was calling Atlanta.

In the Techwood newsroom, Rick Brown was booking a satellite feed when he got summoned to go up and see Burt Reinhardt.

"I'm busy," Brown said.

"No. Right away. It's very important."

In Reinhardt's office, on the couch, were Paul Amos and Peter Vesey. They had blank expressions.

"What's up?" Brown said.

"Listen," Reinhardt said as he walked around the desk and came toward him, "I have something terrible to tell you. There was a tragedy in New Orleans." Brown stared as Reinhardt continued, "There was a death."

Brown fell backward, slumping against the wall. "What?" he said. About to pass out, he felt himself slide toward the floor.

"No, no!" Reinhardt cried. "It wasn't Jane!"

Still dizzy, Brown caught himself and stood again.

In the hotel suite, Jane Maxwell went to the door of the bedroom but could not go any farther. She saw that Nagle was in the same position he had been in the night before. She gave a statement to the hotel manager and to the police. Apparently, it had been a heart attack. Maxwell placed a call to Atlanta.

"Did you hear?" Brown asked.

"He died in the suite," she said.

Even the police and the Marriott security people were speaking in low, discreet voices. Now off the phone, Maxwell sat on the couch, waiting — but for what?

There was a question about what to do with Alec's body and his belongings, but neither Sam nor she could deal with that kind of thing yet. Suddenly the door burst open and Ted Kavanau bounded in holding his bags and, like an eager sergeant ready to lead the charge, shouted, *"So what's goin' on!"*

Maxwell stared at Kavanau. He was jabbering away and it was obvious, unbelievably so, that he hadn't received the news. He had brought Nagle into the company, he adored him, loved him . . .

"Ted," Maxwell snapped. "Sit down."

Kavanau stood there. He had a bewildered look on his face as if his circuits were crossing but he didn't know why. He could tell there was something wrong but didn't have a clue what it might be.

"What's goin' on? What's up?"

"Sit down. Put your bags down and sit," she commanded. Kavanau obediently took a seat. She watched him looking around as if, by now, he could sense the danger.

"Alec's dead."

Kavanau's shoulders snapped forward and he caved. At the same time his face turned white. He sat hunched over for a full minute, in silence.

Then, beaten, he whispered: "What? How?"

That night at a New Orleans restaurant, Jane Maxwell sat between Zelman and Kavanau. She had not wanted to go anywhere for dinner, but Zelman had insisted. Earlier she had called Reinhardt to say she was closing the hospitality suite; and when he'd started to object she had told him, "Burt, the suite is closed!"

Kavanau had gotten into the logistics of everything. He had gone with the police, when they had taken the body away; he would stay behind in New Orleans until he could bring it home.

"Life goes on," Zelman had said. "You have to eat. And we're going to dinner."

Now, at the restaurant, he and Kavanau were acting as if nothing had happened. While they talked, not once did Nagle's name come up. Zelman was talking about the past, while Kavanau was talking about CNN2 and the future. Back and forth they went as Maxwell stared down at her food, holding on to her last shred of composure and wondering if the world had gone mad.

"What do you think, Jane? What I'm gonna do is . . . ."

"That sounds like a good idea, Ted."

"It's a *great* idea," he said, drawing an invisible CNN2 news-room with his finger. "We could put the edit room here, that way, and then we could streamline it this way . . ."

"I remember," Zelman said, "when I worked at CBS . . ."

So this is how these people grieve. This is the only way the strong, tough Ted Kavanau knows how to mourn — by putting himself into his work. He's talking about some news network and Sam is talking about twenty years ago, and this is how they can deal with it. . . .

After dinner she called the newsroom in Atlanta, but Rick and Jim Shepherd had already gone to Harrison's to deal with *their* grief by drinking it away. She got through to a bartender, who put her husband on the line. After listening to him slur about Alec, she spoke to Ken Dickman.

"Kenny," she said, "I can only deal with one death at a time. Please take Rick home."

In the morning, she received a frantic call from Kavanau in the Marriott's lobby.

"There's a fire!" he said.

"A fire in the building?"

"There are several big fire trucks outside! Come down the stairway! Now!"

Maxwell grabbed her things and ran down twenty-seven flights of stairs, crying most of the way, to the lobby.

"It's all over," Kavanau told her. "It was a kitchen fire. They put it out."

In the cab with Zelman to the airport, she felt as if they were leaving the Twilight Zone. At last she broke the silence.

"You know, Sam, Alec really held you in high regard."

"Oh," Zelman said, "really?"

He was smiling politely, as if she had just told him his tie looked nice; and at that moment Maxwell understood some-thing else. Sam Zelman really had seen it all. He had been to Vietnam during the war, he had been in crises all over the world, and he had seen death over a long period of time. To him the tragedy of one young producer was not new.

What did seem to be a revelation to him, however, was that this same young producer had looked to him for wisdom and guidance; and that he, Zelman, had been counted upon to lend much more to the building of CNN than merely his name and credentials.

Much more than he probably knew.

In the newsroom, Jim Shepherd went to one of the writing consoles and began typing words that would be received throughout CNN headquarters and in all its bureaus:

MESSAGE TO ALEC

I KNOW THIS IS A STUPID THING TO DO . . . AND NOW IS NOT THE TIME TO SAY THANKS . . . BUT SOMEHOW THIS GODDAM MACHINE SEEMS THE WAY TO COMMUNICATE WITH EVERYONE, EVERYWHERE.

WE ARE ALL PRETTY MUCH IN SHOCK. . . . I MEAN THE PILLS WERE MORE OF A JOKE TO US THAN A REMINDER THAT EVEN NEWSPEOPLE ARE FALLIBLE, MORTAL AND CAPABLE OF PROBLEMS OTHER THAN EX-WIVES AND HANGOVERS.

IN SHORT, WE'RE GOING TO MISS YOU . . . YOUR ENERGY AND VISION MADE US WHAT WE ARE HERE AT CNN . . . AND THAT WON'T LEAVE . . . BUT DAMMIT, OLD FRIENDS HAVE NO BUSINESS BEING LEFT BEHIND WITHOUT EVEN A GRIMSBY STORY TO HOLD US OVER UNTIL WE GET TOGETHER FOR THE BIG PRODUCTION NUMBER.

IN SHORT, WE LOVED YOU . . . AND WE MISS YOU ALREADY.

JIM S.

In New Orleans, Kavanau waited behind to fly with Nagle's body to New York, where the funeral would be held; but he also wanted his friend to be remembered by his peers. So he persuaded the news directors to share the cost of hiring a jazz band of eight black musicians who would lead a funeral march through the streets.

He went to the morgue, where he cajoled the coroner into releasing Nagle's driver's license; then he had the photograph of Alec's face enlarged for the traditional poster to be carried aloft during the parade.

In the Marriott's lobby on that Friday evening, a loudspeaker announcement addressed the news directors: "Mr. Nagle's party is leaving from the Canal Street entrance!"

On hand was columnist Dick Williams, who observed that what followed was "surely the most incongruous New Orleans funeral in Bourbon Street's storied history. . . .

The marchers, 250 of them, were predominantly white, middle-aged, suited and vested, tassled and shaved. They may have been the first New Orleans funeral procession that couldn't walk and clap at the same time. . . .

The eight men of Dejan's Olympia Brass Band marched down Canal to Bourbon, with the news directors walking slowly behind. As the procession passed Vieux Carée and other familiar spots, they were joined by natives and tourists who danced while the musicians played "Ramblin'" and "Saints" and "Back Home in Indiana" and "Tiger Rag." With the sight of drunks and strippers' tassels on either side of the street, amid the jazz music and dancing and awkward marching, while many of the news guys avoided reality by scoffing, joking and making plans for drinks back at the hotel bar, Ted Kavanau grimly carried the poster with Nagle's face on it. There were tears in his eyes, but, he knew, this crazy funeral march was the perfect tribute to his young friend, who had always looked squarely at life to see its lunacy and absurd contradictions and to laugh at its pain.

A letter arrived in the newsroom "to Alec's friends" from Harry Fuller of San Francisco, who had worked with Nagle at KGO:

> I cried when Alec Nagle died. . . .
>
> I valued Alec as a co-worker for his intelligence, energy, determination and professional thoroughness. He never said, "Can we do?" but always, "We gotta do!"
>
> Yet he was never cruel, never afraid to explain his purpose. In the ego-strewn landscape of a TV newsroom, Alec was one of the few people you could always count on to be primarily concerned with the news, not personal gain or comfort. . . .
>
> His humor and depth of feeling were central to his work and his success. . . .
>
> Alec did not accept cowardice or bullshit. Shortly before he left the employ of KGO, he doodled onto a piece of notepaper the following line about somebody:
>
> "How can anyone go through life being this chickenshit?"
>
> Alec did not go through his life that way, and he did not leave it that way. . . .

On September 17, 1981, a young man named Tom Todd, who had been working at Turner Broadcasting for several months, wrote up a "personal and confidential" memo to Sid Pike, his boss, and sent a copy to Ted Turner. The idea was to carry forward Turner's plan for selling CNN2's half-hour news programs to local broadcast stations — even those affiliated with the Big Three networks.

Here was a new way of marketing, to increase CNN's financial power in the face of the coming cable news war; but the very notion of syndicating to regular TV stations was destined to raise the hackles of cable operators, who figured that CNN would always be theirs and theirs alone.

It would also mean trying to reverse all those reciprocal agreements with over-the-air stations for exchange of news material; because, if the plan went forward, Cable News Network would no longer be offering its side of the bargain for free.

(As Alec Nagle had written in jest, sooner or later local stations would see that CNN "represents the future and they'll come begging" — and, he had added, "That's when we want you to ask them to *pay*." At the time, Nagle could not have known that he would be right.)

"The syndication of a hard news service has the potential of being among the most dramatic events to ever take place in radio or TV program distribution," Todd wrote in his memo. "The availability of 24-hour national news has never before been offered to local stations. . . ."

Under the plan, the service would be offered on an exclusive basis to one outlet in each market. A station could excerpt up to forty-five minutes of hard news per day, for use within its regularly scheduled local newscast; but there would be a "news alert" so the station could use breaking stories as they occurred.

"We are working in unchartered waters," Todd wrote about the syndication plan. "This will be the most revolutionary event since the original concept of network television." When Turner read the memo, he called Todd into his office and gave him the go-ahead. At the end of their meeting he said to the young man, "Whatever you do, don't botch it up!"

Ted Kavanau yelled and screamed at people when things went wrong, but just as quickly the fireworks were over as he pressed on. He did not carry his anger around with him; and later, when he met up with the person whom he had scolded, the whole incident was forgotten. At the same time, as a man of enormous personal honesty, he made little attempt to hide his feelings.

Kavanau did not particularly care for anchor talent. To him, the news was far more important than any male or female reading TelePrompTer copy. "An anchor is an anchor is an anchor," he would say, "just like, you know, a burger is a burger is a burger." Some of the women who anchored CNN shows, among them Chris Curle and Denise LeClair, were convinced that Kavanau enjoyed making them cry — although male anchors often felt that way, too.

In any event, Kavanau tended to keep his deepest emotions to himself; and some of his colleagues were certain that underneath it all, at this point, he was pouring every ounce of his energy into building CNN2 as a way of releasing his grief over Alec Nagle's death.

TED KAVANAU

"It was clear that ABC and Westinghouse wanted to do something that looked totally different than what *we* were doing; and they saw that opportunity because, in fact, CNN had been changing. Reese had sent me over to the Rome bureau for a while, and later I took charge of the national assignment desk, but that began to change the network from my fast-paced style. They had begun evolving into a long-form program, with three-hour shows, so the ABC-Westinghouse guys saw they could come in and, you know, give 'em the world in eighteen minutes.

"We were gonna preempt 'em by moving in very quickly, and grabbing every single cable system we could, with a short-form network of our own. Essentially we were going back to what I had done at the beginning of CNN, with the fast-paced newscasts. The only thing was, now I had to do it with a different format and a new look.

"Actually I wanted to start up in *two* months, in half the time, but Ted Turner said, 'Why are you in such a hurry for me to lose another million bucks a month?'

"They were putting up the building and we were buying all the equipment. I asked for Jim Shepherd as my number-two man, but Reese gave me Paul Amos, which was fine, and I got Fran Heany for graphics. Then it became another mad dash. I guess I'm perfect at making life miserable for myself, because I designed what I considered to be the fastest format in the history of television. . . ."

REESE SCHONFELD

"Ted Kavanau and I were always friends, but we had our share of battles. He was very, very concerned that we would look bad in comparison to Satellite NewsChannels, so he kept asking for more and more and more, and I kept saying no, no, no, we can't afford it. And I made him bring it in on budget. Kavanau wanted a very glitzy service, and I wouldn't go for it. I just would not. And that's where we had our falling-out."

Despite his feeling about anchors, Kavanau was worried about reports (later proved false) that SNC was planning to use "twin anchors" during its news shows; and when he insisted to Schonfeld that he, too, should have more than one anchor per newscast, the CNN president reluctantly gave in.

Schonfeld was not exactly thrilled over having to supervise this second "child" in the house. "Reese did not like the idea of CNN2," one staff member would recall, "and shortly after that he and Kavanau were fighting like dogs. Kavanau wanted his network to be able to go live, but it wasn't supposed to. He felt Reese was blocking him. Reese would say, 'Well, it's not that I don't like Ted,' and Kavanau would say, 'It's not that I don't like Reese,' but the fact was, they had one last shouting match and then stopped talking."

TED KAVANAU

"In my vision of it, there would be nothing like it ever seen before. And I was gonna follow all my personal predilections, my likes and dislikes. For one thing, I just can't stand sportscasters who sit on the camera and groan on and on; but I'll look at the *action*. I'll look at the pretty pictures. So I said okay, we're gonna have sports but it's gonna be all pictures with voice-overs. All you'll see is pictures with a voice. And I don't like weathercasters, either. I don't mind putting the *weather* up, I said, but we're gonna do ten seconds, with a national weather map and a voice-over, and that's the end of it."

*   *   *

Because their building was still being constructed, Kavanau and Amos were forced to use a corner of the CNN newsroom during the overnight shift, when the main network was mostly running tape replays of the previous day's programming. They brought in their new team and began rehearsing with Kavanau's high-speed format.

In his office two floors above the basement, Turner was making new corporate decisions each day. One was to fold the Atlanta Chiefs soccer team, which had lost $7 million over the previous three years. The Braves and Hawks were losing money, too, but partly they were regarded as TBS program costs. Turner also postponed an idea to build a studio that would attract Hollywood companies to Atlanta and turn the city into a powerhouse for cable production. That project would be deferred, at least until current battles were over.

Turner also secured a $50 million revolving credit line from Citicorp Industrial Credit, permitting TBS to borrow in order to repay some $30 million in debt. CNN was still losing up to $2 million a month, but it was now serving 1,373 cable systems and gaining about 450,000 new homes each month, with more than 135 advertisers aboard. The combination of income from subscriber fees and advertising sales would amount to $27 million by the end of 1981 — but the break-even point was a slippery one to reach because, as Turner himself admitted with considerable pride, "Every time we get near it, I just want to plow all the money back into our growth."

By now there were four hundred fifty CNN staffers in a dozen domestic and international bureaus and, Turner said, when funds were available he would open new bureaus in Philadelphia and Detroit and, maybe, even in Moscow.

Turner concluded a deal with Warner Amex Satellite Entertainment Company, based in New York, under which Warner would represent all advertising sales for CNN and CNN2. The deal also involved satellite transmission of CNN2. The main network was now permanently on SATCOM IIIR, which had replaced the ill-fated SATCOM III, and the second news network had been scheduled to use a Western Union WESTAR bird for its distribution; but Warner agreed to lease a newly available transponder on SATCOM I for the headline service. The deal was a shrewd move by Turner in the chess game: Satellite News-

Channels would be carried on WESTAR, which reached cable systems tied to only about a fifth of the viewing homes reached by SATCOM.

Ted Kavanau was playing a chess game, too. His counterpart at Satellite NewsChannels would be Bill Scott, acting as its first president and chief operating officer. Scott, a seven-year veteran of Group W, had run WINS in New York, the nation's first all-news radio station.

Way before that, as youngsters, Kavanau and Scott had been buddies in the Bronx. They had hitchhiked across the country together. Now they were meeting head-to-head as leaders of the "great cable news war," and Kavanau figured that in terms of experience he had the edge.

TED KAVANAU

"Radio was his skill. That was Bill Scott's essential training. He'd had one television job in his whole life, working for *me* at Channel 5 in New York — when he'd been unemployed and needed some money and I'd brought him in. That was the only TV experience he had, working for me as a reporter, although he was a very *good* reporter, it just so happens. And during this war I don't think Bill and I talked to each other, because it *was* a war and I was anxious to kill him. . . ."

What Cable News Network needed least of all was an effort by its technical or operations employees to join a union, but that is precisely what was in the works.

To get around unions in the bureaus, CNN had been using subcontractors who hired people to run cameras and crews — such as Mobile Video, run by Sheldon Levy, who had been CNN's first subcontractor in Washington, D.C. If those employees voted for a union, then CNN could simply cancel its contract (which, eventually, was what happened in the case of Mobile Video) and go to another outfit.

When it came to CNN's technical people in Atlanta, however, there was no subcontractor shielding the network from union recruitment. In this case, the challenge came from a New York chapter of the National Association of Broadcast Engineers and Technicians (which had been named in the ongoing White House pool suit); and representatives from NABET started showing up in Atlanta to hand out cards to CNN employees, asking if they were dissatisfied with working conditions.

"We've been hearing that your pay is real low and that your hours are real long," the union officials would say to the young video journalists.

Even though the sentiments in Atlanta were mostly against unionization, the threat could not be taken lightly. It would undermine CNN's flexibility, which was based so strongly on the VJ program. Moreover the entrance of a union would come at a time when CNN, as Paul Amos put it, was "entering a major war that's going to drain our resources and cost us a fortune while we fight for survival."

The vote was set to be taken in a few months.

TED KAVANAU

"We were rehearsing all night to make this deadline, but now I changed the structure of how I worked. Instead of having people work across all the shows, I began having small units that would do an hour here, an hour there. As we got closer to New Year's Eve, one of my producers became hysterical. He said, 'This can't be done,' because of the speed of the shows, and he walked out. Another one said, 'I need a day off tomorrow,' and *he* never came back. They started disappearing on me! And I'm trying to hold the organization together. . . ."

CNN2 was going to cost nearly $20 million to start up and $1.5 million a month to operate. Turner was offering cable systems a variety of package deals for the headline service if they carried it in addition to Cable News Network itself.

Both CNN2 and SNC1 were going to compete for the same national and local advertising, but the Group W/ABC service was going to be offered to cable systems at no charge. "I'd call them whores," Schonfeld said of the competition, "but even whores don't give it away for free!"

What he didn't know at the time was that Turner's rivals would go beyond *giving* SNC away; they would be *paying* cable operators to take it. They would offer fifty cents per subscriber out of those "much deeper pockets" owned by the two powerful corporations.

Pacing on the sidelines were the network news divisions. Having held back for years on delivering more news, they now saw that they could be overtaken by these cable-TV upstarts. ABC, through its division called ABC Video Enterprises, was entering the fray directly with Group W and its Satellite NewsChannels; and the other two networks were trying to get into cable news programming as well. But their nightly network newscasts were the core of their power in television news. And those evening programs were beginning to seem smaller than ever.

In November, CBS announced that it intended to expand its news to forty-five minutes or an hour; ABC was preparing to offer a one-hour evening newscast; and NBC, despite opposition from affiliates, was planning to pursue the same thing.

"Watching all this with a certain bemusement," wrote Tony Schwartz in the *New York Times,* "are the folks at Cable News Network, which provides 24 hours of news daily, including a two-hour evening program from 8 to 10 o'clock each weeknight. Indeed, on breaking stories, CNN is sometimes the only live show in town."

In discussing Turner's willingness to keep fighting for what he'd started, *Forbes* conceded that he had "done things no one else could do" but wondered what would happen if his financial projections for CNN crumbled as a result of the upcoming competition. "Most men might then sell out and go away, rather than crash in flames," the magazine observed.

By December, a Compton Advertising media research study was predicting that "while Turner will enjoy a short-term advantage, the ABC-Westinghouse venture will dominate by 1990." The study forecast that "the Turner news service will have an edge for, at most, four years" and then "merger or outright sale will be necessary for Turner to keep a competitive position."

On the news front was the Solidarity uprising in Poland and a government shutdown of communication to the outside. Even the wire services were cut off, preventing the rest of the world from knowing what was happening inside the country. Meanwhile, Warsaw television continued with tunic-clad military announcers replacing the local news anchors.

But on an island in the Baltic Sea, a little TV set with "rabbit ears" picked up the news pictures from Warsaw. This video was then microwaved to Copenhagen. From there it was fed by land line to Rome. From Rome it was up-linked to a satellite and beamed back down to Maine, then sent via land line through New York and Washington to Atlanta. Finally the same pictures of Warsaw television — with the audio portion translated into English — went up to the RCA satellite and then to CNN's audience. Whatever the Polish people were seeing and hearing about the fate of their country was being monitored, day after day, by a pair of rabbit ears linked to the world.

On the night of December 31, 1981, outside Techwood, the fireworks were ready to go off when the new CNN2 rang in the New Year. Fewer than a million cable homes had subscribed. WTBS and CNN were going to be carrying the opening show live.

"Let's rehearse our first half hour," Ted Kavanau said to Paul Amos, "and then we can lead with that show, so at least we'll get started. After that, we'll be going forever."

"We'll try to pattern ourselves after the old theater newsreels," Kavanau told a reporter, "and to keep the screen as full of action as possible. In one half-hour program, you'll see an anchor for only two and a half minutes. They'll be *there*, but they're not preeminent."

While the dry run (taking viewers "around the world in thirty minutes") was going on, champagne was being uncorked in the Techwood conference room. Media people and guests clustered around Schonfeld and Turner as eyes focused on a giant TV screen on the wall. At 11:45 P.M., the room erupted into cheers as CNN2 hit the air with a live report from Times Square in New York, where James Alan Miklaszewski surveyed the pandemonium from a rooftop. Then it was back to Atlanta for a videotape tour of CNN2's news facilities by Lou Waters: "Once again, the experts said it couldn't be done . . . just a few moments from now, you'll be part of television history . . . starting at midnight, this control board will be alive with news every minute of every day. . . ."

When the tape ended, the picture on screen returned to the live countdown to midnight in Times Square. As the giant apple drifted slowly downward, the fireworks outside Techwood were readied. In CNN2's new studio, Denise LeClair and Chuck Roberts got set at the anchor desk, waiting for their camera cue.

Midnight.

The fireworks went off, spelling out a giant "CNN2 — 1982" as Roberts said, "Hello again and happy New Year. In the news,

Poland's military regime will force the unemployed into compulsory labor in an effort to put Poland's economy back on its feet . . ."

"What'd I tell ya?" Turner exclaimed as he strode around the conference room, beaming and shaking hands. "I knew we could do it. Happy New Year! What a network!"

TED KAVANAU

"Something happened that night — I've never told it. To this day nobody — not Ted, not Reese, nobody — knows what happened that night in our newsroom. I still get pains in my chest whenever I think about it. The sweat breaks out on this head. . . .

"Turner shows up with an army of his friends. He comes in with about thirty people, with drinks in their hands, and they're all standing against the wall, packed into the place. The show is going on over here, and they're all standing over there. . . .

"But before that, without me being aware, Amos had seen a whole bunch of new stories on the wires. And without asking me, Paul had changed the entire show! We were in a state of chaos. It was completely out of control, because things were not written or assembled, with again the whole nation watching for this sign-on.

"I looked at Paul and said, '*Paul*, what are you *doing?* I can't *believe* it, Paul — you gotta get this thing into shape,' I say, and he's running around, we're desperate, and that's when Turner comes in with his party and I'm looking at 'em with this fixed smile on my face, saying to myself, *I'm finished, washed up, there's no possible way of bringing it on the air, the worst disaster in the history of television is about to befall me, and I'm responsible for it.* . . .

"So what happened, while Paul was desperately racing around trying to get the show together, I remembered that for some reason I had *taped* the show that we had *rehearsed.* Meanwhile the opening show went on, because Paul and the others were moving with lightning speed. About two-thirds of the way through it, Turner said to his guests, 'Let's go,' and they all trouped out of the studio, not knowing that we had nowhere to go from there! If they had stayed much longer, they would have seen that there wasn't any second show.

"They left and I said, 'Go to the tape! Put *that* on!' So we ran the tape of the show we'd rehearsed *before* the opening. And during that time, we were able to recover. I was able to regroup everything and get the network started. And from then on, it never stopped."

Once the second all-news network was on its feet and running, the pressures on both Ted Turner and Reese Schonfeld began to build. The upcoming cable news war with Satellite News-Channels was going to be expensive and there was no assurance of victory. For Turner the goal was corporate survival, at the very least, while for Schonfeld the task was to make sure that CNN itself would be unbeatable.

For a long time Schonfeld had maintained his own working space in the newsroom, to be next to the action. Offered a bigger office upstairs, next to Turner's, he had refused. He was an "instant man" who operated in much the way that Turner himself did — impulsively. In meetings that were never boring, he could handle five people at once with rapid-fire reactions, cutting right to the issues requiring immediate decisions. "I don't want to hear about that," he'd snap, moving quickly onward and remaining unaware that he might have offended someone. He listened to those who disagreed, but made his own choices without wasting time in wishy-washy discussion or debate.

Even when he began using the upstairs office, Schonfeld would fly out the door and bound downstairs with ideas: "Can you fly to Israel tonight? You don't have a passport? Can you get one tomorrow?" When the Tylenol scare took place, he ran down and shouted, "We've gotta have a Tylenol desk! Let's put it over here and set up a hotline so people can call in!" While admiring Schonfeld's energy and drive, some staffers were amazed by his capacity for hatching off-the-wall ideas or schemes. One time, after three CBS employees had been shot in a New York parking garage, Lou Dobbs was sitting in Schonfeld's office when the CNN president suggested that the network offer a million-dollar reward for the capture of the gunmen. It was a great story, he added, and this way CNN would get momentum going.

"Reese," Dobbs said, "are you sure that's a good idea?"

"It's a *terrific* idea," Schonfeld said.

"I don't think so," Dobbs cautioned. "I can see it if they were *our* employees, but don't you think it would be a little sensationalistic?"

Schonfeld dropped the idea, but he was the same man who had jumped to buy a satellite feed from Italy when a child had fallen into a well — way before the similar story, of young Jessica McClure in Texas, occurred later in the decade — and when the live Italian coverage had come up, Schonfeld had put it on a quarter-screen during CNN's other programs. The impact on viewers and ratings had been enormous, the way all that live coverage of the Titan Missile story had received so much attention.

But now Schonfeld no longer had Ted Kavanau and Alec Nagle in the CNN newsroom to spread that kind of energy. Kavanau's time and effort had been redirected into CNN2, while Nagle's death had been a serious blow to everyone. The latter's gift for making others feel special, for creating a sense of teamwork and fun, was irreplaceable. At a time when Schonfeld needed both men to help him, they were gone.

Another problem for the CNN president was that it cost more and more money to keep finding ways of giving viewers a different fare than what the commercial networks delivered. "Reese never overspent," John Baker said. "He spent money on things that didn't work, and wasted money on stories that didn't pan out, but the philosophy that he was following *did win* a lot of times. And being the fledgling network, we needed that kind of excitement." Although Schonfeld was cutting costs everywhere he could do so, he knew that his mandate to give CNN a special identity required those financial risks.

He and Turner were in agreement on that point. Schonfeld was not being told by Turner to pull back on expenditures. If he was going to make a major, costly decision, however, Turner did want to know about it beforehand; and by the same token, if Turner was going to try to influence the network's editorial policy, Schonfeld wanted the power to agree or disagree. Such built-in tension had existed between them from the beginning and it was still necessary in order to maintain a working balance between these two strong individuals, but under the growing pressure that balance was being strained.

The heart of the matter was whether they could trust each other. They had been somewhat wary at all times, but so far neither man had crossed the invisible line to make the other's alarm bells go off. From Schonfeld's side, the alarm nearly had sounded back in September 1981, when Turner was scheduled to appear before Congress to give his views about violence on network television. Schonfeld had agreed that CNN would cover the hearing, but not live. They would tape it and produce an edited version for the newscasts. The night before, however, Turner called him and said he wanted CNN to carry it live.

"Look, Ted," Schonfeld said, "I'm sorry, but it's too late. There's no way we can get things ready on time."

Attempting to maintain control, he had given Turner the best excuse he could muster; and then, to bolster his position, Schonfeld called the Washington bureau, ordering the staff to "make sure you don't get any line up on Capitol Hill so we can go live." He went back to sleep, confident that he had "outfoxed" his boss.

That night, however, Turner walked into the Washington bureau full of enthusiasm. "Hey," he shouted, "do you guys know I'm testifying to Congress tomorrow? You're gonna be covering it, right?" He gave no order but, as soon as he left, the bureau quickly arranged to carry the hearing live — without letting Schonfeld know about it.

The next morning, the CNN president was flying to New York. When he landed he heard himself being paged. He called the Atlanta headquarters and listened to a furious Jane Maxwell: the commercial networks were carrying President Reagan live from the White House while he clarified some earlier remarks about the possible use of nuclear weapons by the United States, but CNN was stuck in its own live coverage of Ted Turner at the congressional hearing. For one of the few times in his life, Schonfeld was speechless. Then he called the New York bureau and heard Mary Alice Williams complain that she was unable to break into the network's coverage to give bulletins on the recent Brinks truck armed robbery and shootout. Major developments were occurring, but the live line from Washington to Atlanta was being used.

Finally Schonfeld called the Washington bureau and ordered an end to the live coverage from Congress. When there was hesitation he screamed, "*I'm* the boss and *I'll* take the heat if there is any, so just do it!"

It was a borderline case, because no one had heard Turner actually dictate that the congressional hearing be covered live; but it made Schonfeld more sensitive about the potential threat of his losing control. The bottom line was the image of CNN as an objective entity free of any dictates or whims coming from its owner, not to mention Schonfeld's own image as a president who was fully in charge.

At the same time there was much to celebrate. After nineteen months the network was reaching over ten million households and a new market study showed that CNN's subscribers were using it as their "primary source" for national and international news. Also Schonfeld had extended *Moneyline* to the weekends, with Lou Dobbs producing and hosting; and deservedly Turner would get credit for having had the foresight to want separate categories of news created around subjects involving business and finance. Turner's hand could be seen in the creation of *Moscow Live*, moderated by Stu Loory and carrying weekly two-way exchanges between the United States and the Soviet Union by satellite. The new Tokyo bureau, run by John Lewis, was expanding its coverage of the Far East; and as the Solidarity movement grew in Poland, CNN still was taking live satellite feeds for "simulcasts" of Warsaw television, with immediate translations into English.

While the network was growing, expanding and taking root as a fact of TV life, it was also winning its "pool suit" against the White House and the networks. At one point the Reagan administration had attempted to eliminate all television coverage of so-called limited-access presidential events, but that was followed by a predictable outcry from the news organizations. Then in a landmark decision, the U.S. District Court in Georgia held that exclusion of TV representation from White House pool coverage "denies the public and the press their limited right of access" guaranteed by the First Amendment. When the White House implemented a new policy that included CNN, it was a springboard for settlement out of court. By early 1982, Turner's all-news network was on its way to gaining recognition as a member of the White House pool, with all parties acknowledging "no inequality of personnel, equipment or competence as among CNN, ABC, CBS and NBC."

At least a million dollars had been spent by Turner on legal fees; and with official status as "the fourth network," CNN would have to purchase more than a million dollars in new equipment for coordinating duties out of the country. The victory would be expensive in other ways, too. By having to prove it was one of the "big boys," CNN would be paying sixteen percent of pool-coverage costs. And some staff members wondered if winning the pool suit would have its down side: instead of "traveling light" all the time, with its reporters and crews "jumping in and out" of stories, now CNN would have to *help* the commercial networks.

"Now that we're one of them," a CNN staffer wondered, "will we have to turn into a dinosaur, too?"

On its front page of February 13, 1982, the *New York Times* carried the following story:

> President Reagan ordered an investigation today into why five American advisers in El Salvador apparently violated United States policy by carrying M-16 rifles in what may have been a combat zone.
>
> A videotape broadcast by the Cable News Network showed several men identified by the camera crew as Americans in civilian clothes carrying M-16 rifles and .45-caliber pistols. . . .
>
> Today, Senator Paul E. Tsongas, Democrat of Massachusetts, went to Cable News Network's Washington headquarters to see the videotape. He said later that he intended to challenge the Reagan Administration under the War Powers Act of 1973, which prohibits a change in status of American forces without consulting Congress. . . .

The carrying of M-16's by American officials in Central America was the opposite of what the White House had been telling the public; but the story would not have appeared in any media if CNN had not been committed to covering El Salvador in the first place. As a result of James Alan Miklaszewski's reporting, which included being pinned down by gunfire from Salvadoran troops, CNN found its name on front pages all over the country; and other broadcasters were running its videotapes, giving full credit.

"The disparity in the time that the Cable News Network and the networks devote to Central America was graphically reflected," the *New York Times* observed, "when CNN devoted the first seventeen minutes of its evening newscast solely to

Central America. The major networks' entire evening news programs run just twenty-two minutes after commercials."

The days of being called "Chicken Noodle News" were over.

Ted Turner and CNN were making a different kind of news. Just when conservatives in the Moral Majority were thinking they had Turner for themselves, based on his plea for "family values" in TV and movies, he was flying down to Cuba to hang out and go duck-hunting with Fidel Castro. As the *Atlanta Constitution* put it, here was a "visit by one of America's most fiercely independent capitalists to the most famous communist leader of the Western hemisphere."

"Castro has an earth station and he watches CNN all the time," Art Sando told the media. The Cuban leader was "apparently a bootlegger" because he had never become a paying subscriber.

At Castro's invitation, Turner flew down to Havana on a commercial charter flight out of Miami, accompanied by reporter Mike Boettcher and a camera crew. During their interview on tape, Castro said in Spanish, "When there's trouble in the world, I turn to CNN." Afterward Turner said, "I'm no communist, but he's a pretty nice guy, actually. You have to look for the good in people and nations."

When Turner got back to Atlanta, he remarked that his visit to Cuba had been "the first time I'd ever been in a communist country, and I was just interested in learning a little bit how it worked. He was very nice to me," Turner said, "and I certainly think he'd like to have good relations with the United States. He said it's hard to understand that America can trade with Russia and not trade with them. After all, he's just a knothole on the log. I told him, 'Well, you're always saying bad things about us. Ease up a bit.'"

ARTHUR SANDO

"Ted came back with a promotion tape showing Castro saying how much he liked CNN. We had a meeting of the vice-presidents and he showed us the promo. He solicited our opinions. I said I didn't think we should use it. I thought it would be a short-term gain for a long-term loss. It was still that early time of Reagan patriotism and doing a promo by Castro for this new network was not what we needed to do. We put it to a vote and

Ted lost. So the promo never aired and we didn't have another meeting for about five years."

The union vote was set for the evening of the last Friday in February, at the Atlanta headquarters. The National Labor Relations Board had installed a "voting booth" in the conference room on the first floor, adjacent to the newsroom.

"We couldn't operate here if we were unionized," Turner said before the vote. "But it's not going to happen. I'm not that worried about it. I don't blame the union for trying — they try and unionize everything, right? And that's fine. Unions have a great place, they've performed a great service in certain companies. But we don't need one here."

There had been five or six months of campaigning on both sides, directed at members of the operations and production departments. Bill Shaw, in charge of personnel, was in the conference room along with about thirty other employees (pro- and anti-union) who watched as the votes were tabulated. Turner was out of town, but Schonfeld and Reinhardt were waiting in their offices upstairs.

The vote was 156 to 53 against joining the union.

Schonfeld came down and shook hands all around, thanking people for their support. Then he and Shaw went back up to Turner's office, where Dee Woods put the boss on the speaker phone. Turner expressed his delight and issued a statement, which Woods typed for release to the press.

Years later, Schonfeld would have his own memory of the events of that night. His recollection, although contradicted by others, reveals the kind of tension that was building. In a nutshell he was certain that Jim Kitchell, now in charge of TBS technical operations, was gunning for him.

REESE SCHONFELD

"Kitchell had inside information from somebody who was feeding him the union stuff, and he was not delivering it to me but to Turner or his people, in order to heat up whatever battles there were between Turner and me. It was kind of 'Look, Reese can't get along with his people, and they're trying to unionize 'em, but I know how to handle these people.'

"So the day of the union vote, I was there and Dee said, 'Don't leave before this is over. Ted wants to talk to you. Be sure you don't leave.' Then Kitchell shows up with his wife and I couldn't understand why they were there. The vote was announced and we won by a big number. There were a lot of cheers in the newsroom, right in the middle of *Moneyline,* so Lou Dobbs had to stop and tell viewers the reason for the cheering. . . .

"Immediately afterwards, Kitchell and his wife walked out without a word of congratulation. I talked to Turner and he said his congratulations in a very sour way. I couldn't understand it. Later that night, I realized that if we had lost that vote he had been prepared to fire me on the spot and name Kitchell as president."

Years later Jim Kitchell would not remember being present for the union vote that evening, while Bill Shaw would swear that Kitchell hadn't been there. The important point was that Schonfeld had come to the conclusion that Turner no longer wanted him as president; and that he perceived, on the night of the union vote, that his days in charge of the network were numbered.

Cable News Network had succeeded so far, in the face of all predictions that it would fail, precisely and paradoxically because there had been no chart by which to guide it. No one had really known how much it would cost (and they still didn't know), nor did anyone really have a firm idea of what CNN was supposed to be. The network had sprung forth from nothing more than the mind of Ted Turner and Reese Schonfeld's ability to implement that vision with a bunch of other mavericks. Turner had needed someone who knew how to do it without spending $100 million and bankrupting him; and while Schonfeld was certainly accomplishing that, his mandate was to cover national and world events no matter what the cost and to find ways of getting into line financially by trimming elsewhere.

Two particular pressures had arrived: the threat of yet another cable news network on the scene (in addition to the upcoming offering from ABC and Westinghouse) and the prolonged Falklands War between Great Britain and Argentina.

It was CBS that was planning to start its own cable news network in competition with both CNN and Satellite News-Channels. Drawing up the strategy and budget was Ernie Leiser, a veteran CBS newsman, under chairman William Paley's directive to jump into the fray while it was still possible. "All you people can do is say, 'No, it can't be done,'" Paley told his executives — and in fact, Leiser helped to draw up figures showing it would take 359 additional people and cost about $50 million a year to operate CBS Cable News. "That was the idea-killer," Leiser would write about the experience, because it came "at a time when CBS had lost more than $30 million on a financially disastrous cultural cable network." Red-faced and furious, Paley rose from the conference table and stormed out of the final meeting, never mentioning the project again; but until it was scrapped, the threat of this further competition from a major network was an additional burden on both Turner and Schonfeld.

So was the war in the Falkland Islands, which began in early April and promised to continue for several weeks. Schonfeld ordered massive coverage, taking live satellite feeds from both Argentine and British television. At times he used a split screen to cover each side of the war simultaneously. "We'll be all right," Turner had told an interviewer before this time, "as long as Schonfeld doesn't come up with some riot in Europe that we have to cover." He had been half kidding, but those earlier fears of not having *enough* news to fill twenty-four hours had been totally reversed by now. (Before CNN had gone on the air, Turner had joked with Gerry Hogan and Terry McGuirk that maybe they'd have to buy up some old, abandoned hotels around the country and "blow them up" to create news on slow days; but now they were concerned that *too much* news to cover might drain the financial resources being provided by the SuperStation. Already being phased out by Schonfeld were those commentators he had hired in the beginning to fill airtime; and a so-called evergreen tape, which had been created by Ted Kavanau before CNN's launch to provide a source of general stories playable in a crunch, had *never* been used by the network.) The Falklands War was not the "riot in Europe" that Turner had feared, but it was just as expensive.

"We spent an awful lot of money on satellite time," Don Lennox recalled, "and I think that had something to do with Reese's problems because I heard the company nearly went broke afterward. The news events kept getting bigger and we kept trying to cover them, but it became an incredible logistics problem along with those bills."

The money was a factor, but it was not the specific issue that began to make Turner believe (as Dee Woods did) that Schonfeld was a "two-year player" who could not make the transition from entrepreneur to manager of daily operations. That issue had to do with Schonfeld's style of running CNN "out of a hip pocket and a hat, with scraps of paper," as Ed Turner described it. "That's really the way Reese ran things. You'd come to work and find out that he'd sent anchors off on some assignment when they were supposed to be on the air in the next hour, but he'd forgotten to tell anybody that they needed to be replaced. In his enthusiasm to get people to stories, he'd do it and then have no follow-through to figure out how we would do everything else we needed to do. There was no support mechanism for people in the field, no plans for their motel rooms — all the stuff you need as an organization gets larger and more complex. That didn't retain Reese's interest. It wasn't in his makeup."

The CNN president's style was also to run on lots of pent-up, nervous energy that would often erupt in front of his staff. (Rick Brown recalled that before CNN was launched he had told Schonfeld not to worry, only to be told by his boss, "No, no, I've *got* to be worried.") Under increasing pressure now, Schonfeld appeared to others to be completely indifferent to corporate concerns; and he began to drive his own staff so hard that Lou Dobbs sent him a note: "Reese, you have forgotten who your friends are."

Dobbs was asking to have his time on air reduced. "By then I was on camera six hours a day," he said, "and being worn to a frazzle. All I wanted was some kind of adjustment, but Reese was getting very angry that I would even suggest it. He was reacting very badly to lots of people who were his great fans, his great supporters."

Then three more incidents served to drive Schonfeld into a direct clash with Ted Turner over which man controlled the network.

One issue revolved around an anchorwoman, Marcia Landendorff, whose contract came up for renewal. Discussions centered on her salary, about $45,000 a year. Schonfeld had had no plans to fire Landendorff, but when her agent announced that she could get $85,000 from CBS, he replied, "Mazeltov!" He was offering what he considered to be a "fair raise" for her to stay at

CNN, but if she could get nearly double the money, he wasn't going to stop her.

The trouble was, Ted Turner wanted Landendorff to stay.

Next came contract talks with Sandi Freeman. In trying to keep her nightly talk show as "topical" as possible, Schonfeld had made frequent changes of guests at the last minute. Sometimes the lineup was switched just hours before airtime and, by now, the host had been worn down. Freeman had brought in her agent, Al Geller, to participate more actively. Geller, whom she later married, was exerting more and more influence over his client, to the point where Schonfeld was struggling with him over control of the show itself.

Schonfeld was clashing so much with Geller that Ted Turner, who liked Freeman and wanted to keep her, felt he was losing his objectivity. "Business is business," Turner told him. "Don't let personalities get involved when you're making judgments." At one point he said, "You know, Reese, my father always wanted me to read *How to Win Friends and Influence People*, so I read it and it changed me." Turner handed Schonfeld a copy of the Dale Carnegie book, suggesting that it might help him get along with Freeman, Geller and others.

Not only did Schonfeld not read the book; he went ahead and fired Sandi Freeman, after coming to the conclusion that *Freeman Reports* was suffering in the ratings because of her. When Lou Dobbs and other anchors had guest-hosted the show, its rating had gone up. "For the first year she had shown enormous promise," he said, "and she'd really wanted it to work. But the ratings weren't there and by this time I just didn't want her at all." After refusing to renew Freeman's contract, Schonfeld continued negotiations to pick up *Crossfire*, a local Washington, D.C., show with political commentators Pat Buchanan and Tom Braden.

That move alone might have made up Turner's mind to fire Schonfeld; but when the network president hired Mike Douglas to replace Lee Leonard as host of the showbiz interview program from Los Angeles, there was no more question about it. Schonfeld hired Douglas at an annual salary reportedly of about a million dollars — and he did so without informing Turner, who felt slighted. "Ted felt he should have been talked to," Ed Turner said, "not so much to overrule it but, if nothing else, as a courtesy. Reese, on the other hand, felt that he had absolute authority to do what he wished."

Soon after, in early May, Schonfeld and his wife, Pat, took their first real vacation. They spent a week in Martinique, generally hating it because of poor treatment they received at the hotel and elsewhere, and returned on a Sunday. That night Ted Turner called and said he wanted to speak with Schonfeld in person the following morning. Early on Monday, Schonfeld went to see Burt Reinhardt and, when Turner arrived, he followed him into his office. "I've decided to make a change," Turner said, explaining that there was "bad morale" in the company. To Schonfeld it was clear that the complaints from Jim Kitchell and others, including those from Freeman and Geller, finally had hit their target. One way or another, Turner was letting him go.

But not altogether: Would Schonfeld consider moving to Europe and heading up CNN operations over there? Two days later, Schonfeld returned for another meeting with Turner and declined. Would he become a consultant on a newly formed CNN board of directors in Atlanta? Yes, Schonfeld said, he would accept that role.

Meanwhile, Turner went forth personally to sign new contracts with both Marcia Landendorff and Sandi Freeman at higher salaries.

Among those on the news staff there was shock, sadness and even bitterness over Schonfeld's departure as president. "It's over," an emotional Mary Alice Williams told John Baker, meaning that the era of CNN's wild and crazy days had passed. When Schonfeld hosted a party at his Atlanta home, it was difficult for friends who felt torn between loyalty to him and to CNN. "Reese *made* it difficult," said Diane Durham, who remained one of his big admirers, "because if you weren't on his side and you stayed with the network, it felt as though you were going against him. He's very loyal and would say, 'If you come with me, I'll find something for you.'"

Some people did leave the network, but not many; and in any case, Schonfeld was still around as a consultant. At one of the first board meetings he attended after his firing were Ted Turner, Bob Wussler, Ed Turner, Burt Reinhardt and Ted Kavanau. A major topic of discussion was the fact that Kathleen Sullivan had received a good offer from ABC and wanted to accept it. The question, Ted Turner said, was whether they should let Sullivan out of her CNN contract.

Wussler was unsure, but Reinhardt made it clear that he'd be happy to avoid paying Sullivan more than $100,000 out of his budget. Kavanau, the man who supposedly had so little respect for anchor talent, blurted out, "Ted, everywhere I go in the country there's only one person they want to hear about. Every time I make a speech, all they want to know is what Kathleen is really like. You *can't* let her go." At this point, Turner asked Schonfeld for his opinion.

It was an opportunity for Schonfeld to try a don't-throw-her-in-the-briar-patch routine on Kathleen Sullivan's behalf. He wanted to do her a favor by having the board let her go to ABC. "I think you should keep her," he said. "I think she's much better than Landendorff. But, of course, I had that argument with you and I lost. If you were right," he told Turner, "and Landendorff is better than Kathleen, then let Kathleen go. If *I'm* right and Kathleen is better, then make her stay."

Turner took the bait. "She goes," he said. "We're letting her out of her contract."

On the corporate side, there was considerable relief that Reinhardt had become CNN's acting president. "We've gotta fire the clowns," someone said, "because the circus ain't funny anymore." When Ed Turner spoke with Bill Bevins, the TBS financial wizard, and with Ted Turner himself, he heard that CNN was "at the very edge of bankruptcy." It was urgent, he was told, to establish to creditors at the banks that the all-news network could be run as a "real business" from here on.

So the transition to Reinhardt was a move to extremely careful, bottom-line management of daily cash flow. The result, as Reinhardt stayed behind the scenes and gave Ed "No Relation" Turner the job of speaking for the network in public, was a tremendous pull-back. Instead of chasing after "minor" stories, they would wait for the big ones before spending money. Even when some major event took place, there would be a period of deliberation by Reinhardt before committing to full-scale coverage on a mad-scramble basis.

TED TURNER

"I knew Reese was a competent newsman. I had no intention of having to part company with him and I didn't want to. I liked him. There's no question he's a great person. But it was obvious to me, with a number of management problems, that he just hadn't had experience with a large organization before. I was concerned about his management skills with a big operation, not about his journalistic skills.

"It came back to me, from a number of sources, that he was making all the decisions, and most of the journalistic decisions, and really trying to do too much, rather than do the kind of delegating needed. He wasn't as good a 'people' person. Basically, running CNN is a job of people motivation and management. At the time it was only three hundred people, but I wanted them to be given the opportunity to grow as the organization grew.

"You can't have a twenty-four-hour news network that's totally run by one person. There has to be lots of people involved in the running of it, and you want the decisions to be made as far down the line as possible. You don't want to totally centralize the situation, where everyone else is afraid to make any decisions unless that one man is consulted at home in the middle of the night. That's crazy.

"And Reese wanted to make every decision himself. It just wasn't the kind of management style that was going to make the organization strong in the long run."

ED TURNER

"Reese may contend that he was not over budget overall, but I'm tellin' ya — in the view from the top, he sure as hell was. I didn't have access to the books, so I can't tell you from my own knowledge that he was right or wrong. What I suspect is that Reese was juggling figures in his head, saying, 'By the end of the year I'll make all this up, but right now we've got to establish by razzle-dazzle, by the big event, that we're here, to give people an excuse to tune in.' That's a perfectly rational and solid form of programming. But if you're in danger of taking the whole ship down by doing it, then it loses some of its merit.

"Bevins was not a person to panic. He's a very sane, no-bullshit kind of guy. And Burt knows how to read figures, if anyone does. So if they said we're in trouble, I would tend to believe 'em. Reese may have had a master plan to recover by year's end, but only he knew that.

"Burt and I were told, 'It's your job to save the company.'

"That was pure and simple and those were the words. We acted accordingly, and what followed was a very difficult six months. . . ."

One of Ted Turner's key strategies for "turning the corner" with Cable News Network had been put into motion a few months before, in March 1982. The plan, outlined months earlier by Tom Todd, was to create a separate "network" by marketing CNN2 to broadcast stations. "I had figured it would take us six months to have a service that was syndicatable," Turner said, "and when I went over to my plantation and watched CNN2 the first week it was launched, I said, 'Hell, we're ready to go right now.' And we had our first meeting of the broadcasters in March, less than ninety days later."

Here's how *New York* magazine described it:

> Ted Turner . . . struck again.
>
> Turner invited — at their own expense — the network affiliates of ABC, CBS and NBC to come down to his Atlanta headquarters. He told them he had an announcement that would interest them: CNN2, originally designed for cable delivery, was being made available to the broadcasters. Speaking for many at the networks, one senior CBS News executive groused to a colleague, "Turner not only wants the cable audience, now he wants our over-the-air audience as well!"
>
> The Atlanta meeting caught the networks off-balance. And when hundreds of local broadcasters showed up, it became all too clear that the broadcast-news game was changing in a major way. For those slow to realize it, Turner was happy to be helpful. An ABC station executive who attended the affair remembers that "one of the things Turner threw out was that CNN2 was better than ABC, CBS and NBC News. 'Why don't you blow them out and put CNN in?' he asked. People in the audience chuckled, and Ted chuckled, but Ted never chuckles without having a certain seriousness underneath the chuckle."
>
> Needless to say, no one was chuckling at the networks. . . .

The syndication team for CNN2 was headed by Henry Gillespie, with Henry Rierson and Bob Schussler as chief lieutenants. They were reversing the old "reciprocal agreements" with about eighty TV stations across the country. "We're converting freebies into paybies," they said as a kind of missionary slogan. (Within a few years, more than two hundred stations would be paying Turner Program Services to receive cable news coverage, mostly in half-hour packages, via satellite.) "We're giving them an alternative to the networks now," Ted Kavanau said that spring. "The stations can take our stuff and replace CBS News if they want."

It was a tough sell in those first several months as the syndication team hit the road, but as Turner put it, "We've already done the impossible. From now on, 'difficult' to us is easy."

On March 15, 1982, the *Atlanta Constitution* carried this story:

> CBS News will begin in September to offer an all-night news service to its affiliated stations. . . .
>
> The news service will run from 2 to 5 A.M. on weekdays, and will be the first entry of one of the three major networks into the all-night news field.
>
> The CBS announcement came a week after the start of a campaign by Ted Turner to sell his Atlanta-based Cable News Network to broadcasting stations.
>
> Many local stations are expected to run Turner's 24-hour news channel in the early-morning hours, between sign-off and sign-on, and CBS's move is seen as an effort to prevent Turner from signing up any CBS affiliates for his service.
>
> ABC is said to be planning a similar all-night news service. . . .

So the networks were reacting, by expanding their news operations from both ends of their daily programming schedules. To compete with CNN and with the syndication of CNN2, they were going to be giving news later at night and earlier in the morning. There was talk of a new TV era for the networks. The age of Television I was passing, making way for Television II. And the reason was Ted Turner.

In May, just as Schonfeld was leaving as president, CNN gained viewership in more than fifteen percent of all the country's television households, qualifying for "national metered measurement" by the A. C. Neilsen Company. It was another reason for CNN people to say, "We've arrived."

Near the end of May, Turner called Schonfeld and said he was thinking of doing an "editorial" on CNN. The trial of John

Hinckley, Jr., had confirmed Turner's view that movies and TV shows wielded enormous influence on young people's behavior; and in this case, it was clear that the movie *Taxi Driver* had directly motivated Hinckley to try to assassinate President Reagan.

"I'm not president of the network anymore," Schonfeld replied, "but my advice to you is not to do it."

Turner went through Reinhardt to make arrangements for appearing on CNN to give his opinion. It was the first time he had delivered an editorial, but to many it appeared to be an ominous sign. Now that Schonfeld was gone, would Turner increasingly use his network as a personal forum?

Before that question could be answered, he went into the studio and spoke in an off-the-cuff, conversational style. Turner's editorial was broadcast on May 29, 1982:

"I would first like to point out, and make very clear, that I am against news censorship of any type. But after watching the last few days the trial of John Hinckley, Jr., for the attempted presidential assassination of Ronald Reagan, I am very, very concerned that this movie, *Taxi Driver*, was an inspiration to Hinckley and was partially to blame for his attempted assassination of our president.

"Many years ago I stumbled into that movie almost by accident and was absolutely appalled by the blood and the gore and I knew, at that time, that that movie was going to have its effect on young people. . . .

"Columbia Pictures produced and distributed that movie, and in my opinion, the people that were there at the time, and were responsible for this movie, should be just as much on trial as John Hinckley himself."

Turner criticized *The Deer Hunter* and *The Warriors*, before concluding:

"These sorts of movies must be stopped. And if you're concerned, as I am, you should write your congressman and your senator, right away, and tell him that you want something done about these destructive motion pictures. Thank you very much."

Over that Memorial Day weekend, his *Taxi Driver* remarks appeared on CNN eleven times and on WTBS three times. Then came Dan Schorr to the rescue of the First Amendment. Although agreeing with Turner about the effects of violence in the media, and stressing that Turner had every right to express his opinions on the network, Schorr felt he had a "duty" to reply. In a commentary aired Monday night, he said that if Turner was advocating legislation against movie or TV companies, "I must respectfully disagree" because it would interfere with the constitutional right of free expression.

("Hey, Reese," Turner asked Schonfeld, "is Dan Schorr a liberal?")

The exchange of views between CNN's owner and its chief Washington correspondent had been lively but harmless. A flap did occur, beyond the control of either man, when the usual replay of Schorr's commentary was canceled the following morning. Nobody on the outside (and very few on the inside) knew where the cancellation order had come from; but Ted Turner, who'd had nothing to do with it, took the heat.

Later, in fact, Turner would cite Schorr's commentary as evidence of CNN's openness to all points of view. "You want to know how we run this shop?" he'd say. "Well, there's Dan Schorr, and if he doesn't agree with his boss, he says so right on my network! What *more* can you ask?"

LOU DOBBS

"Ted wanted to do another editorial, this time about Gandhi, and it was a heartfelt expression of enthusiasm. As I picked up the telephone at home I said to my wife, 'You might as well know that when I get off this phone, my relationship with CNN will probably be over.' It was a Friday, so I called the plantation and said, 'Ted, you simply can't do editorials. It's not appropriate. It's not what we're about. It's a terrible risk.' I fully expected the worst. He said, 'Be in my office Monday morning and we'll discuss it.' So I was in his office at ten o'clock and we sat and talked for an hour. We talked about the distinction between editorials and commentary, about news analysis, the role of a columnist, and the importance of not using CNN as a platform. He sat there and did something that most people don't give Ted Turner credit for — he listened. And, to my knowledge, no one had ever talked to him about editorials in those terms before. He said, 'Thank you,' and he has never done an editorial again."

Turner had been expanding his perspective of the world. In August of 1980, a few months after CNN had gone on the air and while he was losing in the America's Cup trials, he had met a young woman named Barbara Pyle, a photographer on assignment in Newport, Rhode Island, for *Time* magazine; and when Pyle expressed her concerns over environmental threats to the planet, Turner realized that he had found a kindred spirit. Over dinner he produced a copy of "The Global 2000 Report to the President" and proceeded to read it aloud:

"The available evidence leaves no doubt that the world, including this nation, faces enormous, urgent and complex problems in the decades immediately ahead. . . ."

Turner himself had given speeches about the need to replace outmoded practices: "What is a newspaper? You cut down a tree, mash it, make paper, deliver it by truck to somebody's house, then another truck takes it away — and every stage requires fuel!" He had argued that electronic communication should replace newspapers, to save energy; and now he was worried over the population growth amid systematic destruction of the earth's resources.

BARBARA PYLE

"The report affirmed Ted's darkest fears about the future of the planet. He had been a closet environmentalist. He'd never had anyone to listen to his concerns. We had long talks and he offered me a job in Atlanta, to make documentary films for WTBS, but I told him I was not qualified. 'I don't care,' he said. 'Teach yourself to make movies, the way you've taught yourself everything else.'"

Turner encouraged the SuperStation to pursue documentaries on major problems, from nuclear weapons to overpopulation to environmental destruction, and Barbara Pyle went on to produce many of those films. Otherwise he expressed his views in public speeches, describing himself as a "wide-eyed do-gooder" — who, on business matters, was "conservative," and who (without changing his views on television's responsibility to the public) was "liberal" when it came to the big social issues.

But the power of CNN, in terms of its ability to shape public opinion, was both paradoxical and elusive. It gained respect in proportion to its objectivity. By including as many points of view as possible, from more and more corners of the world, *without* editorial comment, the network could be trusted as a source of information. Viewers would form their own opinions, Turner realized; and, he felt, if people were given *enough* information they'd come to the same conclusions as he did — by themselves.

It was an amusing irony, for Turner, that his competition in the news war involved Westinghouse Broadcasting — which, after all, had bought his station WRET in Charlotte for $20 million, providing him with the seed money to begin financing Cable News Network back in 1980. If not for Westinghouse, he might never have gotten CNN off the ground in the first place.

In a letter to cable operators he took aim at ABC, charging that the network was trying to destroy the cable industry even as it vied for a piece of the action. He quoted the chairman of an ABC affiliates committee who was urging the local stations to run stories about the "threat" that cable posed to "free, over-the-air television broadcasting."

"With one hand," Turner wrote, "ABC outwardly is embracing cable with its proposed Satellite NewsChannel. In the other hand is a dagger to put us away."

The news war officially began on June 21, 1982, when SNC launched its service from Stamford, Connecticut, with a staff of two hundred fifty people working in shifts of seventy at a time. The headquarters facility was touted as "the best in the country." Circulation at launch was 2.6 million subscribers, compared to CNN2's current count of 1.2 million cable homes.

SNC was receiving its ABC News video (and Metromedia's WNEW-TV news feeds) from New York via terrestrial microwave. And its own earth stations were able to grab WESTAR-satellite news feeds from more than twenty "regional" broadcast affiliates. A significant difference was that SNC was "all live, all the time," as its advertisements said, while CNN2 (although *capable* of breaking in live) repeated itself on tape every other two-hour period. The setup looked formidable.

"If it turns into a battle and drags on," *Broadcasting* observed, "Westinghouse and ABC would certainly seem to have the finances to outgun Turner if they have a mind to."

And on the horizon was SNC2, the more in-depth channel that would compete directly with CNN. The second service was going to be produced entirely by ABC News, meaning that it would become the first cable network to employ a commercial network's programming experience and reportorial depth.

That, too, looked formidable.

But when the people at CNN tuned into SNC for their first look at the competition, there were sighs of relief. The rival headline service was not as impressive as they had feared. There were more similarities than differences, but one day they recorded both channels at the same time and found that Kavanau's fast-paced style delivered a lot more stories.

JOHN HILLIS

"People gathered around the monitors, watching, and after ten or fifteen minutes they just walked away shaking their heads, saying, 'Is that the best they can do? Where's the secret weapon?' By then it was clear that once again Kavanau had been able to smash something together incredibly fast, with incredible intensity. He had outfoxed them at their own game, before they'd even gone on the air. If SNC gave thirty-seven stories in eighteen minutes, then he gave at least thirty-eight."

Kavanau took nothing for granted. He was so involved in the cable news war that he put sliding steel doors at both entrances to the CNN2 building — "with the very real fear in his own mind," a colleague said, "that terrorists would try to take over the network." When they arrived, Kavanau would still be on the air behind those steel barricades.

When Stacy Jolna joined CNN2, the new producer noticed that Kavanau was always there during the daytime but also might drop by at nine o'clock at night or at two in the morning, to pump everybody up and make sure things were going the way he wanted them to.

STACY JOLNA

"He wanted that level of excitement to be maintained. He once told me that fifteen minutes before going on the air I should rip up the first news segment and start again from scratch, just so everybody would stay on their toes.

"At four in the morning he'd come in and walk around the horseshoe where the writers and producers and copyeditors were, and he'd go around emptying wastebaskets. Just looking for something to do.

"He might look at a script and chat with an anchor person or go into a control room and start yelling orders at the producers and directors. During airtime. Most of the people would gently and affectionately ignore him. He just loved the place and had all this pent-up energy. . . ."

In July 1982, a Pan American jet crashed after takeoff in New Orleans, killing 154 persons. It was the second worst single-plane disaster in United States history. And for staffers at Cable News headquarters, it also provided one of the most heart-pounding experiences. In the journalistic contest with SNC, they were suddenly getting beaten; and worse, the shellacking seemed to be portentous: "Now that Reese isn't here, is this what we have to look forward to?" In the future their fears would be proved wrong, but the frustrations of the moment seemed ominous.

JOHN HILLIS

"That was the crystalizing moment after Reese's departure. I was watching the monitors, searching for video like crazy, and we're dialing around the satellites. All of a sudden on a monitor I see the plane crash, so I grab the phone to Jane Maxwell and I holler, 'Okay, I got the plane crash. Is it ours?' And there was this hesitation! If Reese had been there, it would have been, 'Take it and we'll worry about whether it's ours later.' After five minutes of scouting around, it winds up that the video isn't ours and we *don't* take it. But that seemed to me the difference between the old CNN under Reese and the new model. Now we were more careful, no longer shooting first and asking questions later."

JANE MAXWELL

"Burt was standing at the assignment desk saying we shouldn't send a crew to the plane crash. Had it been Reese, there never would have been any deliberation. It would have been, 'Go!' I wouldn't have thought to ask. So it became a discussion of how much it was going to cost. We had always been cognizant of how much we were spending on something, but under Burt you had to know it going in."

JIM SHEPHERD

"We were crushed. It was maybe six o'clock at night when I said, 'Dammit, we're gonna have the video by eight, no matter what.' We got our nose bloodied. I told everybody, 'I'm getting these pictures and they can take me to court if they want! If you want to blame somebody, blame me. I don't care if I get fired! We are not gonna get beat just because Reese isn't here to make a decision!' SNC had a station in New Orleans that was sending pictures to 'em, while I sat there banging by hands bloody on the desktop."

Burt Reinhardt and Ed Turner were struggling to bring CNN's budget under control and to reduce the chaos. In due course, CNN's crew got to the scene and started sending back pictures; but amid the reverberations in the newsroom, it was clear to Reinhardt and Turner that only future performances would dispel fears that a critical "watershed" had been reached.

Around this time, during a private meeting at the Stadium Club, Ted Turner asked Reese Schonfeld to consider returning to the network as president.

Schonfeld was still miffed over the press release that CNN had given to the media after his firing. At first, the release was going to say that he had quit over differences in "philosophy" between him and Turner. Then it was changed to "policy" disagreements; and finally the release quoted Schonfeld as saying, "Business differences make impossible my continuing. . . ." That one change to "business" made it appear as though he had been fired because of overspending; and it had been picked up by others as the company line.

Schonfeld kept delaying his answer about returning. At one Stadium Club meeting, with Bill Bevins on hand, Turner remarked that CNN's viewership ratings and audience shares had gone down. "Yeah, the ratings are down," Bevins said, "but not the share."

"Yes," Turner said, "the share, too."

Once again he asked Schonfeld if he'd come back at the helm.

"Well, Ted, do I get to fire Sandi Freeman?"

"No," Turner said.

"Well, if you control the talent, then I wouldn't be running the network."

It was another standoff between two men with towering egos and pride. Bevins, reminded of how New York Yankee owner George Steinbrenner was fond of hiring and firing and then re-hiring Billy Martin as manager, turned to Schonfeld and quipped, "You could be his Billy Martin."

Burt Reinhardt would take over officially in January 1983.

Despite their power, ABC and Westinghouse could not compete with Turner for publicity; and in August 1982, it was *Time* magazine's turn to put him on the cover:

THE BIG TV NEWS GAMBLE
Ted Turner Shakes Up the Networks

And inside, above a seven-page article:

Outrageous As Ever, Ted Turner
Is Changing the Face of TV News

Time was fairly ecstatic over Turner's news channel, calling it "a catalyst for a burgeoning revolution in television" and adding, "By any measure, CNN is in the big leagues of news. . . . Until recently the offices of news executives at the Big Three networks each contained three monitors tuned to ABC, NBC and CBS. Now in many there is a fourth, tuned to CNN."

Turner was also way ahead when it came to the loyalty of cable operators. As *CableVision* wrote, "The high-profile maverick is a sentimental favorite who endeared himself to an underdog industry when — remember? — it had no broadcast friends." Just to make sure, however, Turner was now appearing at cable conventions with placards, buttons, T-shirts and a giant 3-D billboard of himself in a cowboy hat, playing a guitar, all inscribed with a slogan paraphrased from a country music song title: I WAS CABLE WHEN CABLE WASN'T COOL.

He even went into the studio to record part of a music video whose lyrics went this way:

Turner: When are we ready?
Singer: Down in Atlanta, Georgia,
        There's a legendary dude.
        In New York they say he's crazy,

In Newport they call him rude.
And to those Bel Air mansions,
Where Cadillacs all go,
He never gets invited,
'Cause he's just a good ol' boy.
Though society may shun him,
'Cause he won't toe their line,
To the people across the country,
Teddy Turner's doing fine.
He was cable when cable wasn't cool.
When he went cable,
They called that boy a fool.
The experts said his time ain't come,
And in the end, he's number one —

Turner: Heck, all I did was jump the gun.

Singer: In those network ivory towers,
They still look down their nose:
"How can anybody start a network
Down where the cotton grows?
You gotta be near Broadway,
Or at Sunset and Vine.
You gotta be sophisticated
To program that prime time."
But this is their perspective,
They're bogged down in the past.
And NBC, CBS and ABC won't last.
He was cable when cable wasn't cool.
The Captain Outrageous,
He's broken every rule. . . .

Loyalty was one thing, but economics was another; and in their quest for cable systems, the sales teams for CNN2 and SNC got into a literal rate war, whittling each other down until it became mutually destructive. With SNC's people paying cable operators to carry their service, CNN's subscriber fees kept plummeting to keep pace; and neither side was above cutting special deals.

TERRY MCGUIRK

"We were spying on each other like crazy, trying to find out everything we could. When Christmas of 1982 came along, our guys found out that SNC was going to shut down its sales operation for two or three weeks. That was typical for a big, major company. So they sent all their marketing people home. On the day their people took off, we came up with a plan. . . .

" 'If you sign up for our two news networks over the next three weeks,' we told the cable people, 'we'll pay you a dollar a sub for the next three *years*. When you have our two networks, there'll be no reason for you to take the other guy. Even if you *did* take him, there's no way he's going to get large enough distribution to compete with us.'

"So it was a grand, grand play by us, because there was a damned good chance this war was going to drive us both out of business. We were killing each other, barely hanging on. We figured it was gonna wind up with both of us dead. We couldn't coexist. We knew we were within probably a year of going under, maybe less.

"We telexed all the cable operators and sent our people out to follow up. By the time the other guys came back from their little vacation, we had signed up most of the country. That was a key move."

On a Monday morning, Tom Todd arrived at his office to find that the place had been burglarized over the weekend. The syndication staff's papers had been taken out of each desk and stacked neatly on the floor. There were piles of paper and, it seemed clear, someone had photographed them before sneaking out in the middle of the night.

TED KAVANAU

"The fight got uglier, because they were raiding our *people*, too. It became very bitter. After the union struggle, many of the people at CNN who had been behind the union were picked up by Satellite NewsChannel. SNC was doubling their salaries to get 'em. We had trained those people, so they were very valuable. You couldn't get people with that kind of experience from anywhere else. So the war was draining us. But here was Ted Turner, once again, ready to lose the whole barrel over it. . . ."

Turner called Tench Coxe into his office and said he wanted to sue the competition. When Coxe said he didn't have a decent suit to file, Turner said, "Well, dammit, *find* one."

Coxe found one.

He brought an antitrust suit against SNC and Group W, arguing that they were making secret deals to keep CNN and Headline News from being accepted by Westinghouse-owned cable systems. The lawsuit proved to be a brilliant tactic, because ABC and Westinghouse found themselves having to explain to stockholders why they should spend even more money in court while already predicting losses of $40 to $60 million that year. On the New York Stock Exchange, ABC's stock began to fall; and as a widely owned public company, its directors found themselves under far more pressure than Turner, who still owned eighty-seven percent of TBS stock.

In the fall of 1983, tired of waiting for ABC and Westinghouse to admit defeat, he gave a helping hand by offering them $25 million for SNC. And they accepted. *Time* proclaimed: "David conquered Goliath with his checkbook."

ED TURNER

"Everybody was telling him that if he would just hold on another month or two, SNC would fold of its own accord. But he didn't want to wait. I think he wanted the gratification of being able to buy them out and shut them down. That was worth $25 million to him.

"I happened to walk into his office the instant he was hanging up the phone, after being told by his lawyers that SNC was his to shut down.

"He was putting the phone down and there was this look on his face, not of smugness but of elation, as if he was wondering how he had done it. How had this little Atlanta company taken on those two giants and beaten them?

"He hung up and I said, 'What is it?'

"He said, 'We won.'

"I said, 'What do you mean?'

"He said, 'I just got SNC.'

"It was over."

TED KAVANAU

"It was a great triumph and a great relief. I, personally, thought that SNC had a very good show. My feeling was that their product was first rate, and if they had not been so afraid they probably would have succeeded. Instead they decided to cut their losses and they collapsed. It just demonstrated what an entrepreneur like Turner could do against a corporate bureaucracy. They were a bunch of frightened guys. They blinked and folded."

All during the cable news war, Rick Brown had viewed the strengths and weaknesses on both sides from his perspective on the satellite desk. The story of why SNC failed, he felt, said something about why CNN was succeeding. SNC's so-called regional system, relying almost totally on stations rather than on its own bureaus or crews, was a complicated monstrosity. It also required the use of ten transponders on WESTAR IV — a bizarre waste, costing a fortune each month, and a blatant violation of the "KISS" rule that Ted Turner had not invented but had cited often: "Keep It Simple, Stupid!"

RICK BROWN

"SNC seemed to be spending too much money in almost every area. It was typical of the problems the networks had always had. They couldn't imagine anything being done right without overspending on it. . . .

"They were paying outrageously tremendous salaries. Some of us were amused when one of those who had led the push to unionize Atlanta said, on his departure, that SNC was going to walk all over us. Jim Shepherd wondered out loud how long it would take the competition to find out they had stolen away all our union organizers. . . .

"Our magic was cutting down the bureaucracy, keeping things simple. In many areas, we combined functions. All the experts were saying that if anyone ever succeeds at twenty-four-hour news on cable, it won't be this little guy because he's underequipped and doesn't know what he's doing — if anyone can do it, it will be someone bigger, someone heavy on resources and experience. But they mistook the network bigness and experience for advantages instead of disadvantages. CNN succeeded because it wasn't carrying all that extra baggage; ABC/Group W failed because it was. . . .

"So as for that old saw that 'the new kid on the block finally grew up and showed it could play with the big boys,' the opposite turned out to be true. In the long run, the other networks had to learn how to do things like we did."

In one of the most bizarre episodes of television history, the shutdown of Satellite NewsChannel took place live for its viewers to watch. On the evening of October 27, 1983, in Stamford, Connecticut, the SNC staff held a party at its high-tech facility while anchors continued to deliver the news. In Atlanta, a crowd gathered in the conference room at Techwood to witness the end. Champagne was served, but for many of the newspeople it was not a joyous occasion. As one said, "It could have been us." On the television screen, the SNC crowd was throwing confetti and cheering — as if trying to turn a funeral into a celebration.

At the same hour, Turner's legal and financial people were still tying up loose ends of the deal.

STEVE KORN

"Satellite NewsChannel was going off the air at six o'clock in the evening, but the deal was not signed. We were down to negotiating the fine points. Dee Woods had planned a party at Techwood to celebrate. They were in the top-floor conference room and I was in there with the ABC-Westinghouse lawyers. We were negotiating while the party was going on all around us and SNC was signing off the air. The other lawyers knew they didn't have a deal yet, even though they were watching their client go out of business. In fact we ended up working through the night and signed it at eight in the morning."

PAUL BECKHAM

"It was an exciting time, because Bill Bevins and the lawyers were at Techwood negotiating with SNC relative to the buyout and I was over at Citicorp finalizing the loan for the $25 million. It was sort of a race, because I had to get my deal done in order to have the money so he could get *his* deal done. And the switch was going to be pulled at six. Everybody gathered to watch 'em go dark — and there wasn't much happiness, because the battle was over. It's sad to see something like that go under, even though it's your competitor. We had to do it, but the moment when you thrust the sword in — that's not a pleasant thing."

*　　　*　　　*

"Give us eighteen minutes and we'll give you the world," came an announcer's voice, but there were only ten minutes left to go.

"That's it for now," an SNC anchorman in Washington told viewers. "In fact," he added with forced bravado, "that's it, period. And now, Ted buddy, it's in your hands!"

Then, like a drumroll, came the sound of a news ticker as hundreds of SNC employees' names were rolled in alphabetical order; and at last, the screen turned to hash.

SIX

"'If we fail' does not exist in my vocabulary."

CAN IT BE DONE?"

In October 1983, Ted Turner's victory in the cable news war was the final answer to his own question, put to Reese Schonfeld back in November 1978, five years before. CNN might have died at birth or during infancy; it might have been killed in childhood or early adolescence; but after Turner shut down Satellite NewsChannel, the field was open for his network to build up self-sufficiency.

Yes, it could be done; and it *had* been done because Turner's appetite for risk had enabled him to be the first one on the scene; because he had been backed by a bunch of *other* mavericks who had dropped everything else in their lives to make it happen; because, in the beginning, CNN's ratings had meant nothing; because nobody had really known, or cared, how much it would cost; and because, in the face of competition, Turner had chosen to press forward rather than back down.

Now CNN could handle any problem or threat that might have destroyed it earlier; the only question was what it would become in the fullness of maturity.

A direct result of winning the battle against ABC and Westinghouse was CNN's pickup of several million new subscribing households that SNC had been serving. Operating losses still ran over $9 million for the year, and CNN lost another $6 million in 1984 — in all, Turner had sunk $77 million into it — but then in 1985 his Cable News Network sailed into the black with a net profit of more than $20 million!

The rest is epilogue.

But for the future of telecommunications, the story of Cable News Network until its tenth birthday on June 1, 1990, is a prologue.

* * *

Although CNN was in the White House pool from 1982 on, it still had a junior status. Union crews from the Big Three refused to accept video pictures from CNN's nonunion crews, so the cable network could not operate pool cameras covering the president of the United States, except when he visited abroad. (The situation would not change for several years until August 1989, when labor roadblocks would be eliminated to give CNN equal status.) Meanwhile, the network's first "transmission pool assignment" outside the country was during President Reagan's trip to Mexico in 1984.

Ted Kavanau was in Washington, D.C., leading a new team of CNN investigative reporters. The K-Team! Having built and nurtured Headline News during the SNC war, he then surrendered the reins to Paul Amos in Atlanta. Now the bundle of energy known as Mad Dog was sending crews across the country to produce reports on the steel industry, pollution and so on. CNNers thought the unit was composed of "paramilitary oddballs" landing in Nicaraguan jungles and on Grenada beaches. Most stories were broken down into as many as thirty segments of three to four minutes apiece. Kavanau was running wild again, heading for burnout.

* * *

In March 1984, Ed Turner set off on an adventure that became a "personal watershed" in his life. When word came that Jerry Levin, the CNN bureau chief in Beirut, Lebanon, had disappeared, the network waited for messages that he was being held by kidnappers. None came. Meanwhile, as CNN's senior vice-president, Turner took it upon himself to make a journey to the Middle East to search for Levin. Over the next two months he went from one clandestine meeting to another in Beirut and Damascus, making contact with 147 different factions of the Islamic Jihad (Holy War) to try to learn Levin's whereabouts. With a man's life at stake, public comments from Atlanta were held to a minimum. Ted Turner made calls to the State Department while keeping abreast of Ed Turner's daily reports to Burt Reinhardt on a secure phone line.

ED TURNER

"I went all through Beirut and Damascus, meeting people at midnight in the mountains and at three in the morning in back alleys. I had a guard with me and most of the leaders spoke English. There was no call from any group saying that they had him. There was silence. No demand for anything. And that was the most maddening part of it. We didn't know who we were *not* dealing with, nor did we know what the price tag was. I never got a 'yes' or 'no' answer. When they mentioned currency, they spoke in terms of numbers of Mercedes — each was the equivalent of $5,000. But there was never a Hollywood opportunity to sidle up to someone at a bar and offer $10,000 for Levin's release.

"We were prepared to do whatever was necessary. One of the factions asked me for tank and airplane parts, but I had to explain that Ted Turner didn't have any of those. I did pay tipster money, just nickels and dimes, and at one point we provided food and shelter money.

"It was the kind of experience that made it possible for us to be less deceived on hostage stories in the future. We learned more about the Arab mind. And for me it was the experience of seeing the trauma of Beirut and Lebanon at first hand, of living potentially in harm's way. We were shot at, in the middle of firefights, and it's like a private test to see how you'll react in life-threatening situations. It turned out that I loved the exhilaration of the chase. I absolutely loved it."

That summer, after Ed Turner had called off his mission and returned to Atlanta, the amir of Kuwait received a short videotape of Jerry Levin demanding the release of a dozen Islamic terrorists. The tape was the first sign that he was alive. There were no efforts by the terrorists to demand airtime on CNN, nor did the network contemplate using the tape in its newscasts. In February 1985, eleven months after his ordeal in captivity had begun, Levin escaped by lowering himself on blankets from his makeshift cell and wandering through Lebanon's Bekaa Valley until reaching friendly Syrian troops. He returned to the United States, where he would remain with CNN until 1988; but the network would never learn who had kidnapped him or why.

Bob Furnad, a veteran from ABC, was heading up a new CNN political unit in 1984. He led his team through the conventions into the reelection victory of Ronald Reagan over Walter Mondale. At the Democratic gathering in San Francisco, CNN broke the story that Geraldine Ferraro would be Mondale's running mate. All logistics for full-time convention coverage were handled by Jane Maxwell, director of special events.

The network used some new toys: a $300,000 anchor booth overlooking the convention floors and a $2.5 million state-of-the-art production truck. Big stars in the coverage were Mary Alice Williams, Bernie Shaw and Daniel Schorr, along with Don Farmer and Chris Curle. The point of all this: in just four years, Turner's brainchild was no longer the new kid on the block. "CNN beat the well-tailored pants off the broadcast networks," the *Miami Herald* said.

The outreach extended that year to twenty-two countries. Already in Australia, CNN made its debut on Japan Cable TV. Feeds to Europe and Africa were on the way. Sid Pike, president of Turner Program Services (and the man who once told Reese Schonfeld that "Ted will *never* do news"), was talking about the creation of a global TV news service. Turner himself flew to Moscow, hoping to get CNN behind the Iron Curtain, on his way to the launch in Tokyo.

Courtroom coverage was controversial when CNN went live from the Fall River rape trial in Massachusetts. Six men were tried for gang-raping a woman in a New Bedford bar. For viewers it was better than a soap opera. "Whatever the prurient may find interesting in this," the *New York Times* said, "may be overshadowed by an opportunity to see the judicial process at work." CNN aired thirty-five hours of live coverage, getting a big ratings boost from what *Newsweek* called "turning an eye on the lurid."

"I tried to buy CBS to strengthen my company," Ted Turner would say afterward, "so I'd be strong enough to continue in business. I felt like I was very, very vulnerable because I was too small."

To get stronger, Turner had been looking ahead toward merging with one of the major networks — but only if he could control it. By now he had shopped CNN to all three commercial networks, wanting to be paid in stock so he could be the major shareholder in either company. He and Bob Wussler had met often with the heads of CBS, ABC, NBC, Gannett, Metromedia and others to try for a merger. By March of 1985, after years of talking about how he'd love to run one of the Big Three, Turner finally decided to make an unfriendly move on the country's top-rated network.

On Wall Street, there was laughter and derision. Ted Turner? Trying to take over the broadcast home of Bill Paley, Ed Murrow, Walter Cronkite and Dan Rather?

"It's the fantasy of the Mouth of the South," said John Reidy of Drexel Burnham Lambert. After all, CBS's current market value was about $2.6 billion; it would take at least $1.5 billion more than that for anyone to get hold of the company; so how could Turner Broadcasting, valued at $500 million, carry out such a takeover? In 1984, CBS revenues were $4.9 billion, compared with TBS revenues of $282 million; and CBS posted a net income of $212 million, more than twenty times the $10 million earned that year by Turner.

Could a minnow swallow a whale?

"Okay, wow!" Turner exclaimed when he faced reporters at a Manhattan news conference. Even he could hardly believe what he was about to do: announce a bid for CBS that bordered, most felt, on the preposterous. He was offering a complicated package of securities (including low-rated certificates called junk bonds) worth $5.4 billion, in exchange for all thirty-one million CBS common shares.

"I've never called them junk bonds," Turner said, grinning. "That's what the doomsayers call them. CBS pays a dividend of two to three dollars, but I'll pay twenty-one dollars in interest. Call them anything you want to. I like to call them *high-yield*."

In effect, his money would be borrowed from the network's own stockholders; and to help carry the enormous debt, he would sell off all the CBS radio stations as well as its nonbroadcast operations involving records, magazine publishing and toys.

Precisely because he was taking such a long shot, Turner once again captured the public's attention and imagination. Out came the old David-Goliath headlines, referring to Terrible Ted and Captain Outrageous; and despite a general consensus that this time the biblical tale would be reversed, with David being crushed, few analysts were willing to count him out too soon.

CBS filed a lengthy petition with the FCC, arguing that Turner's takeover bid should be denied because it threatened the network with "high risk of financial ruin" by adding $4.5 billion to its long-term debt. The petition quoted Turner himself when he appeared before Congress: "I'm eventually going to go broke, but so is our federal government. That's why I love it up here in Washington so much. You operate at massive deficits every year and keep smiling, and so do I."

Aside from using Turner's sense of humor against him, CBS ironically paid him a compliment by admitting that CNN was beginning to challenge the other network news operations — and if the cable network lost its independence, CBS continued, the country would suffer!

Wall Street stopped laughing when it became clear that Turner's strategy could work. By selling off the parts of CBS that he didn't want, he could raise more than $3 billion; and cash flow from the network and its stations would be able to pay the interest on the acquisition's debt. Even if Turner wound up paying more than $7 billion for CBS, his method was viable.

Moreover, although CBS chief executive officer Tom Wyman had called Turner "unfit" to run a major network, members of Congress now regularly watched CNN (courtesy of a dish installed by Turner on Capitol Hill) and most felt it was being run quite well.

Finally, CBS countered Turner's hostile bid by offering to buy back twenty-one percent of its own stock. In the process, the network would voluntarily lift its debt from $386 million to $1.3 billion and make itself too expensive for him to buy. Turner responded by asking the FCC to speed up its consideration of his own offer, so that CBS shareholders could vote on it at the same time.

TED TURNER

"As far as CNN is concerned, trying to take over CBS made sense from the standpoint that you could consolidate your national and international newsgathering facilities. You could gather the news for both CBS and CNN with one organization. That's $100 million in savings right there, if you wanted to save. Instead of two bureaus in Moscow, say, you could have just one. But if you wanted to keep spending nearly the same amount of money, you could have twice as big a newsgathering organization. Instead of having twenty overseas bureaus, you could have thirty-five. You could have bureaus virtually everywhere in the world."

*   *   *

Turner called CBS's buy-back plan "the culmination of its entrenchment efforts" against him. He accused the network's directors of showing "blatant disregard for their fiduciary duties to CBS shareholders," whose right to determine the future of their company had been "usurped" by the latest corporate maneuvering.

Facing defeat without being able to wage a fair fight, Turner went on what some called "the Ted Offensive" against CBS executives Tom Wyman, Gene Jankowski and Ed Joyce. He appeared before the National Press Club in July 1985 and, quoting Wyman as having said "I don't think you'd characterize CBS as a lean and hungry, skeleton-crew corporate operation," he retorted, "It's an *admission* that they're wasting money!" He quoted Jankowski as saying that CBS "threw away" much of the $150 million a year it spent on program development and added, "We at Turner Broadcasting, to my knowledge, don't throw a *nickel* away." And Joyce, the president of CBS News, came within range of Turner's fire for having said that his operation was "not very good" at getting a variety of voices on its air. "After forty years in the news business," Turner declared, "they *admit* that they're not very good at it. I think it's high time there was a change!"

That was for starters. "There is no corporation in America that's as arrogant as CBS is," Turner told the Press Club, aiming his fire at *60 Minutes* for its treatment of individuals and institutions. He cited an interview on that show with former president Carter: "The first question was, 'President Carter, you've got the image as a *loser*. What do you have to say about that?' A loser? The president of the United States? I mean, how many elections has *Mike Wallace* stood for? You get beat once and you're a loser in their image? When we take 'em over, we'll see who the *losers* are!"

Turner said he wouldn't cancel *60 Minutes* but would "try and increase the objectivity of it." And no, he replied to another question, he would not fire Dan Rather. "I'm looking forward to meeting him one way or the other," he said. "I mean, he doesn't seem like such a bad guy to me."

"It's exciting," he said of his hostile bid to take over the CBS network, "and I've really enjoyed it." So far the effort had cost him $15 million, he added, "but I'd really say it's been a lot of fun." In the end, however, CBS's defense tactic of buying back more than a fifth of its own stock was too strong, and Turner dropped his attack.

But defeating him in this manner carried a steep price. CBS was forced into a major cost-cutting program to offset the new debt, selling off its magazines and records and dropping a tenth of its CBS News employees around the world.

Turner took a call shortly afterward in 1985 from Kirk Kerkorian, majority shareholder of Metro-Goldwyn-Mayer/United Artists. "I've been watching what you're doing," Kerkorian said, referring to the CBS affair, "and it's very interesting. Maybe it's time for us to do something."

They'd been talking informally for about three years, but suddenly Turner got approval from stockholders to take over MGM/UA. Out came the headlines about Captain Outrageous again. He switched from being the scorned suitor of a powerful TV network to the warmly welcomed, would-be sovereign of a big movie studio. The folks in Hollywood were not frightened by Terrible Ted the way the CBS crowd had been; and in fact, most welcomed the news that another self-made maverick was on his way.

But because the price was $1.5 billion or so, MGM/UA would be divided back into its original components. Turner would spin off UA for $470 million and resell it to Kerkorian. (With MGM in his fold, Turner would gain a valuable library of films including classics such as *Gone With the Wind* and *The Wizard of Oz*.) The rest of the financing, this time with cash, would be done through sale of the studio's real estate, along with bonds and notes. The price itself seemed insanely high. "Unless Turner has found oil on MGM's property," one investment banker observed, he was taking much too great a risk. How would he possibly repay the debts? If he fell behind, he could lose everything.

The consequences of the battle against SNC were still being felt by both sides. By 1985, it was being reported that ABC and Westinghouse had amassed losses of $85 million; and Bob Wussler estimated that the competition had cost Turner Broadcasting as much as $100 million. One reason was CNN's offer, at the height of the struggle, to pay some cable operators one dollar per subscriber to carry WTBS, CNN and Headline News as part of their basic services — during 1984, 1985 and 1986. That incentive was quickly dropped after SNC had been shut down, but the resulting payments over those three years would cost Turner $17 million.

Revenues earned by CNN and Headline News in 1985 totaled about $115 million, fifty-five percent from advertising and forty-five percent from subscriber fees. As the News Channel turned the financial corner, Turner boosted its program spending from $65 million to $84 million. (The three major commercial networks were now spending about $250 million each to program their news shows.) While CBS was laying off people and ABC's new owner, Capital Cities, was trying to cut its costs for news, Turner was opening bureaus in Nairobi, New Delhi, Frankfurt, Paris and Beijing — at a cost of about $600,000 to open and staff each additional office overseas.

"Ted can't stand to see a company make a big profit," Ed Turner told the *Washington Journalism Review.* "He's always spending money to get bigger, to improve."

NBC News president Lawrence Grossman, seeing cable TV's growing importance, tried "to move heaven and earth" to get his network to buy into CNN before Turner saw black in 1985. Years later, Grossman would also tell *Atlanta* magazine that he had been intrigued by Turner's "guts and outsized vision." It had taken "an entrepreneur and an individualist to pull off something like CNN," Grossman said. "A dreamer. That's the way all great new projects operate."

Turner had thought about selling a minority interest in CNN as part of his attempt to raise money for the MGM deal, but talks with NBC broke down. So Grossman began to encourage his network in 1985 to start its own all-news cable operation in competition. The fact that Turner's service had been in jeopardy until just a short while ago was suddenly forgotten in the face of his success: "Nobody likes a monopoly," Grossman complained, "and that is what CNN and Headline News represent in cable television."

"CNN has become a major force in the industry," Grossman went on. "It's amazing what Ted Turner has accomplished in such a short time. But Turner's rather steep subscriber-fee increases may have made CNN vulnerable. Our plan at NBC is a longshot, but we're looking at it."

Ironically the man who came up with a blueprint for NBC Cable News was Reese Schonfeld, who was no longer consulting for Turner; but when the network failed to get enough commitments from cable operators, the project began to founder. Schonfeld attributed the failure to two factors: Turner's business acumen and NBC's inability to act quickly and quietly.

"The networks tend to be elephants," he said. "It's tough to teach elephants to dance. It's impossible when the elephants insist on leading."

Schonfeld also felt that NBC had played into Turner's hands by talking to him about buying half and controlling interest in CNN, for $250 million. The talks had destroyed much of NBC's credibility with the cable industry, enabling Turner to tell the operators, "See? NBC can't be trusted!"

NBC Cable News disappeared before it could get off the ground. In the cable news field, the third of the Big Three had fallen by the wayside.

Even while his MGM purchase was in the works, Turner announced a groundbreaking deal between TBS and Soviet officials. They would coproduce and broadcast an Olympics-style competition, the Goodwill Games, from Moscow in the summer of 1986. The event would be repeated every four years. Turner wanted to help improve relations between the U.S. and Russia; but he was striking back at the Big Three networks, too, after being unable to compete with them for TV rights to the regular Olympics. And the Soviets, stung by the U.S. boycott of the 1980 Moscow Olympics and having pulled out of the 1984 Games in Los Angeles, jumped to agree. Ted Turner and the Kremlin would go forth together.

CNN had been pursuing the right to broadcast from courtrooms, attempting to broaden the definition of the word "public" in the constitutional guarantee to a "speedy and public trial." The biggest test case was an unsuccessful effort to televise the libel-suit trial of General William Westmoreland against CBS. Bob Ross, attorney for Ted Turner, worked on that case as it went to the Supreme Court; and although it was a losing effort, he became convinced that TV cameras ultimately would be admitted into all courts of the land. More than half the states were allowing coverage in 1985, but no federal courts permitted it.

Ed Turner had become CNN's chief spokesman on the matter: "People have a right to a public trial. You can't avoid it under the Constitution. And people have a right to know what's happening in their courtroom. The camera is far less intrusive than a sketch artist, and able to bring a more full and complete record than you would read in any newspaper. . . .

"We don't sensationalize cases — some of the cases are sensational. We see nothing wrong in reporting about crime. One of the public's main concerns is crime. For every hour of a crime trial, we have tenfold carried dull hearings. We have paid our dues. . . .

"It's impossible for most people to attend trials that may be of interest to them. To a large extent, we as a society have let trial coverage get away from us. So, when a case comes up that's of national interest, we try to get in there with our camera."

Another big TV trial for CNN was in Rhode Island, where socialite Claus von Bulow was being retried on charges that he attempted to murder his wife by arranging for an overdose of insulin. CNN devoted sixty hours of airtime and, to many viewers, it seemed like a real-life version of *Dynasty.*

The hijacking of a TWA jetliner in 1985 captured the attention of the world. Terrorists holding passengers hostage demanded the release by Israel of several hundred Lebanese Shi'ite Muslims; the ordeal of Flight 847 became a theatrical event as well as a news story. It was gripping and painful when the pilot, in desperate communication with the Beirut airport, reported that "they are about to shoot a passenger" and then that "they just shot a passenger."

"There was no way to be fully and immediately informed about any of this without CNN, Ted Turner's scruffy little all-news network that has grown up to be indispensable," Howard Rosenberg wrote in the *Los Angeles Times.* "Unlike the other networks, CNN's entire business is news, so there was never a decision to make about when to interrupt regular programming for a hostage update. The hostage story *was* CNN's programming."

There were jokes that CNN should be called the Crisis News

Network; and with each new terrible event in the world, someone else announced that its coverage and audience respect had "come of age." Ed Turner said those who thought his network went overboard were full of hogwash: "That is the worst kind of elitism. It implies that when given the information, the audience may do the wrong thing with it. Who's to say what we don't give? Where do you stop? I think viewers are tough enough and have the ability to sift through the news and separate the wheat from the chaff and pick out what's important. And what use they make of it is their business. I would err on the side of giving them too much rather than too little."

"For CNN, the release of the hostages, and the events before and after," observed the *Los Angeles Herald Examiner,* "gave the fledgling network perhaps its greatest coup since its birth just five years ago."

By 1985 Turner had expanded the reach of CNN into virtually every continent and many world capitals. Henry Gillespie was the main architect of the push into Europe; CNN became the first transatlantic channel. Sid Pike negotiated to have coverage fed into the People's Republic of China. Bob Wussler, who spent two years negotiating exchange agreements with the Soviets, talked about his boss: "Ted is an internationalist. Ted believes very strongly in one world, that we are all citizens of the planet Earth. He wants his company to be as global as possible. He wants to prove that private industry can sometimes do things quicker, better and easier than governments can."

Turner donated half a million dollars as seed money for the Better World Society, a group founded to use television as a force for improving life throughout the globe. It had the support of people like Jacques Cousteau, whose deep-sea adventures were aired on WTBS, and Russell Peterson, head of the National Audubon Society. Although he often still wore the same J. C. Penney–style sport coat day after day, Turner began adding some worsted suits to his wardrobe. Newspapers and magazines stopped referring to Terrible Ted, and headlines proclaimed him a "Maverick with a Mission" and a "Crusader by Satellite."

In May 1985, CNN decided not to renew Sandi Freeman's contract at the network. She was replaced by Larry King, the popular Mutual Radio talk-show host, who made his debut in June with a one-hour interview program from Washington, D.C., at 9 P.M. Eastern Daylight Time on weeknights. In the first five weeks, *Larry King Live* saw its ratings surpass those of its predecessor; and it would become one of CNN's highest-rated programs from then on.

Cable News Network celebrated its fifth anniversary on June 1, 1985, at Harrison's on Peachtree Road in Atlanta. Burt Reinhardt, the mostly invisible CNN president, stood before the crowd to make one of his few speeches. It consisted of two words: "Let's party!"

> JAN. 28 (UPI) — The explosion of the space shuttle Challenger today was carried live nationally only by Cable News Network. . . .
>
> The Challenger blasted off at 11:38 A.M. and CNN cameras followed in closeup as the spacecraft slowly rolled, banked off and then burst into flames. . . .
>
> None of the other networks — ABC, NBC and CBS — was live.

For CNN, live coverage of the shuttle launches had become a habit. When the Challenger disaster occurred in 1986, there was an echo of Reese Schonfeld's voice arguing that you never know if the two-alarm fire will become the one that burns down Chicago. . . .

At the Executive Mansion in Washington, D.C., Nancy Reagan watched the liftoff on CNN and gasped, "Oh, my God! No!"

Tom Mintier was the lone network journalist on the air at that moment. With coanchor Mary Ann Loughlin, he stayed on all day, for a total of thirteen hours, while all around him in the Techwood newsroom there was a combination of grief and excitement, a controlled form of pandemonium.

CNN's jump on the other networks gave it an immediate breakthrough into the European market. It had been available to networks across the Atlantic on a free-trial basis since the fall of 1985, but only now did these clients see it to be "the first electronic equivalent of a wire service," as *Variety* put it. The trade paper reported: "As the story came up on monitors around Europe, TV news execs scrambled to get the CNN feed on the air."

Now clients from Austria to Britain were eager to sign up for Turner's all-news network and to pay for it.

*   *   *

A technological advance for CNN was the development of new, highly portable "satellite up-links" able to be disassembled, checked as baggage and flown to the site of a breaking story in order to feed back live reports. They cost about $250,000 apiece. A "flyaway" dish could become a temporary CNN bureau in just the time it took to get one to the scene. Ed Turner exclaimed that the up-links would "change the face of TV journalism."

Atlanta columnist Dick Williams found himself watching CNN in his Tokyo hotel room during the U.S. raid on Libya in 1986. This was his moment to write home that "the marvelous creation of Ted Turner and Reese Schonfeld has come of age, without question or reservation." He was joined by others, including anonymous newspeople from the Big Three, who now admitted that they, too, had watched while CNN correspondent John Donvan reported on the bombing from a balcony of his hotel in Tripoli. At about 10:30 P.M. Eastern Daylight Time, when the other networks had switched back to their sitcoms and melodramas, Donvan was the only reporter on TV as the shooting unexpectedly started up again. "If it wasn't so horrible it would be beautiful," he said as anti-aircraft fire lit up the Tripoli sky.

The commercial-network news departments rushed to get back on the air.

At three o'clock on the morning of July 13, 1987, Headline News went on the air from its new headquarters in the CNN Center, the former Omni International office complex in downtown Atlanta; and, also without interruption, Cable News Network switched over from Techwood just before dawn. Now the CNN newsroom was part of a huge complex of hotel rooms, offices and retail shops, with the atmosphere of a space station. Turner had purchased seventy-five percent of the complex in 1985 and the remaining interest in 1986.

The changeovers under Gene Wright and CNN's chief engineer, Jack Ormand, took place during two-minute commercial breaks, as staffers and technicians bunched together in front of the monitors. Cheers rang out when the transfers were accomplished without a hitch, culminating a $30 million move from the cramped facilities on Techwood Drive to more modern ones with 200,000 square feet of space — twice the size of the news-room at the former Progressive Club's brick mansion.

"The switch to the spacious environs," the *Atlanta Constitution* reported, "means the one-time underdog has achieved technological superiority over its network news competitors."

Next door to CNN Center was the large arena, now managed by Turner, where the Hawks played and where the 1988 Democratic convention would be held the next year.

PAUL AMOS

"One of the real milestones was our moving to this building, which is the first facility designed from scratch to really handle what we're doing. When we built the facility at Techwood, we kind of had an idea of what we needed to pull it off, but this one was built based on the experience of that. It's the most efficient television newsgathering system in existence. Before we moved here we were a small company, but after July of 1987 our culture dramatically changed. We went from being all cramped together, as a family, into an environment that completely changed us. And it would be difficult ever to go back."

The high-tech architecture was a symbol of CNN's new corporate culture. More than fifty thousand visitors would take a forty-five-minute guided tour of CNN each year, beginning with a ride up a long escalator to the eighth-floor level, where a sign proclaimed that "The World Is Watching." The tour group was led through a labyrinth of gray and white hallways and stairs, into the bowels of the complex, arriving at a glass wall over-looking the newsroom. Down below, in what looked like NASA's control center, there were no ragged edges or crazies or misfits in sight. It was a clean, polished, glossy, quiet factory for news, dedicated to the onrushing present, with no discernable history.

At one point in the tour, however, some visitors noticed a photograph on the wall. As if hung there by mistake, it revealed the front view of an old, ramshackle, white house. . . .

Saddled with a $1.4 billion debt as a result of the MGM/UA deal, Ted Turner completed the sale of thirty-seven percent of Turner Broadcasting System to a group of twenty-six cable operators and Time Inc. If the $525 million deal hadn't gone through, Turner would have been out of cash. He would have been forced to issue some 800,000 shares of common stock to preferred shareholders, in lieu of cash owed to them, and to sell off more assets to retire additional debt. As a result, his stake in his own company would have fallen below fifty percent, and he would have lost control of it to Kerkorian.

Bailed out by the cable operators, Turner went from owning more than eighty percent of TBS stock to maintaining from fifty-one to sixty-five percent, depending on upcoming maneuvers. The new stockholders, led by Time Inc. and Denver-based Tele-Communications Inc., immediately appointed seven directors to join Turner's eight board members; and they would have a lot of power over big decisions in the future. Turner had lost his firm grip on the empire he had built from his father's billboard company.

"Every time he did something, he put all his chips on the table and rolled the dice," said a friend. "Sooner or later he had to crap out."

"It was the ultimate tradeoff for the MGM film library," Art Sando said, "but the cable guys didn't want a noncable interest to control Turner Broadcasting. They figured it was better to do it themselves and keep TBS cable-loyal."

Meanwhile, Turner was going through a divorce from his wife, Janie, reportedly costing him more than $40 million. He was spending much of his time in California with another woman, J. J. Ebaugh, who was once his pilot. (A previous companion had been Liz Wickersham, coanchor with Bill Tush of *Showbiz Today* on CNN.) He devoted more energy to the Better World Society. Nearing fifty, Turner seemed to be fleeing at last from his old roots, personal and professional. The prophets of doom were projecting images of Turner winding up on an island in the Pacific. Even Woody Allen shook his finger at him, telling Congress that it was "sinful" for Turner to think about adding color to the old MGM black-and-white movies.

The fun days appeared to be over.

President Reagan told his aides to call in "all four networks" for an Oval Office chat in October 1987. Showing up with Dan Rather, Tom Brokaw and Peter Jennings was Bernie Shaw. In

CNN's history it marked another turning point, which Shaw summed up in just three words: "We have parity."

By November there was a power shift at the top of Turner Broadcasting. Bob Wussler, who had been considered second to Ted Turner, was shifted from president of WTBS to the role of overseeing its international expansion. Wussler was on the losing end of a struggle between himself and Gerry Hogan, who emerged on top with responsibility not only for WTBS but for a proposed new network to be called Turner Network Television or TNT, set to make its debut in the fall of 1988.

Wussler had brought Turner some valuable smoothness and class, as well as alliances with senior executives at the Big Three networks; and for the next two years he would continue to help build TBS into a $4-billion-a-year international broadcasting presence. Some people felt he had lost ground in the corporation as a result of a few public displays of fisticuffs; as evidence they cited a barroom argument at Harrison's, when he had punched out financial chief Bill Bevins — who, now in the midst of working to restructure the company's enormous debt, suddenly resigned.

Cable News Network started airing *CNN World Report*, produced by Stu Loory. The program, conceived by Turner, consisted of three-minute news reports from local broadcasters all over the world. The pieces were neither censored nor edited — whether received from Israel or Kuwait, from Russia or South Africa — and aired on Sunday nights.

Dr. Don Flournoy of Ohio University wrote in *Broadcasting* that it was "the first truly planetary newscast to which any country in any part of the globe is free to contribute and use as it will." He called it "the biggest breakthrough in international news flow, ever."

Eighty-seven countries had signed up by December 1987. Each broadcaster was responsible for its own up-link and down-link costs, but no money changed hands with Cable News Network. Lots of countries receiving CNN were airing *World Report*.

"We've finally got 'em talkin' to each other," Turner said, "instead of just fightin'."

*   *   *

In 1988, Jane Maxwell was named a vice-president of CNN. For six years she had been coordinating live coverage of special events such as the 1985 Geneva summit, the visit of Pope Paul II to the United States and the Statue of Liberty centennial. This year she was handling logistics for the political conventions in Atlanta and New Orleans.

When the news divisions of ABC, CBS and NBC converged on Atlanta for the Democratic National Convention, they hardly needed to be reminded that they were in Ted Turner's terrority. In eight-foot-high blue lights, the letters CNN dominated the skyline as visitors approached the Omni Coliseum. Once again CNN's "gavel-to-gavel" coverage was unbeatable in terms of airtime.

In the Headline News headquarters, a new organization sprang up: Noticiero Telemundo-CNN, with a staff of twenty-five bilingual members, transmitting CNN news (reworked and translated into Spanish) to a United States Hispanic audience and to eight Latin American countries. As Bob Schuessler said of Turner's ability to continue finding new markets, "We keep cutting the hog and selling it again."

Bernie Shaw became visible to millions of additional viewers when he moderated the second presidential debate of 1988 from Los Angeles. He asked Michael Dukakis if his views on capital punishment would change if the candidate's wife, Kitty, were "raped and murdered." It was generally agreed that Dukakis's cool, detached answer was what finally ended his chances in the race. He asked George Bush if he'd worry about the country under President Dan Quayle if he, Bush, suddenly died. Not all of his new viewers were pleased.

Rick Brown, who had left CNN's satellite department in the mid-1980s, was fulfilling one of his dreams. At home in Atlanta — while his wife, Jane Maxwell, was at her CNN office — he was cranking out his own trade paper, *TV News Journal*, which he called "a weekly digest of industry scuttlebutt." In one of his December 1988 issues, Brown noted some changes in senior management: Ed Turner became executive vice-president for newsgathering, Paul Amos got the same status for news programming and Jon Petrovich took charge of Headline News. Brown, who insisted that none of his tips had come from Maxwell, added that insiders felt Paul Amos was "being positioned to take over Reinhardt's job as head of the network within a year and a half."

So the race to see who would lead CNN in the 1990s had begun. Ed Turner had been an apparent choice to succeed Schonfeld and Reinhardt, sixty-eight; but now the younger man, Amos, was moving upward. Also rumored as contenders were Petrovich and Stu Loory, although they were seen as being longshots. In fact, the man with the inside track was Bob Wussler — but after having lost to Gerry Hogan in the recent power shift, Wussler was looking for opportunities outside Turner Broadcasting.

(In September 1989, Wussler resigned to become chief executive officer of Comsat Video Enterprises, a player in the pay-per-view market for satellite-delivered sports and entertainment to hotels and homes.)

The only certainty was that Ted Turner felt it was good for his company when various executives were jockeying around trying to prove themselves. When the pot had been stirred long enough, and when Reinhardt decided to step down, Turner would make the decision on a successor himself.

Turner Network Television took almost everyone by surprise. In less than three months, from its launch in October 1988 to January 1989, TNT's circulation climbed to more than twenty million homes. It was the quickest start in cable network history; and TNT already qualified for those all-important Nielsen ratings, critical for drawing advertising support. The New York brokerage firm of Donaldson, Lufkin & Jenrette reported: "We believe that Wall Street has not yet recognized the transformation of Turner Broadcasting. The common view is still that of a company tottering on the financial edge with an unpredictable and sometimes rash chief executive. The truth is that the company is rapidly becoming one of the dominant media empires."

After coming perilously close to losing his company, Turner was suddenly "Captain Comeback — back from the brink," as *Business Week* put it later in 1989. The investment in Turner Broadcasting by cable operators, who had bailed out Turner by putting up a total of $568 million, had meant the difference. On the downside, it meant that Turner no longer could make all major decisions on his own — twelve out of fifteen votes by board members were required, now, to approve any expenses exceeding his budget by $2 million. Otherwise he was still at the helm of his own company, making it grow.

With a library of 3,300 vintage movies — from MGM, RKO and pre-1950 Warner Brothers productions — to get TNT rolling, Turner had maintained the strategy of continually increasing the value of his product. In this case, he was sinking money into production of new films and programs for the network. He now envisioned TNT becoming the biggest channel for sports and entertainment in the world — yes, bigger than the major broadcast networks, he predicted, adding that he might beam it internationally by the mid-1990s, and no one was laughing this time.

He would enter the 1990s with $1 billion in yearly revenue.

It was Turner himself who had remarked, as a joke, that he went to Hollywood in a Brooks Brothers suit and left a few months later hitchhiking out of town in a barrel. "But I saw those old films as worth more than anybody else did," he told *Variety.* He had seen the profit in colorization, too — "I had looked at some tests, several years before the opportunity to buy the MGM and Warner libraries became available" — and by distributing the films himself, Turner said, he had known he would make double the normal profits.

"So the main thing is," he continued, explaining his approach to business, "you don't pay too much for something if you see what the current owner of it doesn't see. Every time something changes hands, every time there's a willing buyer and a willing seller, the guy that's selling thinks that he can do better by reinvesting his money in something else. The guy that's buying thinks that it's going to be worth more than it was to the previous owner.

"I have absolutely no bad feelings about colorizing the films whatsoever. We're not interfering at all with the original black-and-white negatives. They're available. Anybody who really wants to see the movies in black-and-white can buy a videocassette of the film. They're all available. So what's the big deal? Those movies would have all been made in color. All movies today are made in color. We're making those movies very valuable, and we're letting young people see them who wouldn't watch them in black-and-white. . . ."

(While Turner managed to colorize such classic films as *The Maltese Falcon* and *Casablanca,* he was unable to do the same with Orson Welles's 1941 epic *Citizen Kane.* Welles, in his 1939 contract with RKO Pictures, had gotten a guarantee that he would retain full control over the film's black-and-white photography. Welles died in 1985, but that stipulation remained; so Turner, avoiding a possible court fight, abandoned plans to colorize *Citizen Kane.* "It was a victory from the grave," *Time* magazine quipped.)

"I'm very ambitious," Turner told *Variety,* "and if I wasn't, we wouldn't be where we are now. Our hope is to be the leading producer and distributor of news and information and entertainment programming to television audiences around the world. One thing that people don't understand is that money never has been what motivates me. I was willing to take chances because I didn't think the money was that important. The challenge and the adventure were the main things with me, and the sense of achievement and accomplishment, and wanting to do something in my life that would really be spectacular. I've always had grandiose schemes. . . ."

Turner was back in full swing. As his corporate strength expanded, he raised his long-range vision again. He still saw himself as David against Goliath: "It'll take a number of years" to beat the networks in ratings, he told advertisers, "but that's not so bad. I want them to suffer slowly. I like being the little guy on the way up."

When NBC launched its around-the-clock Consumer News and Business Channel (CNBC) to a cable-TV audience in April 1989, Turner saw it as a kind of Trojan horse. Underneath was an NBC plan, he felt, to turn the new channel into a direct competitor of his Cable News Network. (Ironically a few of CNBC's most prominent anchors were former CNN people: Dave Walker and Lois Hart, who had left a while before, and Mary Alice Williams, who made a celebrated leap back to NBC in 1989.) In a speech to cable operators, Turner lambasted General Electric, NBC's owner, by calling it "the most corrupt corporation in America" because of its defense-contracting problems.

His remarks made some members of his new board of directors shudder; and when Turner planned to strike back at NBC by purchasing part of Financial News Network (FNN), he called a special meeting of the board. His proposal called for TBS to pay up to $110 million for the forty-five percent of FNN owned by Infotechnology Inc., a New York investment group, and for the right to buy the remainder of FNN in the future. (FNN also had some former CNN people, including Jim Shepherd.) The purchase would give Turner a way to take on CNBC directly — but the board voted him down.

Turner could not play the chess game with the same free-wheeling management style as before. Some of his colleagues, like financial chief Paul Beckham, felt he actually relished the challenge of having to persuade the new directors to accept his ideas; but that may have been putting the best face on what others saw as a crucial turning point for the man who loved to take on "impossible" goals.

TED TURNER

"I'm not sure it was such a setback. I knew what I was getting into when I made the deal to be partners, rather than basically an entrepreneur, and I had every reason to anticipate what's happened. On balance, it's been a big plus. We got TNT as a result of it. We wouldn't have gotten that otherwise, and that alone made it worthwhile. . . .

"Convincing the board certainly adds another challenge. It's like getting married. You give up some independence when you get married, but you gain a wife. If it's a *good* marriage, you get a companion. If I could go back to the way it was before, I wouldn't do it. I had high expectations — and I can actually say that a partnership with the cable operators has been better than I thought it was going to be."

In the spring of 1989, in New York City, Ted Kavanau spoke for several hours almost nonstop, recalling his CNN days as if they had happened the day before. "I played my little role," he said, "but as far as I'm concerned it was those kids, the video journalists, who were the key and the backbone and the inspiration. I mean, mention those kids, because without them we couldn't have done it."

Kavanau had stayed with CNN until 1987, but after building Headline News and making sure it was running well he had gone to Washington, D.C., as leader of the Special Investigations Unit. It was his feeling that by being away from Atlanta for so long he had removed himself from the center of CNN's leadership; but in any event, his four years of doing investigative reports took their toll on him. "I was so angry at the Washington bureau," he said, "through all those years of watching them put on just standard stuff, not breaking any news at all, that I told myself I'd go there and hire a bunch of investigative journalists and turn Washington upside-down."

One reporter whose work he admired was Larry Woods, husband of Dee Woods, who helped Kavanau's team from Atlanta. Most of the others were based in the nation's capital. They were "crackerjack" journalists, Kavanau said, but it was difficult to transform them into television performers as well. It was rough going, all the way, with Burt Reinhardt threatening at one point to close down the unit altogether while Kavanau kept defending his people. "I was prolonging the agony," he said. "I held it together under extreme pressure and it was killing me. Those were four of the worst years of my life. Burt finally decided to give our unit the ax and offered me the job of chief of all the European bureaus."

When Kavanau couldn't make up his mind, Reinhardt let him go. He had wanted to stay at the network but was going through personal problems at the time. "I had helped to form CNN and it was part of my blood," he said, "but in the end I was shoved out. That's the way fate is. I mean, look at Reese — one of the unsung stars in the history of American television. After CNN he went out and started a 'shopping' network. He started Cablevision on Long Island, a huge success. He started a 'book' network. Now he's working on a CBS show called *People Magazine on Television*. They're all big concepts, and that's Reese — very daring, risk-taking, and, in his way, almost like Ted Turner. But we all have endings."

He and Schonfeld had ended their long silence; and, in fact, Kavanau was joining Schonfeld to produce a syndicated show, *Crimewatch*, based in New York. The two friends, who had given so much of themselves to CNN's founding and early years, had not lost their zest for breaking new ground.

Dan Schorr was in Washington when he talked about why he left CNN in 1985. "I was unprepared for it," he said, recalling that Burt Reinhardt had removed the original contract clause that had allowed him the freedom to refuse any assignment he deemed unsuited to his professional standards. Schorr had objected to appearing as a co-commentator with former treasury secretary John Connally, a Republican, at the 1984 GOP convention. "I made a big fuss about it," Schorr said, "and Reinhardt was clearly furious that I had thrown my weight around."

Later, after Schorr left CNN, he met up with Ted Turner, who said, "Hi, Dan. Listen, I can't remember — are you mad at me or am I mad at you?" The hatchet, which had never really existed, was buried; but Schorr admitted that he "hadn't been ready to move on" from the network he had helped so much to start up and survive.

Dave Walker and Lois Hart were at the CNBC office in New Jersey, just over the George Washington Bridge from Manhattan. A warm, friendly couple, they had left CNN in 1987 after having felt that their services were no longer appreciated as before. Anchors at CNN are not as highly prized (or paid) as they are at the commercial networks; and when they start costing too much money, they often get the message that they can be replaced. An anecdote going around CNN was that when an anchor once went into Ted Turner's office to argue for a raise, Turner went to the window and started gesturing. "What are you doing?" the anchor asked. Turner replied, "I'm shaking that tree out there and I see anchors falling all over."

At CNN the news gets star billing, and no Dan Rathers need apply. From the outset, the network avoided any of the "happy talk" formats devised by local stations — the boom in local news had never been a sign of sudden viewer demand, but a result of marketing strategy to boost audience shares — and so CNN normally downplayed the element of personality when it came to its anchor people. Back in 1984 John Baker wrote a long memo to Burt Reinhardt saying, in effect, that the policy had been taken too far: "We at CNN have not concerned ourselves with producing interesting, compelling television. We have depended on the news itself to do our producing for us. When the news is dramatic and compelling, CNN is. When the news is not, CNN is not."

The subject of how to utilize anchors will be debated at CNN for years; and the strategy will keep changing as the network continues to evolve. Meanwhile, Walker and Hart said they preferred the policy at CNN of "playing it straight" even though markets across the country were looking for pizzazz. Did they miss being at CNN? The answer was that, like so many others, they missed those early, crazy days.

"The whole upshot is that it was an exciting, high-energy place," Walker said, "and then, like most corporations, it got big and bloated. That happened shortly after the ABC-Westinghouse war when Ted shut down SNC. Then CNN became more financially stable and we got respectable." What's more, the network had become a genuine syndicator of its news to broadcasters. "It seems like every station in the country is using CNN," Hart said. "The upshot is that it has made all these affiliates much more powerful against the networks. Now they have CNN and can tell their network to take a hike — and as a result, the networks are suffering. Ted Turner has changed the business of television."

Don Farmer and Chris Curle had left CNN in 1988. Now they were "local stars" on WSB-TV in Atlanta. They, too, used the word "respectable" in referring to what CNN has become. "There's a level of respectability which nobody ever expected," Farmer said. "When Reese was there, we didn't have any of that. We didn't have respectability or a widespread audience. It was exciting."

The watershed, Farmer felt, was the transition from Schonfeld to Reinhardt. "The way to explain it," he said, "is that when Reese came to an intersection, the lights were all flashing and cars were coming from every direction and nobody knew what to do, but he went on through it even though fenders and egos got bruised. When Burt came to the intersection, all four lights were red for about a week until they turned green and then he made the decision to proceed."

In other words, Farmer added, "Burt saved the network by cutting costs, pinching every penny and mulling things over. He let others speak for him while he sat back there and tried to figure, 'How in the hell am I gonna pull this off?'"

Bill Zimmerman had left CNN in May of 1984 and, soon after, had begun anchoring for Cablevision, the regional cable-TV news operation on Long Island, New York, which Reese Schonfeld had helped to start. Zimmerman was critical of how CNN had developed, complaining mostly about the depth of its information and analysis. "When Alec Nagle died and Reese left," he added, "the life and soul went out of that place."

Also at Cablevision was John Hillis, who had left CNN after the 1984 elections. "The people at CNN were no longer scruffy," he said. "Now there were more who'd been at the networks, with network mentalities, so it was a different place, just as a natural consequence of getting bigger. God bless them for making a profit, but it had begun to cease being fun, so it was time to move on."

Jim Shepherd, now directing the Financial News Network in Manhattan, also left CNN in late 1984. To him, the early days were still vivid. "That time of my life was special," he said. "I'm still closer to those original people at CNN than I am to the people I went to college with. I miss that time and I miss the feeling of comradeship. It was like giving birth — or more painful — and I wouldn't have missed it for the world. I still get emotional when I think of Alec. Well, I guess I was among the last of the original fire-breathers. . . ."

In the spring of 1989, Mary Alice Williams was at her new NBC office in Rockefeller Center. Surrounded by still-unopened boxes, eager to get on with this new phase in her career, Williams nevertheless wanted to talk about the CNN days that had just ended for her. After nine years as the main New York anchor and chief of the bureau, she was replacing Connie Chung at NBC for an estimated $400,000 a year — about double her CNN salary — and scoring a personal victory after having been fired by the New York NBC station more than nine years before. At the moment, however, Williams was complaining about having to ride back and forth to the CNBC studios for anchor chores.

"Those early days at CNN were the ones I cherish most," Williams said. "Now it's a big, credible news organization, it's awesome, and since 1984 people have joined CNN in the same way they might have joined NBC or ABC or CBS News. They don't have the benefit of knowing what it was like before, and why our loyalty and spirit and guts went into it. My heart is still there and it always will be."

Williams recalled a time when she couldn't stop laughing while delivering the stock market report. It had taken place in

1984. Told that anchor Stuart Varney was stuck in traffic, Williams had raced down the hall to the studio while ripping rollers out of her hair; and when she sat down and went to put the mike on, her entire dress fell open. She was facing the camera wearing nothing but a black bra.

"They zoomed in extremely close while I was holding the dress up along with the mike," she recalled, "and I just couldn't stop laughing. I couldn't tell that story on the Johnny Carson show."

She also couldn't tell about the other most embarrassing moment in her life, when she accidentally "mooned" thirty thousand Republicans during the 1988 convention in New Orleans. Williams was in the anchor booth, visible to all on the convention floor, when a wire caught hold of her skirt and ripped it right up the back as she bent over.

On a more serious note Mary Alice Williams added, "What separated CNN from all other places was that everybody had an investment in everybody else's success. We weren't competing with each other. We had twenty-four hours to fill, so we needed every story to get on the air and we needed everybody to succeed. That's something you don't see anywhere else. When I started at CNN I was twenty-nine and among the oldest people, so it was truly a children's crusade. And I think it was important to the planet, really, that we did it."

Of the three veterans — Sam Zelman, Jim Kitchell and Bill MacPhail — who had taken their "last fling" by joining CNN before its 1980 launch, only MacPhail remained at the news network. He was still head of the sports department, which had grown to a staff of sixty-six. "The days of 'poor old CNN' are gone," he said, "and now we're very sophisticated and knowledgeable. I think our sports coverage is just as good as any. We're respected, both here and abroad. When we first started, sports was just a necessary evil and we were pretty amateurish. But it's not that way anymore and we're carrying our weight. We hold our head up high."

Jim Kitchell, directing operations for TBS (but not involved with the news network), was up in his corporate office at CNN Center. He had been an integral part of CNN's early history and, like the others, he saw that time as a high point in his life. Kitchell spoke enthusiastically about the video journalist program, which still offers an unequaled training ground for young people starting in television news; and he gave examples of those who had started by running cameras, writing stories, becoming field producers, learning how to edit tape and so forth, as they had progressed through the ranks to top-level positions either at CNN or elsewhere.

(One young man, the late Tommy Murphy, had started as part of the construction crew in 1980 before taking on many roles and eventually becoming a supervisor at Headline News. In the summer of 1988, he was killed in a car accident.)

Sam Zelman was still living in Atlanta, even after leaving CNN to enter a "second retirement" in 1985 at age seventy. In his opinion, the future of TV news will include an "interactive" relationship between viewers and screen. "You'll see people punching up individual stories to see and hear," he said, "as if they were turning pages in a newspaper. Somewhere, in some central core of the local cable company, there will be tiny reels of tape with thousands of accumulated stories. You press a button, like on a jukebox, and your selection of a story comes up. Otherwise, the information glut is terrible. Our circuits are overloaded. We need time to be interested in reading and in going to plays and ballgames — in being with the kids and doing a thousand other things that make up life."

One of Zelman's last contributions to CNN had been a report on his own generation of senior citizens — the fastest-growing segment of the American population. Although he was not accustomed to working in front of a camera, Zelman went off with producer Stacy Jolna to be the correspondent focusing on life in an Arizona retirement community. "What a great play this would make," the older man remarked. "It's got all the elements of great comedy and drama, joy and sorrow." Jolna suggested it would make an even better novel; and after they got back to Atlanta, while working on their series about the aging, Zelman announced he had decided to write it. That same week he submitted his resignation. Four years later, he was still writing.

In the New York office for his new TV shows, Reese Schonfeld admitted that he was more of an innovator than a long-term player. "I knew I was going to leave CNN," he said, "and I think

Turner was aware of that. In my own mind there was always a question of how long I should stay." But he was wistful. "I felt that for CNN to really work I probably should have done one more three-year contract. I didn't want to stay there forever, but I would've had one year to get it started and then five years of running it."

He'd had the startup year but only two more years, not five, as CNN's president. In his view, he would have "shaped it" differently so that it would make more of an impact on public opinion. Schonfeld would not elaborate, but he clearly felt that CNN had not yet reached its potential and wondered aloud if it ever would. Reading between the lines of his conversation, it appeared that he had dreamed of CNN as providing even more breaking news from all points on the globe, with perhaps less emphasis on features. Schonfeld left no doubt that he saw the network's immediacy as its heart and soul, and that he felt it could assume a more "influential" (and even possibly "dangerous") role in world affairs.

He felt that CNN had the potential to become the most important instrument of communications in the world, for its leaders and people — and the thought of the network becoming so powerful was even frightening.

At the helm in Atlanta was Burt Reinhardt, who had never given an interview during the entire decade. He was still the second president of CNN in the fall of 1989, still making virtually all decisions. He remembered sitting in the old white house, wearing rubbers while the rain leaked from the roof, and he recalled going over to Techwood each night — in the spring of 1980, before CNN's opening day — to remove dust from the cameras.

For all his zealous privacy and reputation for being a grouch, Reinhardt is an affable man with a great sense of humor. After an interview, he asked, "Did I tell you anything?" No, he was told. "Good!" he snapped back, grinning.

"This isn't just a news network anymore," he said. "It's a news and *information* network." That, to him, was obviously a big point. As an example, he cited various feature-type programs on health, medicine, science and even nutrition — "just about everything of interest," he said, adding, "I think we're really in our infancy. We're only just starting. It's really part of Ted Turner's dream of giving information to help the world."

But when Reinhardt was asked about the main thrust of CNN's future, he replied that it was "to be as live as possible" while news is breaking. The old, original theme was still alive; and there was, unmistakably, the echo of Alec Nagle's voice: "We committed television!"

Mikhail Gorbachev was going to China in May 1989 for the first Sino-Soviet summit meeting since 1958.

The Soviet president would meet with China's Deng Xiaoping, age eighty-four, to review key issues that first divided the two communist giants after Mao Zedong's victory over Chinese nationalists in 1949.

Gorbachev knew he would find himself smack in the middle of a democratic awakening. His own *glasnost* had brought political openness to the Soviet Union; and for some weeks now, he had been the focus of a push by Chinese university students for democratic reforms. They saw him as a hero whose policies should be adopted by their own country; but Chinese officials were determined to keep the Soviet leader away from the students, who had been insisting on their own meeting with him.

The summit meeting, by itself, would be a historic occasion; but the growing demands by Chinese students provided a backdrop of unknown, possibly volatile dimensions. Among the Big Four networks, only two were sending their top anchors. Tom Brokaw of NBC and Peter Jennings of ABC were staying home. Going to China were Dan Rather of CBS and Bernie Shaw of CNN.

Shaw was backed by a crew of forty, with four correspondents helping him: Mike Chinoy, the Beijing bureau chief; Steve Hurst, the Moscow bureau chief; John Lewis, head of the Tokyo bureau; and Jeanne Moos, based in CNN's New York bureau, assigned to provide the "wide-eyed perspective" of an American who had never visited China.

The coverage, set to run from May 15 through May 18, was being coordinated from Atlanta by Jane Maxwell. Her chief liaison in China was producer Alec Miran.

Bernie Shaw would anchor CNN's newscasts from an outdoor studio amid a Chinese garden in back of the Great Wall Sheraton Hotel in Beijing. A satellite signal would be sent to Atlanta from CNN's flyaway earth station set up at the hotel.

One of the most dramatic television-news stories ever was set to begin.

When CNN got permission to bring in a flyaway dish, it gained twenty-four-hour access to a satellite transponder for seven days; and so, when Gorbachev left after six days, the network argued that it still had another day of transmitting to go. By now the story had switched to the million Chinese demonstrating for democracy in Tiananmen Square. (Again, in the most surprising way, it was a case of Reese Schonfeld's two-alarm fire threatening to burn down Chicago.) Of course, the Chinese government was horrified that a worldwide television audience was witnessing all this turmoil as it unfolded moment by moment. Word came that CNN would be forced off the air.

The news "process" itself, in the midst of a totalitarian regime, now became the focus of attention, as Alec Miran attempted to delay the shutdown of CNN's satellite signal. President Bush's aides rushed to watch CNN's drama at the command post by his home in Kennebunkport, Maine. When Miran stalled, the press corps broke into cheers. The White House issued its official reactions to the events in China on the basis of what the president was watching as he stayed glued to CNN. The Kremlin was watching CNN, too.

It was Saturday morning in Beijing and Friday evening in the United States. Most of the commentary was heard while CNN ran continuing live pictures of Tiananmen Square.

> Shaw: Overnight the capital of this great country did not sleep. People were in the streets throughout the night, as we were, covering what they were doing, talking to them. The troops just sort of stood there as the people moved in and went to work on them. Talk about psychological warfare. The people appealed to them, "You are a part of us, you are a part of our family." They told them, "Don't do this. Don't go to the square." In twenty-two minutes we will be commanded off this satellite, so we won't be able to transmit to you any more, as we've been saying. The latest word we received from the government of the People's Republic of China here in Beijing, CNN was told,

"You are here to report on Gorbachev. Gorbachev is gone. Your task is over". . . .

Chinoy: I think we are in the middle of a serious revolution. We now have to ask the question, Can this government survive? Can it stay in its present form? The men who rule China and the Communist party are used to having their orders obeyed instantly. The notion that their armed forces would refuse to obey orders is mindboggling, breathtaking. The implications are staggering. Never in a communist country has such an event taken place. And it's so fluid now, we really don't know which way it will go. . . .

Shaw: I want to report to our viewers that CNN president Burt Reinhardt in Atlanta has passed word to us here in Beijing that the network of record, Cable News Network, will stay on the air right up to the last second, until the Chinese authorities pull the plug on us. . . .

Hurst: It is an incredible scene, Bernie. The thing that struck me when we just left the square, and obviously there have been massive developments since then, is that you have the Chinese army on the outskirts of the capital and they can't get to town. I don't know how the leadership hopes to resolve that. It's an incredible problem for them. . . .

Chinoy: The students have been very, very skillful. They have been very disciplined. They have been very peaceful and they have been at pains to stress they are patriotic. They love the country. They do not want physical confrontation. They do not want a revolution in a violent sense. . . .

Moos: We are getting some conflicting information . . . but student leaders are under the impression that at ten o'clock our time, in just ten minutes from now, there might be some police activity. . . .

Shaw: Hold on, just a second . . . a Reuters bulletin out of Beijing is that martial law has been imposed . . . this is very sketchy. We'll try to clean that up for you. . . . The lead says that martial law has been imposed on portions of Beijing. . . . We have five minutes on the satellite or the bird, as we call it. Things that are rushing through all of our minds — one thing, to all of our families and to all of our friends watching anywhere in the world, are we endangered? No. . . .

If you're wondering how CNN has been able to bring you this extraordinary story . . . we brought in our own flyaway gear, about eighteen oversized suitcases with our satellite gear . . . we unpacked our transmission equipment and our dish. So whatever you've seen in the way of pictures and, indeed, in the way of words, came from our microwave units at Tiananmen Square bounced right here to the hotel, through our control room on one of the upper floors — I won't mention the floor for protective reasons — back down through cables, up on the CNN satellite dish, up on the satellite, and to you across the world . . . and I have to say this, for those cable stations that want to cut away, and I can't believe that any of you would want to cut away, you're gonna risk the anger and angst of all your viewers if you do . . . we have about two and a half minutes left on the satellite. . . .

Hurst: How in the world the government let us keep reporting out of Tiananmen Square with all our paraphernalia, watching what was going on . . . why they didn't shut us down right from the very beginning when it was clear that this was out of hand. . . .

Lewis: It is just unbelievable to me that we were allowed to continue to do what we were doing for so long. . . . They can stop us, but I don't know how they're going to stop these hundreds of thousands or million or so people in the streets right now.

> Shaw: We're counting down. We have about twelve seconds left on the satellite.

> Chinoy: I think there is tremendous risk now in this situation and tremendous possibility of confrontation, if the government actually moves to carry out martial law. . . . I think there is now a great danger of bloodshed.

> Shaw: One of our producers just said in my ear that we now are on borrowed time. . . .

> Chinoy: Now, clearly, the iron fist is about to come down. . . .

But from Tiananmen Square, and from outside the hotel where Shaw was anchoring, the live video pictures continued. Instead of the iron fist, a Chinese official appeared in CNN's makeshift control room inside the hotel. One crew member happened to have a personal video camera, which was quickly connected to the network's transmission cable so the confrontation between CNN and the Chinese government could be sent live to the earth station and the satellite. As it became clear that this event was a news story, ABC sent a crew to the hotel room. For those CNN staffers who had been through all the battles to achieve equality with the other networks, the sight of ABC covering CNN during this remarkable moment in Chinese history was a supreme irony. Now the events in the hotel room were paramount.

> Hurst: I would like to know what is going through that official's mind. Does he want to pull that plug? In his heart of hearts? I think that is the issue going right top-to-bottom through this story. . . .

> Shaw: The government officials are now in our control room up on the ninth floor and they are telling us to stop transmission. . . . On behalf of all of us, goodbye from Beijing as you watch and hear what's happening. . . .

But the plug was not pulled. The video, now from Tiananmen Square, continued. A voice was heard in the background: "Keep talking, Bernie."

> Shaw: We are still watching what is happening in Beijing and it's fair to report that instead of going away from the square, this place is filling up as each hour unfolds. . . .

> Chinoy: This is unprecedented in the world of news coverage. . . .

> Shaw: I am being told that the Chinese government has closed the city of Beijing and no journalists are being allowed. . . . Unbelievably, we all came here to cover a summit and we walked into a revolution. . . .

> Chinoy: I think it is a clear sign that we are going to have some bloodshed here . . . and that contrary to what you said a little while ago, Bernie, all of us . . . are now in some risk.

> Shaw: Well, that's reality. When we signed on, in this profession, we knew that we would be in place where not always would there be safety and comfort. We're all veterans. We've all covered upheavals and civil wars and we're big boys. . . .

Again, the CNN viewers were watching events taking place inside the hotel room, where Alec Miran was receiving a visitor from the Chinese government. Shaw himself was watching on a monitor while he narrated.

> Shaw: This man with a piece of paper in his hands, I'm certain it's not a party invitation. Let's just watch what happens. . . . The gesturing hands on the left side of your screen belong to Alec Miran. . . . I'll just use my reporter's instincts. It seems to me that this official has come and officially told CNN . . . and Alec Miran is appealing to this official, who is calling his bosses. . . .
>
> Now ABC News is covering what's happening before your eyes and ears. They're covering this as

> a news event . . . now we are being told that if we
> don't stop transmitting the Chinese government
> will take our equipment. It will be interesting to
> see what happens. . . . President Bush is being
> quoted by reporters covering him in Maine and it's
> being relayed to us. He is saying, "Word of the
> news blackout is very disturbing."

The video on CNN switched to pictures taken by the camera
outside the hotel, where the correspondents stood, showing the
movable earth station.

> Hurst: It is interesting to me, looking at that flyaway
> dish sitting there as we are about to be unplugged,
> knowing that such a small piece of equipment did
> so much and showed the world so many pictures,
> so many images so quickly. Can you imagine,
> some years ago, something like this happening in
> Beijing? . . . It might have been days before these
> pictures would have gotten out of this country. . . .

As CNN showed more pictures of the crowded square, the
screen froze. Lou Waters, at the anchor desk in Atlanta, suddenly
appeared. He did a quick wrap-up, reporting a new White House
statement: "We urge that the news blackout not signal an end
to appropriate restraint or dialogue with the students." Waters
added that the declaration of martial law and the lining-up of
police officers on both sides of Tiananmen Square "does signal
some sort of government movement on the students."

Now, in a complete surprise, the live pictures from China suddenly came back after two minutes. The blackout had been
caused by a technical problem in the United States, not by the
Chinese government. The coverage continued, with analysis
from Shaw and the correspondents, until CNN switched to the
scene in the hotel room again. Alec Miran was on the phone
with the Chinese ministry and CNN viewers could see and hear
him: "You're saying we are only allowed to cover the Gorbachev
visit? How about all the other stories we did about China that
didn't concern Mr. Gorbachev? That has nothing to do with you?
Then why does *this* have anything to do with you? What is the
government afraid of? They are not afraid? Stand by, sir. . . ."

On another phone, Miran told Jane Maxwell in Atlanta that

he was "trying to make it very clear to him that we require a letter. That is our company policy, correct?"

As Maxwell replied, the CNN viewers could hear her voice saying that the network required something "in writing" about why it no longer could use the satellite, which had been leased for several hours more of transmission.

"Did you hear that, sir?" Miran said into the phone.

The correspondents resumed their coverage of Beijing before the events in the hotel room heated up again. The Chinese official now wrote his letter to CNN, in his own language, on a yellow legal pad. Maxwell appeared on a split screen with a translator in the hotel room, who read it over the phone: "As an observer of the Ministry of Telecommunications of China, and according to the directive from the superiors, Mr. Gorbachev's China visit is over. Now I am here announcing that CNN should stop the movable earth station and its transmitting frequencies right away. Mr. Chou Yin Juing, 11:02, 20 May 1989, Beijing Summer Time."

Miran and Maxwell appeared on either side of the split screen as they spoke on the phone.

> Miran: Jane?
>
> Maxwell: Well, the government has ordered us to shut down our facility. I guess we'll have to shut it down.
>
> Miran: Okay. Our policy is, the government has ordered us to shut down our facility. We are shutting down our facility. Okay, Bernie, sign off.

The CNN picture switched to the correspondents outside the hotel.

> Shaw: Okay. We've heard the orders. We have our instructions from headquarters in Atlanta. For Steve Hurst —
>
> Hurst: Goodbye. It's been lots of fun. It's been very interesting. I've never seen anything like this.
>
> Lewis: Interesting hardly describes what we've seen, Bernie.

> Chinoy: The most extraordinary event I've ever wit-
> nessed in twenty years of following China.

> Shaw: In my twenty-six years in this business, I've
> never seen anything like this. The situation in
> Tiananmen Square is that it is a standoff.... For
> all of the hard-working men and women of CNN,
> goodbye from Beijing.

It was 10:06 P.M. Eastern Daylight Time.

The Chinese pulled the plug from CBS News after Dan Rather
appeared briefly in a hallway with government officials, before
leaving the air for good. CBS had scored a victory over ABC and
NBC, but CNN's suspenseful coverage of itself being thrown off
the air had been unique.

"CNN performed a great national and even international service," said former CBS executive Fred Friendly. "CBS did more
than anyone else among the commercial networks, but they
didn't have what CNN has, which is unlimited airtime."

"What I found fascinating," commented Ed Joyce, former president of CBS News, "was that the competition was between CBS
News and CNN. ABC and NBC were just not factors. This was
a watershed."

"It was an historic piece of television," wrote the *Orange
County Register*, "providing the most graphic illustration imag-
inable of a repressive government in action.... For CNN, the
disappearing coverage was a coup for the ages.... The sense of
foreboding, of imminent bloodshed, was palpable. Nothing in
recent TV history could equal it. For pure live drama, it's difficult to imagine that anything will ever surpass it."

In a story with the headline KARL MARX, MEET MAR-
SHALL McLUHAN, Jonathan Alter wrote in *Newsweek* that if
television's presence "doesn't actually aid democracy, it may
make the cruelest of repressions harder to inflict. Eventually, the
whole world will see. Even in China, long oblivious to outside
opinions, that makes some difference."

ALEC MIRAN

"We would go down to Tiananmen Square . . . and we would say,
in Chinese, 'Foreign journalists.' Those were about the only two
words I knew. Not only would they let us through, but they

would start cheering. They were putting their lives on the line, and they're cheering for us! That was embarrassing . . . but the night before we were shut off the air, a couple of Chinese employees at the hotel came up and said, 'Thank you very much for what you did.' We said, 'Oh, we were just doing our job.' They said, 'No, you kept the soldiers out of the square.' I said, 'Well, I think that's a little much.' They said, 'The soldiers weren't going to come in while you were watching.'"

After the plugs were pulled, they were restored by the Chinese government — and then pulled again. From May 24 on, with no live video from Beijing allowed, networks relied mostly on reports by telephone and videotaped reports shipped out of the country to be transmitted from Hong Kong. The Chinese capital returned to relative normalcy, even though some 250,000 troops were poised on the Beijing's outskirts. Premier Li Peng appeared on government television and declared that the soldiers would enter the city soon. In the second week of June, Communist China experienced its worst day of bloodshed ever. No longer with the world watching, troops under the sway of their government's power of persuasion moved into the center of Beijing and massacred hundreds, perhaps thousands, of protesters.

———

Meanwhile, other developments took place in 1989:

CBS and Turner Broadcasting announced an agreement giving TNT exclusive rights to about fifty hours of the 1992 Winter Olympics — the first time the international sporting event would be available on a basic cable network. Terry McGuirk, president of Turner Sports, said the rights were purchased from CBS for $50 million. Back in 1979, Burt Reinhardt had explained to Turner over lunch that coverage of the Olympic Games in 1980 and 1984 had been bought respectively by NBC and ABC, at prices CNN could not afford; and Turner, stunned, had replied, "That ain't fair!" But now, ten years later, he had a big slice of the action, and those same networks were the ones in shock.

The agreement had no bearing on the TBS-produced 1990 Goodwill Games in Seattle, to be carried by the SuperStation. Turner had lost money on the 1986 Goodwill Games in the Soviet Union and was budgeting "a substantial amount to lose" the second time around. "I didn't do it to make money," he said. "I did it to get the two countries on the playing fields again. I could just tell the Soviets were looking to be our friends."

Instead of counterprogramming, CNN went "head-to-head" against the half-hour evening newscasts of the other networks with its one-hour news show *The World Today*, anchored by Bernie Shaw in Washington and by Catherine Crier, an attractive and articulate Texas judge, in Atlanta. It was showmanship on CNN's part. But Shaw was not happy about the decision to hire an inexperienced person to coanchor the news with him, as though his own years of experience meant so little; and, in fact, he flew down to Atlanta at his own expense to try to change Burt Reinhardt's mind about it. He was unsuccessful.

Pam Hill, the preeminent documentary maker in network television, left ABC News to take charge of a new CNN investigative unit. Her move was made amid a trend by Big Three networks toward "recreating" or "simulating" real events by using actors. Of CNN she said, "There's a respect here for the old, fixed ethics of journalism, while the networks are moving in the opposite direction." By now, Ed Turner was no longer referring to ABC, CBS and NBC as the "other" networks but, simply, as the "entertainment" networks.

Ted Turner sent down an order banning all "commentary" by CNN on-air persons. Among those affected were Rowland Evans and Robert Novak, Linda Ellerbee and even Flip Spiceland, who occasionally did humorous essays during his weather reports. (At the end of the decade, Spiceland had delivered close to forty thousand weathercasts.) Staffers debated whether the policy was good or bad; but as if in reply, a U.S. poll conducted for the *Times Mirror* Center for the People and the Press revealed that CNN was "the most believable" of the networks. It had scored second only to the *Wall Street Journal* in terms of public confidence. The news channel's believability had risen five percentage points since a similar survey had been taken in 1985; the commercial networks had lost ground during the same period. And one reason, according to the poll, was CNN's delivery of hard news and coverage of live news events.

As for Nielsen figures since 1985, the shares of American television sets tuned to news had dropped for ABC and CBS and NBC, while CNN and Headline News (combined) had risen from 16.5 percent to 24.7 percent in 1989. Turner's networks were behind CBS (30.2 percent) and ABC (26.5 percent), but in third place ahead of NBC (18.6 percent).

Nicholas J. Nicholas, president and chief operating officer of Time Warner Inc., confirmed that TWI would love to buy CNN as soon as Ted Turner was ready "to hang up his cleats." Time Warner, with nearly eighteen percent of Turner Broadcasting stock, had gained right of first refusal on any sale of CNN. Nicholas said Turner was spending more time on his Montana ranch and seemed "more disposed than ever" to selling out.

TED TURNER

"They aren't the only ones that want CNN — they just talk about it more. In the event that I retire or when I die, the cable operators as a group have the first option to buy my interest; and in their agreement, *Time* would be the manager of CNN. They've got a very good journalistic heritage, one of the best; and it's nice to know that if anything does happen to me, it will be operated by substantial and respected journalists. But CNN is not susceptible to a takeover, not unless I want it to be, and I have no intention of that."

When the SuperStation was scheduled to run an abortion program with a pro-choice angle, Turner was anything but apologetic: "You bet your bippy we're taking a position!" At a gathering of TV critics in Los Angeles, he criticized anti-abortion activists for trying to impose their views on others: "I don't want anybody else telling me what my daughter's got to have, or my wife or my girlfriend. We live in a free country. There is absolutely no way that that's anybody's business but the person involved. That's my opinion." The TBS program would be followed by a panel discussion with voices on both sides of the issue. "We'll give the other bozos a chance to talk back," Turner said — but then he couldn't resist a parting shot: "The pro-lifers say they don't want people to have sex for fun, only to have babies. 'Sex is sinful.' Well, that's fine if those people don't want to ever have sex. Swell. I happen to enjoy it. I don't get near as much as I want to."

Cable News Network had become the "jewel in the crown" of Turner Broadcasting, earning $89 million in 1988. In early 1989, CNN and Headline News had an estimated value of $1.5 billion, higher than that of the SuperStation.

CNN's growth and expansion, as the network approached its tenth anniversary on June 1, 1990, was one of the great success stories of American business. By the tenth year, its coverage was being received in fifty-three million homes in the United States, more than half the total market, and in eighty-four countries. There were eighteen hundred staffers in nine domestic and eighteen overseas bureaus (seven of which were coming on line), all feeding their reports through Atlanta to CNN's ever-widening world audience. What Marshall McLuhan had envisioned as an electronic "global village" through television had arrived in its most concrete form.

During the final year of the decade, nearly all the experts had publicly reversed their opinions about CNN. Among them was Ed Joyce, former president of CBS News, who observed in *TV Guide* that while the news divisions of CBS, ABC and NBC had been closing their bureaus and cutting back, Turner by contrast had tightened the budget of CNN while continuing to expand.

"Ironically," Joyce wrote, "the individual once portrayed as a bogeyman by CBS executives, myself among them, has shown a commitment to his news organization sadly lacking at the three commercial networks."

William Small, former president of NBC News, wrote in the *Washington Journalism Review* that "the major networks' monopoly on national and world news is a shattered memory," implying that CNN had done most of the shattering by itself.

Meanwhile, the *New York Times* reported in August 1989:

Early last week, when the administration was immersed in deciding how to respond to the threat to American hostages in Lebanon, a Bush aide was asked how the president was spending his day. "He's been in his study a lot watching CNN," the aide replied.

Marlin Fitzwater, the president's press secretary, told the *Times:* "CNN has opened up a whole new communications system between governments in terms of immediacy and directness. In many cases, it's the first communication we have."

"Even the CIA analysts gather during crises in the library of their Virginia headquarters to watch CNN," the *Times* said, adding that the network was popular with many heads of state, including King Hussein of Jordan and Margaret Thatcher of Britain. King Fahd of Saudi Arabia not only watched CNN but placed middle-of-the-night calls to his Washington ambassador, based on developments he saw on the network.

ED TURNER

"In the early days we set out to establish our credentials worldwide, and one of the world figures we went after, for a simple interview, was Margaret Thatcher, then the new prime minister. We were turned down. We went back and we were turned down again. And then again. I couldn't figure out why. . . .

"We found out indirectly that one of Mrs. Thatcher's advisers had told her that because we were cable we were probably pornographic. We got word to her, through her press secretary, that no, we weren't pornographic yet — although if the ratings stayed where they were, we might have to be. Subsequently she had a dish put in. She and her husband began to watch CNN in the family quarters at number 10 Downing. Fade to the present. . . ."

BERNIE SHAW

"We came out of the NATO summit and the president stopped off in London, so I went to number 10 Downing to do my anchor bridges. We wanted to wait until the Thatchers said goodbye to President Bush and his wife, so the house would seem empty and quiet. So we're waiting and the president came out. . . .

"He came across the back of the limo and I yelled out, 'Mr. President, will you favor us with a few words?' My voice boomed across the street. He stopped and said, 'Who's that? Bernie?' He's shielding his eyes from the TV lights and he says, 'Well, I'd rather talk to you about China.' I asked him, 'Do you think Gorbachev is trying to drive a wedge between the United States and the Alliance?' He said, 'Lighten up, Bernie. It's time to go to bed.' Then he got in the car and left. Meanwhile, Margaret Thatcher is over there, in the door, watching all this. And she discreetly waits until the Bush limousine pulls away. So here comes Mrs. Thatcher in her lovely dinner dress, right across the street and up to the camera. . . ."

TED TURNER

"Every day we reach more people as more satellite dishes and cable systems hook up in the United States and over the world — and the more people we reach, the more influential we'll be. We're a long way from peaking in terms of influence. But there's no question in my mind that we've been a force for moderation and intelligence in the world. We've interviewed world leaders on a global stage for the first time. And every leader wants to be favorably thought of. Everyone wants to be popular. Even Adolf Hitler wanted to be popular. He thought he was doing the right thing. But there's a growing consensus of what the right thing is. And the right thing is peace and moderation and human rights, and you see it popping up all over the place — even in South Africa, in the demise of the Berlin Wall and the freeing up of Eastern Europe, in Vietnam pulling out of Cambodia. I mean, it's just good news — the rising environmental and population concerns all over the world — and it almost makes you think that humanity has a chance.

"Some old sage said years ago that a problem recognized is a problem half solved. And I really do think that that is true. You've got to basically believe that human beings, when confronted with the information, will choose the intelligent course. If they don't, then there really was no hope for them in the beginning. . . . With the right information, we hopefully are going to make the right decisions."

In the fall of 1989, Ted Turner received the prestigious Paul White Award from the Radio-Television News Directors Association, becoming the first "entrepreneur" to win the RTNDA's highest honor for broadcast journalism. On hand to receive the award in Kansas City, he addressed a banquet hall filled with news directors.

In his extemporaneous speech, he admitted that CNN's newscasts were low rated and said that one of the best things about his network was that half its revenues came "from the subscribers, rather than all of it coming from advertisers." He said the highest rating CNN had received was when little Jessica McClure was pulled out of the well in Texas in 1987 — a 6.6 rating. "Nobody in this room could keep his job," he said, if they got CNN's normally low rating of less than one point or an audience of around half a million viewers.

"It's not right when all of television's money comes from advertising," Turner said. "It puts too much pressure on the ratings. Then when you get to the news part of the programming, you could be asked or told to do things that don't really make good journalistic sense. You get out of the news business and into the ratings business."

Turner used a humorous example from the days when he had owned the Charlotte television station. He referred to Bob Schuessler, who was at the head table, and recounted this anecdote:

"I have a great idea," Schuessler told him. "We're gonna do a five-part series during the sweeps week, on teenage prostitution in Charlotte."

"In Charlotte?" Turner replied. "Is that a problem?"

"Well," Schuessler said, "we found five teenage hookers."

"Where'd *that* idea come from?" Turner asked.

"Well," Schuessler said, "from the *sales* department!"

"I'm not even a journalist," Turner told the RTNDA crowd, "but I had enough good sense to realize that that ain't journalism!"

Turner said he didn't think CNN ever went out to do a story just to get ratings, but he admitted that "we love it when there's something like the revolution in Tiananmen Square and when somebody falls in a well."

"After starting CNN itself," Turner said, "I think the best thing we've done is *World Report*. Basically it's just giving people in the smaller countries, and countries over the world, a chance to be heard from. It's just really amazing. As an American, I always thought of the world as 'President Reagan talked to Margaret Thatcher' or 'President Bush talks to Gorbachev,' but on *World Report* you'll see the president of an African country meeting with *another* African leader. And that *never* makes the news here.

"What *is* news? You know what news is? News is what you news directors *interpret* it as. News is what we at CNN interpret it as. The people of this country see the news that we think they *oughta* see. And quite frankly, a lot of that decision is geared to what's gonna keep them interested, keep them at your station.

"And that's the great advantage, the good thing, about CNN. We can live with a .5 or .6 rating. Not a five, but a *point* five. The kind of numbers that would get you fired in five minutes. We can live with it. And we can do well with it. And as a result, we can put on stories that wouldn't even begin to make your newscasts.

"Another thing we're doing that I'm extremely proud of, and that has great potential for the future, is this program we're starting for high-school and junior-high-school kids, called *Newsroom*, that we started a couple of weeks ago. . . ."

(When Whittle Communications started testing a service to be used in schoolrooms, there was criticism that it would include commercials. Turner jumped in to prepare a free CNN service in competition; and, taking his own executives completely by surprise, he announced that the daily fifteen-minute news show for schools would have no sponsors at all. It was the tactic of a leader wanting to win the game first and worry about the price of victory later.)

"And if it works," Turner said, "we're gonna do one for grammar-school kids and for college students. We'll do that very quickly. Because kids today grow up in front of the television set. They don't read. I was a vociferous reader when I was young. I don't know whether your children read as much as you did, but my own five children sure didn't read as much as I did, and I did everything I could to get them to read and couldn't get them to read. So I can see that if we're gonna educate the next generation of children, we're gonna have to use video a great deal to do it. . . .

"I really think we have a responsibility, because television news is so powerful, not to make a lot of money but to have an influence in our communities," Turner went on, launching into one of those long, winding thoughts that have characterized many of his speeches. "And our community, as I interpret it, is not just the local market or even our country, but the world in which we live. And many of our problems are global and can only be solved together.

"I'm talking about problems of the environment, of population, of nuclear weapons and proliferation, of chemical and biological weapons, not to mention the poverty that exists in the world, the homelessness, and the hundred million children that are abandoned in the world today, while the world continues to spend a trillion dollars a year on armaments — enough money where even a half or a third of it, properly utilized, would provide decent health care and education, housing, food for everybody on earth that's living in abject poverty.

"We've got to change the way we're doing things, if we're going to survive. That's the conclusion I've come to, in studying the global situation very, very carefully, which I think, as a news person, we're sitting there with the information right at our fingertips, and we have to interpret it. And I think our major responsibility is to our communities and to our species, and to the other living things on the planet, and to the world at large.

"Because we've been living here on this earth for the last five thousand years, at least in the Judeo-Christian world, with the Ten Commandments, and I think they're obsolete. I *know* they're obsolete. It may be considered sacrilegious to say that, but I guarantee you that if Moses was here today, and went up the mountain, that the Good Lord would give him some different things. I mean, for instance, one of the Ten Commandments is about 'Thou shall have no other gods before me,' because at that time, remember, they built the Golden Calf while he was up there, and there were *lots* of gods then. But there *aren't* lots of gods now. How many people in here believe in more than one god? Not a single person in the room. So that's obviously an obsolete Commandment, because nobody believes in that anymore" — he is being drowned out by nervous laughter, now, from the television news directors, who realize that their award recipient is plunging onward and onward to find the heart of his theme — "and back then they had an Ark but now we run around in planes, and now we have holes in the ozone layer, but back then they didn't even know there *was* an ozone layer. They thought everything up there was heaven, but we've been up there and there's nothing but a void.

"And besides, if you were gonna come up with some new rules, you wouldn't call 'em Commandments anyway, because nobody likes to be *commanded* to do anything. So here's some new ones, the best I could come up with, and they're not written in stone, either. And rather than Commandments, I call them 'voluntary initiatives' — how about that? Here they are:

" 'I love and respect planet Earth and all living things thereon, especially my fellow species, mankind. I promise to treat all persons, everywhere, with dignity, respect and friendliness. I promise' — and listen, I had five children, but I didn't know this ten or twenty years ago — 'I promise I will add no more than two children to the earth. I promise to use my best efforts to help save what is left of our natural world in its untouched state, and to restore areas where practical. I pledge to use as little nonrenewable resources and as little toxic chemicals, pesticides and other poisons as possible, and to work for their reduction by others. I promise to contribute to those less fortunate than myself, to help them to become self-sufficient and to enjoy the benefits of a decent life, including clean air and water, adequate food and health care, housing, education and individual rights. I resent the use of force, in particular military force, and back United Nations arbitration of international disputes. I support the total elimination of all nuclear, chemical and biological weapons, and the entire elimination of all weapons of mass destruction. I support the United Nations and its efforts to collectively improve the conditions of the planet.'

"Last year I spoke to Moscow University and I gave 'em something to really work for. You know, we've got the year 2000 coming and we've got a challenge ahead of us that mankind has never had before. We're really on the verge of having peace on this earth. We really are. There's not a major war going on in the world. Wars don't work. We couldn't beat Vietnam. The Soviets couldn't win in Afghanistan. Iran and Iraq were just losers. Everyone's losing in Lebanon. Everyone's losing in Northern Ireland. It's really time that we put that behind us. And that's really something. If we had peace — that's something we've never had, peace.

"And we really need to have peace, not only man with man, but man at peace with the environment. A tree doesn't have much of a chance, the forest doesn't have much of a chance against bulldozers and chainsaws. So we really need peace with the environment, too, and that's a possibility also.

"And I'd like to see a movement going. The most exciting thing that we could do — the last time the calendar was turned over was two thousand years ago, when we had A.D. and B.C., and Christianity's had two thousand years to solve the world's problems and they're just as big now as they've ever been, and the missionaries have either been killed or eaten, in the Third World, and Christianity is *not* gonna take over the world — so why don't we start over?

"Why don't we aim, during the next ten years, to have peace on earth? And in the Year 2000, turn the time back to zero? And let it be B.P. and A.P. — Before Peace and After Peace. That could be the greatest honor we could bestow upon our generation. So if we do that, then people will *be* here two thousand years from now. If we continue on the course that we've *been* on . . .

"You're the most important people on this planet — we are, in the television news business, because we affect what people think. We run a lot of environmental stories, and population stories, and we should push peace — don't push armament, push peace. Because that's what's going to change the way we've been doing things. We can do it. The most important thing we can do is see that our children live a decent life and live to be seventy years old the way we hope to do. So thanks a lot for the great honor for CNN and God bless you all."

Thus speaks the ol' Mouth of the South, the ol' Captain Outrageous, the ol' So-and-So, as he lifts his broadsword into the wind and bounds on. . . .

Index

Turner, Ted (Robert Edward III)
(continued)
news service concept and early
plans, 180–181, 200; and CBS
takeover bid for CNN, 189; fights
for equal pooling, 193, 196, 197,
231–232; and ABC-Westinghouse
challenge and cable news war, 197–
200, 202–205, 208–209, 228, 247,
251–253, 260; and CNN2, 226–227,
242; and Schonfeld, 229–231, 234–
235, 237–241, 245, 250–251;
influence on programming, 231,
236, 243–246, 299, 300–301, 304–
308; and Castro, 233–234; and
unionization attempt, 234–235;
buys SNC, 254–257; takeover bid
for CBS, 263–267; takeover bid for
MGM/UA, 267, 268, 274, 275;
takeover bid for FNN, 280–281
Turner Advertising Company, 10
Turner Broadcasting System (TBS), 58,
74, 118, 140, 142, 172, 218, 264,
267; and TT's sports teams, 222;
and takeover bid for CBS, 266;
Soviet joint venture, 269; TT sells
stock, 274–275; personnel shifts,
276. See also Cable News Network
(CNN); SuperStation WTBS
Channel 17 (previously WTCG)
Turner Communications Corporation, 5
Turner Network Television (TNT), 276,
278, 279, 281, 298
Turner Program Services, 243, 263
Turner Sports, 298
Tush, Bill, 31, 140, 275
"TV: The Moral Battleground"
documentary, 197
TV Guide, 301
TV News Journal, 277–278
TWA hijacking (1985), 270, 271
Two-Minute Newscast (CNN program),
211

UHF, 7, 15
unionization attempt at CNN, 194, 195,
196, 223, 234–235
United Cable Television, 82
UPI Broadcasting, 41, 45, 46, 51, 52
UPI Movietone, 9, 11–12
UPI Newsfilm, 12
UPI Television News (UPITN), 12, 13,
18, 19, 21, 83

Vallas, Dean, 88, 165
Variety, 131, 156, 272, 279, 280
Varney, Stuart, 157, 286
Vesey, Peter, 98, 100, 113, 115, 116,
135
Viacom, 36
video journalism program at CNN, 121,
122–124, 129, 224, 281, 287
Visnews, 88
von Bulow, Claus, 270
Von Essen, Jeanee, 117–118, 161–162

WABC-TV (New York), 58, 65, 77, 168,
212
Wald, Richard, 210
Walker, Dave, 120, 125; inaugural
newscast, 143–148, 150; as
anchor, 157, 185; opinion of CNN
operations, 161, 283–284; at CNBC,
280, 283
Walker, Wendy, 118
Wallace, Mike, 266
Wall Street Journal, 134, 299
Walters, Barbara, 210
Walton, Mark, 88
Ward, John, 99
Warner Amex Satellite Entertainment
Company, 222
Warner Brothers, 279
Warriors, The, 244
Washington Journalism Review, 268,
301
Washington Post Company, 104, 152
Waters, Lou, 120, 151, 182–183, 226,
295
Waters, Mardy, 120
Watson, George, 88, 100, 118, 135, 148,
151, 176–177
Weine, Tammi, 135
Welles, Orson, 280
WESTAR, 19, 21, 111, 137, 222, 247
WESTAR IV, 255
Western Cable Show, 36–37, 39, 79, 81,
82
Western Union, 24; WESTAR satellites,
19, 21, 111, 137, 222, 247, 255
Westinghouse Broadcasting, 131, 132;
competition with CNN, 152, 176,
197, 254; cable news network with
ABC and cable news war, 185, 197–
200, 202–203, 207–209, 220, 224,
225, 235, 247, 251, 255, 256, 260,
267